THE SOVEREIGN SOUL

By

Gerald N. Wright

ALL RIGHTS RESERVED

First Printing 2016
Second Printing 2017

Copyright 2016, Gerald N Wright
ISBN 978-1-938335-69-3

DEDICATION

THREE LADIES

Well, there's Beulah, then there's Brenda, then there's Lucille: One gave me life, one became my wife, and one showed me the light. These three ladies made me this strong; these three ladies made me sing this love song.

Well, there's Beulah, then there's Brenda, then there's Lucille: One made me, One mated me, and One changed my will. My Three ladies: All Queens of my heart ... Three ladies till death do us part.

Well, there's Beulah, then there's Brenda, then there's Lucille; One left me, One's with me, and One I remember still.
Well, there's Beulah, then there's Brenda, then there's Lucille; Thank God for my fair ladies: Beulah, Brenda and Lucille!

TABLE OF CONTENTS

DEDICATION .... Page 3

INTRODUCTION .... Page 5
"Sovereign Soul Introduction and Test"

CHAPTER ONE .... Page 7
"Sovereign Souls Choose Christ as Creator"

CHAPTER TWO .... Page 24
"Sovereign Souls Choose Christ's Covenant"

CHAPTER THREE .... Page 67
"Sovereign Souls Choose Christ's Cross"

CHAPTER FOUR .... Page 91
"Sovereign Souls Choose Christ's Church"

CHAPTER FIVE .... Page 140
"Sovereign Souls Choose Christ's Companionship"

CHAPTER SIX .... Page 179
"Sovereign Souls Choose Christ's Commission"

CHAPTER SEVEN .... Page 222
"Sovereign Souls Choose Christ's Crown"

SUPPLEMENTAL STUDIES .... Page 273
"Word Study on *Soul/Spirit*"
"Jesus is Jehovah Parallels"
"President Obama Indicts Christianity"
"Jesus is the ROCK" (Matt. 16:18)"
"Peter was not the First Pope"
"Memories of Kaimu Black Sand Beach"

RESEARCH SOURCES .... Page 302
"Books and Commentaries"
"Biblical-books by Gerald Wright"
"Documents and Pictures"

INTRODUCTION

Aloha. Please allow me to introduce myself. I'm the young teenager you see on the front cover of this book... except now I'm over half a century older! Though I preferred to be called "Jerry Neil Wright" (and even "Jerry Neil III") in those days, my given name is Gerald Neil Wright. I have been a **"Sovereign Soul"** all of my seventy-three years of life—even when I didn't know what a sovereign soul was. And some of this book will be about ME ... or about my life as a **"Sovereign Soul."**

But the purpose of this book is not to elevate me above you or anyone else, or even to educate you as to who I am. It is, rather, to enhance your understanding as to who YOU ARE as an equal and/or fellow **"Sovereign Soul"** with me. And, dear reader, whether you know it or not, believe it or not, or even like it or not, you are a sovereign soul ... and you should proudly walk and talk like one. If I can and do, so can you. Actually, so must you!

For though you have a choice as to whether you know, learn and enjoy all the benefits and blessings of living the life of a **"Sovereign Soul"** — which will be discussed at length throughout this book — you do not have a choice as to whether you were created as such a solitary spirit, or sovereign soul, at the beginning of your life, and that you will be judged and rewarded as such at the end of your life on earth.

So with this serious and satisfying study before us, I will now present you with the following **Sovereign Soul Test** so you can see where your understanding, or appreciation, of your being a "Sovereign Soul" is before we begin this journey. Then you can compare that understanding with your understanding at the end of this book ... and more importantly at the end of your life after living as *"The Sovereign Soul"* you were meant to be.

COMPOSITION NOTE: This book, as many of my expositional books, includes a great number of Scriptural References within the text, many of which are repeated a number of times. There are so many references so you may do more research after you read the book. They are repeated so each Chapter and Subject has its own references to support it, making it easier for you to research later.

The Sovereign Soul Test

1. Do you believe you have a divinely created soul? Yes ___ No ___

2. Do you believe your soul is unique amongst the billions of souls who have lived/live on earth? Yes ___ No ___

3. Do you believe you are the highest creature in the Universe? Yes ___ No ___

4. Do you believe your soul is worth more than all this world's treasures and pleasures? Yes ___ No ___

5. Do you believe you are as important to God as any person on earth today? Yes ___ No ___

6. Do you believe you are equal in authority to all religious and moral authorities on earth today? Yes ___ No ___

7. Do you believe your soul will survive the death of your physical body and receive an immortal body? Yes ___ No ___

Now if your answer to any of these seven questions was **"No,"** your understanding of being a "Sovereign Soul" is not what it could be. This book will assist you in your exaltation of yourself as *"The Sovereign Soul"* you will understand yourself to be.

If your answer to all seven of the questions was **"Yes,"** you understand yourself to be a "Sovereign Soul," even if you don't call yourself such. This book should lead you to expand your appreciation of your lofty status and lead you to more joyful exultation in being *"The Sovereign Soul"* you claim to be—unto the glory of your Creator.

CHAPTER ONE
Sovereign Souls Choose Christ as Creator

THE CREATOR'S CHOICE

"Adam and Eve"

*In the **Beginning**, **God created the heavens and the earth** ... And God said, Let **us** make **man** in **our** image, after our likeness: and let them have **dominion** over the fish of the sea, and over the birds of the heavens, and over the cattle, and over all the earth ... And God created man in his own image, in the image of God created he him; **male and female created he them**.... And Jehovah God formed man of the dust of the ground, and breathed into his nostrils the breath of life; and **man became a living soul*** (Genesis 1:1, 26f; 2:7; cf. 2:21-25 for the creation of Eve).

Our Creator herein made it clear to the first pair of Human Beings & Souls — Adam (man) and Eve (woman) — that the Triune God was their only Sovereign Creator (See "Soul & Spirit" in Supplemental Studies). Throughout God's communication with Adam and Eve, and with all humanity through His inspired Bible, Jehovah God made it clear that this Godhead (*"us, our image"*) was the only true God and Creator of all life. We also know from the New Testament that Christ was our Creator (see John 1:1-3,14 below, and "Jesus is Jehovah" texts in Supplemental Studies).

***In the beginning was the Word**, and the **Word was with God**, and the **Word was God**. The same was in the beginning with God. **All things were made through him**; and without him was not anything made that hath been made.... And the Word became flesh, and dwelt among us (and we beheld his glory, glory as the only begotten from the Father) ... {or "God only begotten"}, full of grace and truth.*

7

Thus the **"*Creator's Choice*"** for Adam and Eve and all of us was, and will always be, Jehovah God: also called *"Immanuel"* ("God with us"), the Great *"I Am,"* the God-man in whom *"dwelleth all the fullness of the Godhead bodily"*... **Jesus Christ** (Isaiah 7:14; John 8:58; Colossians 1:19; 2:9). So Christ is The Supreme and Sovereign Creator of all Souls, the *"Prince/Author of life"* (John 1:1-3; Acts 3:15; Colossians 1:15-18; Hebrews 1:3).

It is abundantly clear from the Biblical Creation Account that Adam and Eve had no choice about the matter of their being responsible, free-will, "sovereign souls" from the very first day of their lives. Each had the sole responsibility to obey God's clear commands or suffer the consequences for their disobedience: *"Thou shalt not eat ... or die"* (Genesis 2:17). Both violated this command by eating of that forbidden fruit. Though different influences and incentives led to their rebellion, both were equally accountable and suffered the same punishment.

They were both, as divinely created Sovereign Souls, made just a little lower than angels (Hebrews 2:7), endowed by their Creator with *"dominion over all the earth,"* and thus they each sustained equal rights and responsibilities to know and obey what each knew to be God's will. Saying the *"Devil made me do it"* (an angelic creature coming in the form of a much lower subhuman creature, a "snake," that they had dominion over), or "the women you gave me made me do it" (a human made from your side and not your head), didn't help either Eve or Adam one bit (Genesis 3:12; see Galatians 1:8 for confirmation of this principle). Adam and Eve were each the highest created, religious, moral authority on earth at that time. Thus God's Sovereign Rule was their only Rule. So, therefore, His Choice was their only Right Choice! And it will do us well to remember that this Creator is the Only One we need to obey and please when it comes to our Sovereign Responsibility.

Throughout this entire study of Seven Chapters, we will see that this "Divine Balance of Power" and Revealed Order of Human Responsibility — "God's Word First, You and I as individuals next, then other humans, then animals and nature last — must be respected and maintained in all of our dealings with God's commands, covenants, church, carnal relationships (like marriage), civil governments, and lower creatures. Otherwise, any "Imbalance of Power" will lead to all sorts of evils. The only reason all human beings are equal as sovereign beings is because God Created us that way. Though all human beings are equal **under** God, all of them put together are not equal **to or with** God in person or power. The reason God is Superior over his created beings is because HE IS The Supreme Being. The reason God's Rules make us Sovereign is because God is the Supreme Ruler. The reason God's Word is Authoritative and Infallible is because God is Omnipotent and Omniscient, and man is neither and cannot direct his own steps (Jeremiah 10:23). So now let's look at other examples that reinforce this seminal point about each person's individual sovereign responsibility under and before God.

"In Adam's Family"

This same "Sovereign Soul" status was occupied by Adam's first two sons, **Cain and Abel** (Genesis 4:1-5). A good lesson about true worship of God can be found in this text. We find that God's desire has always been for humans to *"worship in **spirit** and **truth**,"* i.e., from the heart and according to His Word (John 4:24; 17:17). Though unstated in this text, God had revealed His desired type of sacrifice — *"firstling of the flock"* and not *"fruit of the ground"* — to both Cain and Abel. Otherwise, neither would have had the knowledge, right or responsibility to offer anything to God. But since we know that Abel offered his animal sacrifice by ***"faith"*** (Hebrews 11:4), and that *"**faith** comes by hearing the **word** of God"* (Romans 10:17), we rightly conclude that God told both of them to offer an animal sacrifice to Him. That was God's only "expected offering," and thus His only "respected offeror." Yet Cain, like other glory-seeking men after him (e.g., King Saul) assumed otherwise and offered God something different from what God commanded ... and it was summarily rejected by God. This lesson on true and acceptable worship is still timely today:

> *And Samuel said {to Saul}, Hath Jehovah as great delight in burnt-offerings and sacrifices, as in obeying the voice of Jehovah? **Behold, to obey is better than sacrifice**, and to hearken than the fat of rams. For rebellion is as the sin of witchcraft, and stubbornness is as idolatry and teraphim. Because thou has **rejected the word of Jehovah**, he hath also **rejected thee** from being king* (I Samuel 15:22-23).

Another lesson we can learn from this text is how one person's sin is often another person's consequence or collateral damage! And so it was with Cain's sin. For we also know God told Cain that he had the self-control as a sovereign soul to *"rule over"* his sinful, envious and jealous desire to kill Abel because his faithful sacrifice was accepted and Cain's unfaithful sacrifice was rejected. He didn't listen to God on this divine advice, either. He wilfully, with knowledge and malice aforethought, violated Abel's sovereign right to life and killed him! So Cain's sinful and selfish "sovereign-soul" caused collateral damage on earth.

But, in spite of Cain's failure, God's Sovereign Rule over the entire matter brought lessons of justice and hope into our world. We learn that, though Abel's faithful sovereign behavior cost him his physical life, God gave him eternal life because of his faith and trust in Him. Thus Abel still speaks to us about the objective hope behind our faith (Hebrews 11:4). We also learn a lot about God's justice when we see how Cain's unfaithful sovereign behavior of putting his personal choice above God's expressed choice cost him his physical well-being on earth thereafter as well as his eternal life with God. Being a "Sovereign Soul" is of utmost importance to God ... and a matter of life and death to You and Me!

Note: God later protected the "right to life" of each sovereign soul with the death penalty for murder (Gen. 9:6; Leviticus 24:17, 21).

"In Noah's World"

Though the earth's entire population during the days of Noah — save the eight sovereign souls on the ark — was destroyed, each adult responsible person had his own free will and choice life: each person sinned in his/her own way; or each person failed to listen to Noah's preaching; or each person failed to repent and be saved; and each of the eight in Noah's family were actively involved in their own salvation (Matthew 24:37-39; I Peter 3:20; See "Supreme Salvation" in *The Supreme Scientist*, pp. 275-288).

"In The Theocratic Nation of Israel"

The Theocratic Nation of Israel was destined to destruction the day they allowed one rebellious and haughty king, Jeroboam, to lead ten tribes of God's chosen people away from God's written commands concerning true worship (I Kings 12:25-33). Hosea denounced their national ignorance, saying: *"**My people are destroyed** for lack of knowledge.... **Ephraim** {Israel} is oppressed, he is **crushed in judgment**; because he was **content to walk after man's command**"* (Hosea 4:6; 5:11). Indeed, though there was wholesale ignorance amongst the Jewish Nation, each person was still responsible for being ignorant, for allowing the priests to teach error, for failing to teach their children, for allowing their erring brethren to sin without censure, and for personally violating God's commands on where and how to worship because of convenience or, maybe, ancient "ecumenism." We cannot "agree to disagree" on what God has clearly commanded; we must **"agree to agree with God."** Sadly, the same fate would befall the remaining two tribes of Israel within a few hundred years (see Book of Jeremiah).

"In The Church"

On the Great Jewish Day of Pentecost, the remnant of this same fallen nation of Israel was offered salvation by their Great God through their long-awaited Messiah: Jesus Christ (Acts 2:1-47). After the Apostle Peter preached the first Gospel sermon to hundreds of thousands of Israel's Jews — which sermon included their rejection and murder of the Christ, His resurrection, His new spiritual kingdom, and how to be saved — he said this unto them:

> *And with many other **words** he testified, and exhorted them, saying, **Save yourselves** from this crooked generation ...**They then that received his word were baptized** ... And the **Lord added to them** {"the church," KJV} day by day **those that were saved**"* (Acts 2:40-47).

There's Peter's inspired and sovereign way of gospel preaching: offering salvation in Christ to everyone who could hear his voice, and allowing each sovereign soul who heard that Gospel call to reject or receive the word by answering the call, accepting the lordship of Christ in word and deed (thus "confessing his lordship" in the process), repenting of his/her past sins, being baptized for the forgiveness of sins and then being added by Jesus to his *"church"* (Gk., ekklesia, "his called out ones"). All this occurred without any delay due to inquisition, tests, or votes by any "higher human authorities." They had obeyed the Lord, not Peter the man. They were saved by faith in Christ and his blood and not by Peter's Apostolic position or power...nor by their Old Law or meritorious works. Their acts of obedience to his words were all acts of faith in the unseen person of Christ and his forgiving blood and power to add them to His church, not Peter's (see I Corinthians 1:12f). This was the *"Gospel power of salvation"* in action (Romans 1:16). *"There is power, power, wonder working power, in the precious blood of the Lamb"* (one of my favorite Gospel Songs)!

When we human beings bow to none other than our Sovereign God through our Savior Jesus Christ, good things happen. And that, in and of itself, is "Good News!" It was for Israel then, and it is today, and it will be until the end of time. And there will never, ever, be any better news for the Jews at the end of the Christian Age. (As is promised and preached by those who yet believe in Jewish Nationalistic Salvation, e.g., Dispensationalism and Premillennialism.) And it is good news for every responsible soul on earth. And though, one day at the end of time, all human souls — be they saved saints or lost sinners — will bow before the *"name"* (the sovereign authority) of Jesus Christ, that final bow will come after the destiny of each and every individual's sovereign choices are set for eternity (Philippians 2:9-11; Matthew 28:18). That will not be good news for some. I pray not you! The same God and Savior still beckons unto all men, Jew and Gentile and you, through the Apostles' words:

> *We {Apostles} are ambassadors therefore on behalf of Christ, as though **God were entreating by us**: we beseech you on **behalf of Christ**, be ye reconciled to God. Him who knew no sin he made to be sin on our behalf; that we might become the righteousness of God in him. And working together with him we entreat also that ye receive not the grace of God in vain (for he saith, At an acceptable time I hearkened unto thee, And in a day of salvation did I succor thee: behold now is the acceptable time; behold, **now is the day of salvation**")...* (II Corinthians 5:20-6:2). And now is the day for your Sovereign Soul to stand up and be counted. Now is the day of your salvation and others through you.

"In the Pagan/Atheistic World"

Our Creator and Godhead — Father, Son and Holy Spirit — expressed in both the Old and New Testaments that all human beings are to know and obey only this Sovereign God, Creator and Savior (Genesis 1-2; John 1:1-3). Jesus expressed this in his Great Commission when he commanded his Apostles (and all of us by extension) to preach His Gospel, commands and teachings to every *"creature"* (KJV Mark 16:15; cf. Romans 10:17f).

The Apostle Paul, in Romans 1:18-32, pointed out how those who refuse to have this true God and Creator in their knowledge, or refuse others of the same, will not be sovereign souls "doing their own thing"—who live just as healthy, honorable and acceptable lives on their own as those who believe in the true Creator and God. Rather they will either be of the uneducated muddled masses or of the misguided miscreants who have no God to direct their steps (Jeremiah 10:23), no God to obey or thank, and no desires higher than dirt. They will be ungrateful, senseless, dark-minded, sinful idolaters and "fools" (Romans 1:21-22).

Indeed, those who wilfully choose to reject the true God and Creator will worship and serve *"the creature"* and all of his lying ideologies (like evolution"), idols, inventions and evil instincts (Ibid. Vv. 23-32). You can't maintain your declaration of individual independence as a Sovereign Soul with "God-given rights" if you have no Divine Creator. For example, you can't rely on your right to life if you live in in an evolutionary society that believes in the "Survival of the fittest," because those more "fit" than you, having more brawn than brains, might choose to eat you for dinner to aid in their survival! We're Sons of God, not apes!

Joshua made this "Creator Choice" so clear to his people that it's been quoted by Bible believers ever since. Listen and choose.

> *Now therefore fear Jehovah, and serve him in **sincerity** and in **truth**; and put away the gods which your fathers served beyond the River, and in Egypt; and **serve ye Jehovah**. And if it seem evil unto you to serve Jehovah, **choose** you this day whom ye will serve; whether the **gods** which your fathers served that were beyond the River, or the **gods** of the Amorites in whose land ye dwell: **but as for me and my house, we will serve Jehovah*** (Joshua 24:14-15).

As G.K. Chesterton said: *"A man that disbelieves in God does not believe in nothing; he believes in anything."* Or as Bob Dylan sang in his "Gotta Serve Somebody" hit song, that no matter who you are, what position you occupy, or what you do, *"you're gonna have to serve somebody."* If you're not serving the Sovereign God and Creator you're not the "Sovereign Soul" or "Soul Man" you imagine yourself to be — like I once thought I was (next). You are just one more sinful slave amongst "Satan's Slaves" (John 8:34). You're not a Solitary Man; you're just one of the go-along-to-get-along **"Sheeple."** <u>**You**</u> have not accepted **The Creator's Choice** that you should be a **"SOVEREIGN SOUL"** in submission to your Creator and His Word. Now back to me and my Creator Choice.

MY CREATOR CHOICE

As I stated in my introductory remarks, I've been a "Sovereign Soul" my entire life. Of course, I didn't know or understand any of this as a young child. But I did come to believe rather early in my childhood — due to my "Christian" parents and relatives, and going to Sunday School and Vacation Bible School — that the God of the Bible was the Creator of the Universe, Adam and Eve and all human souls. Even a child can grasp this rudimentary belief (II Timothy 3:15). And because of that basic Bible knowledge, I was a good little "religious boy" for the first nine years of my life.

But, in spite of this basic core belief in God as Creator from my childhood, I never was any sort of Bible student throughout my teenage years who understood this adult responsibility. My faith was as shallow as the waters of some of the creeks I swam around in. (One was called "Peter's Creek!") One can sing *Onward Christian Soldiers* every Sunday and not actually be enlisted in the Lord's Army, much less be a "Sovereign Soul" who preaches and defends the Lord's word regardless of the social costs and religious pressures to bow to school teachers, professors, church clicks, creeds, backward collars and big clergies. (Yet, as I stated in my *Supreme Scientist* book, that deficiency still didn't cause me to accept evolution or surrender my little faith in God to any of my Junior and High School teachers, who were Confessed Ape Descendants, aka., public "Evolutionists!")

Because of this shallow faith throughout my early life, and my entrance into the work force as a golf caddy amongst over a hundred older worldly caddies at the ripe old age of nine years old, I was soon being wooed and molded much more by evil companions and their worldly ways than God's word (I Corinthians 15:33). Thus by the age of thirteen I was walking on the wild side of life as a "solo spirit," or "stupid soul," rather than a "sovereign soul," throughout my entire teenage life. Though I didn't believe I came from a monkey, I often acted like one as I imitated those who did believe such and acted like monkeys: "Monkey see, monkey do." But because of the financial necessities of our family and the surrounding richer golf communities and work opportunities, the changes seemed necessary and almost "natural" for me. I mean, "everybody was doing it," and I was not near as worldly and sinful as many of the caddies and golfers. Though I soon quit going to church and avoided talking about religion, I still believed in God and Jesus!

Oh well, though I was obviously following the crowd down that notorious wild and *"wide way to perdition"* that Jesus warned about (Matthew 7:13f), I still felt like I was just growing up, getting "street smart" and pulling my own strings during all my teenage years. Now, looking back on my life and all the temptations I still have to struggle against today, I wish I would've had a working knowledge of "the good life" versus the "bad life" scriptures — like Psalms 1:1-6; 73:12-17; I Peter 3:10-12 — before I took that dangerous detour. Read and heed those three texts and remember these words of worldly advice written in **Ecclesiastes** by one of the world's wisest men, King Solomon, who had experienced all the treasures and pleasures the world has to offer:

> **1:9** *That which hath been is that which shall be; and that which hath been done is that which shall be done: and there is **no new thing under the sun**....* **1:14** *I have seen all the works that are done under the sun; and, behold, **all is vanity** and a striving after the wind...* **12:1** *Remember also thy **Creator in the days of thy youth**, before the evil days come, and the years draw nigh, when thou shalt say, I have no pleasure in them....* **12:7** *and the dust returneth to the earth*

> *as it was, and the **spirit** to God who gave it.... **12:13f** This is the **end of the matter**; all hath been heard: fear God, and keep his commandments; for this is the **whole duty** of man. For God will bring every work into **judgment**, with every hidden thing, whether it be good, or whether it be evil.*

But, of course, we can't relive our lives, and I probably wouldn't have read those gems of wisdom if some "church person" would have advised me to do so because of my already overbooked schedule. Hmmmm ... let's see ... from the age of nine thru twelve, I had a long list of normal, lawful and good demands upon my time. Then I added a lot of abnormal, unlawful and bad deeds to the list as I got older. All of them had an effect on my life ... and some of the bad ones still do! **A short list will suffice.**

JOBS — Making grocery and household money to assist the family from every kind of job occupied most of my daylight hours from the age of seven to nineteen. The jobs included: picking wild berries and selling them door-to-door, digging up sassafras roots and making and selling tea, working in orchards, mowing grass, shoveling snow, helping in concrete work and construction, working on Oscar Jenkins' farm bailing hay and picking corn, stocking groceries at the A&P, caddying at several golf courses, fixing cars and motorcycles, etc. Since my teenage years at home, besides preaching, I have worked in construction, real estate and dozens of lawful jobs. I've always had a "mind to work" (Nehemiah 4:6). The problem was "I worked hard...and played harder!" (Fortunately, I never sold drugs or worked unlawfully.)

EDUCATION — I loathed school as a teen because it cost me time and money away from working. In High School, I would often slip out the back door during the afternoon study hall so I could ride my Harley to the Hidden Valley Golf Course to caddy. In spite of all my class-skipping, I still managed to graduate from Jefferson Senior High School in 1961, albeit with less than what I'd call optimum grades.

RECREATION — I really enjoyed seeking all the lawful pleasures the world had to offer (Hebrews 11:25). Of course there were other forms of recreation that took a lot of my time besides golf: like spelunking at McVitty's Cave, climbing cliffs, and swimming in every creek, river, lake, public swimming pool and even in the sewage treatment plant in Roanoke, as well as at the beaches in Hampton, Virginia. And best of all, from age 15 to 19, I loved riding my motorcycles, which I purchased with my left over caddy fees. My first Harley was a small, slow, old and unattractive bike. Even my paint job didn't help. So I sold it after a year or so, and in 1958 I purchased a like-new, full-race, 1956 KHK Harley Davidson motorcycle, which you see on the front cover of this book, which was just like the one owned by Elvis Presley (See in Research Sources). The previous owner was such a great Elvis Fan that he painted *"Houndog"* (misspelled it) on the windshield. This macho machine made a profound difference in the life of this homely little country boy.

So during this period of my life, I was running from reality, reveling from dark till the wee hours of the morning, competing with the crazies and dancing with the Devil at every opportunity. I was, ostensibly, trying to have "FUN" by: guzzling the booze, siphoning gas, smoking like a smokestack (yet I didn't inhale ... really!), cursing like a drunken sailor (but not in front of my mother!) and running from the law on "Houndog," which I rode at breakneck speed every time I "turned it on" or wanted to get to the sock hop or dens of sin on time. I was chased by the law often, and one night I outran them going over a 100 mph with my lights off! (Idiot!) I was chased by an outraged neighbor with a gun. I often took other old sinners or novice sinners with me on the buddy seat to be partners in crime and sin. They say *"the road to hell is paved with good intentions"* ... but it is usually paved with people with bad intentions! I was dying my Elvis-style ducktailed hair yellow and black, and letting my moral hair down every chance I got (if you know what I mean). I was racing the cars and *"playing the bars"* and getting a *"bad name"* around my home town of around a hundred thousand people (Roanoke, Virginia).

Looking back on my wild life during the "Rock & Roll" era reminds me of one of Elvis' later songs — ***Pieces of my Life*** — that reflected his tattered life at the time when he recorded it. The words tell me a lot about his life, and have some application to my life, as well as to all those whose quest for fame, fortune and fun becomes their priority in life. Here's the song with some of the points which are relevant to my life highlighted.

*A water glass full of **whisky**, and **women** that I never knew too well. **Lord, the things I've seen and done**, most of which **I'd be ashamed to tell**.*

*I don't know how it started, but that's what **makes a man** a man, I guess. Now I'm holding on to nothing trying to forget the rest.*

***I'm looking back on my life, to see if I can find the pieces**. I know that some were stolen, and some just blew away. Well **I found the bad parts**, found all the **sad parts**, but I guess I **threw the best parts away** ... Lord away ... away.*

***Playing the bars**, playing like a star, **anything to get a name**, carrying on, living on songs, my friends wrote for me to sing.*

***I'm looking back on my life, today**. To see if I can find the pieces. I know that some were stolen, and some just blew away. Well I found the bad parts, found all the sad parts, but I guess **I threw the best parts away**.. away ... away.*

***Lord, the pieces of my life, they're everywhere**, they're everywhere. And **the one that I miss most of all ... is you**, and you know who.*

***Looking back, on my life, Lord**, to see if I can find the pieces. Looking back on my life today, to see if I can find the pieces. Looking back on my life, **God help me find the pieces**."*

Well, I've been there and done some of that, especially *"playing the bars."* I suppose some parts of this tragic song fit some parts of the lives of every person who lives a hedonistic life. I know they expose many of the details of my past prodigal teenage years, which I just touched upon. And believe me, I am *"ashamed to tell"* anything more than the basic categories of sin I dallied in. I'm lucky (I believe blessed) I wasn't found in *"pieces"* during any of my many bad motorcycle or car crashes. And most of all, I am glad I didn't throw *"my best part away,"* the one I'd *"miss most of all."* For I kept my teenage sweetheart, who has been my "better half" and beloved wife for fifty-four years. Thank God for you, Brenda Meredith!

Brenda & Jerry
(Circa 1959)

Believe it or not, my reckless behavior did get me a *"name"* back in those good ole days: not a big star's name like "Elvis," but a bad name — "Houndog" — with the cops. For they were lying in wait for ole Houndog and caught him so many times that the City made me sell my speed-demon-cycle! I finally ended up in jail and was so blacklisted in Roanoke that I couldn't get a job.

Well, "I had fought the law and the law won!" But it wasn't the end of the free life for a silly little boy who went by his nickname *"Jerry Neil Wright."* I always preferred my nickname "Jerry" over "Gerald," and even had it on my Social Security card and played golf for the Air Force with "Jerry Neil III" inscribed on my golf bag. I added the "III" because I liked the sound of it and still have it on my bag today (see in Research Sources). Maybe that's what "sovereign souls" do! Well, as we'll soon see, it was a good thing I used this nickname rather than my given name throughout my youth. It not only concluded my teenage life that had just ended at this low point; it was also the name that turned this idiot around and would very soon lend itself to launching me on the way to a better life.

Soon after Brenda and I ran off to Leaksville, North Carolina to get married in November of 1961, I decided that since I couldn't get a job I would enlist in the USAF. However, a glitch popped up in my plans: *"Jerry,"* alias *"Houndog,"* had racked up such a criminal record that they wouldn't allow such a misfit to enlist in the Air force. The recruiter said that because of the draft I would still be able to get into the Army. But I didn't want to go into the Army because of my recent marriage, and I knew I'd be shipped off to the escalating Viet Nam Conflict. So my recruiter reviewed my police record again and, being puzzled, asked me why I went by the name "Jerry" when my given name was really "Gerald." After I told him how I always preferred my nickname, he sent me back to the police station to see what kind of record "Gerald Wright" might have. Much to our surprise, "Gerald's" criminal record was as clean as the wind-driven snow! So he got me into the Air Force by getting me to do what I was good at doing, lying!

So I joined the USAF on January 25, 1962. I went to Lackland AFB in San Antonio, Texas for Basic training ... then to Tech School in Shepherd AFB in Wichita Falls, Texas for nine months ... then almost to jail again! Why? Well, since my new career field required a Top Secret Crypto Clearance, the FBI had found out about my little "Jerry-to-Gerald" switcheroo to get in the USAF. Oops! Caught again!

But to make this long story a little shorter, the FBI decided little ole "Jerry" was more a mischief-maker than a national menace and allowed me to continue my new life in the USAF. (Thank God!) Then, after Tech School, my first duty assignment was not to some cold, isolated, Air Force Radar site in Thule, Greenland or other Bases overseas where my wife wouldn't be allowed to go with me, but to Bermuda: a sweet little tropical island with pink sand beaches and golf courses that was less than a thousand miles from our hometown and families in Roanoke, Virginia. And she would also be able to join me there within a month or so. Lucky me!

When my wife finally arrived in Bermuda, we moved into a house that was beside the steps that led up to the St. George Hotel and Golf Course. Which was also near the house where George Spurgin and his wife Lucille lived on the other side of those steps. George was a Staff Sergeant in the USAF and head of the base gymnasium ... who, incidentally, played golf. Since George and I were neighbors, we soon met each other and started playing golf every Sunday morning with some of his military friends. (He should have been attending church with Lucille!)

George & Lucille
(*Circa 1963*)

George thought I was a better golfer than I actually was and decided to send me to California for two weeks to play in an Air Force tournament to represent Kindley AFB. When I returned, my wife surprised me by telling me she had been attending a Gospel Meeting with Lucille for the last few nights. She then asked me if I wanted to go with her and George and Lucille that night. So the four of us piled into Lucille's little Fiat car that night and went to hear evangelist, Jack Gray (see picture at end of this Chapter).

After the first night's sermon, George asked me what I thought about Jack's lesson (containing over 100 scriptural quotes). I said something silly about the Bible and scoffed at my need to "take a bath for Jesus!" George, whom I respected, said something like this: "Hey, son, you're just stupid and need to go read the Book of Acts and see for yourself." My wife and I did that very thing before we went to sleep that night. Then the next night we both began to make GOD'S CHOICES OUR CHOICES by not only choosing Him to be our only Creator but also our Re-Creator as per John 3:3-5; Romans 6:3f and II Corinthians 5:17. We became New Testament Christians just like the first Christians did in Acts Two.

My wife and I both knew we had made a serious life-changing decision that night, one that we both would have difficulties in keeping. But there was no question that it was THE RIGHT CHOICE. There can't be any logical or scientific argument or biblical controversy about choosing Jehovah God as the only Sovereign and Supreme Creator in Charge of your life. There's no other Creator to choose. I've looked at the so-called pagan gods of this world, including those springing up from beyond the Roanoke River, Rhine River, Euphrates River (Allah) and Wailuku River (Pele) in the land in which I now dwell, and they don't qualify as anything more than manmade, made-up myths, which do not deserve a second of my time, devotion or service. "If El-Shaddai is a lie, every other religious god, life, sacrifice, blessing or hope is pie in the sky." ("El-Shaddai" is Jehovah, Genesis 17:1; 49:25.)

As I stated over and over in my *Supreme Scientist* book, if the Creator of the Bible is not the true Creator, I have no desire whatsoever to even remotely consider wasting my time looking into any other senseless, purposeless and hopeless explanations of this universe and the earth's creatures — whether those causes be the idiotic, unscientific "theory of evolution," extraterrestrials, or any other pagan gods as creators — for such create a life that is so purposeless, hopeless, vain and vexing that I'd rather return to my former life of seeking worldly pleasures and sin (Ecclesiastes 1:1-18; I Corinthians 15:14-19; Hebrews 11:25).

Only the God of Genesis chose to create me and my soul. Only Jehovah God gives me physical life, breath and all things (Acts 17:25). And as we're going to see as we develop this study further, only this God made little "Jerry" a Sovereign Soul in every major aspect of the Christian life and faith. Without God's book, this book could never have been written. And only this God will take Jerry's/Gerald's soul when he dies (Ecclesiastes 12:7).

So this Sovereign Soul, like Joshua, made that sovereign choice for himself — without any coercion, complaints or conditions — and has no regrets ... but a lot of reverence and rejoicing. Makes me want to sing Elvis' personally enhanced version of "How Great Thou Art" (sang during his last concert in 1977). Here it is:

"Oh Lord my God. When I in awesome wonder consider all the big worlds thy hands have made. I see the stars, and I hear the rolling thunder, thy power throughout the universe displayed.

When Christ shall come with shout of acclamation And take me home, what joy shall fill my heart.

Then I shall bow, in humble adoration, and there proclaim, Oh my God! how great Thou art. Yeah, then sings my soul, my soul, my Savior God to thee, Oh how great I think you are, O Lord, how great thou art.

Yeah, then sings my soul, my soul, my Savior my God to thee, Oh How great thou art ... How great! ... How great!! ... How great!!! ... Thou Art!

Jack Gray & Asa Keele at Church of Christ Gospel Meeting

CHAPTER TWO
Sovereign Souls Choose Christ's Covenant

CHRIST'S CHOICE

People can deny the standard Bible of sixty six books, including both the Old and New Testaments, is the word of God all they want. They can debate the Bible is the Word of God all they want. But they can't deny or debate the fact that the Bible records that "God" (or the Godhead) claimed to be the speaker (in the first person) and author throughout the entire Bible. They can't deny this entire Bible has proved to be the inspired and infallible word of God for 3500 years (O.T.) and 2000 years (N.T.). They can't win a debate against a single scientific, medical, historical or religious fact recorded in the Bible. They can't deny that the Bible has been/still is the most widely used, quoted and Best Selling Book of all time. Therefore, the Bible is the World's Choice. No one can deny that our Bible was/is God's only inspired Choice of Scientific, Historical and Religious Truth. Notice that Peter agreed:

> *knowing this first, that no **prophecy of scripture** {Old and New Testaments} is of private interpretation. For no prophecy ever came by the will of man: but **men spake from God**, being moved by the **Holy Spirit*** (II Peter 1:20-21).

The Old Covenant

The Old Covenant/Testament contains all the history of God and mankind that we need to know from the Creation till Christ. I say this for three reasons: **First,** because the Old Testament tells us: Who our Creator-God is; Who we are; What God requires of us; What sin is; Why we need a Savior; How God promised, provided and prophesied our Savior. **Second,** because the Old Testament is the only inspired, infallible and proven historical record that God chose to give us to reveal all of the things listed above. **Third,** because there are no other books from which to choose. There's not one book that claims what it claims, reveals what it reveals, or compares with its proven accuracy and infallibility.

The Old Testament was man's *"tutor"* to get him to see his need for Christ and verify Christ's fulfillment of all the Old Testament's sin requirements and Messianic prophesies (Galatians 3:23-25; Luke 24:44). The Old Testament is Christ Concealed; the New Testament is Christ Revealed. The Old Testament was God speaking through men; the New Testament was God speaking through His Son (Hebrews 1:1-2). The Old Testament was to last until Christ, and then be replaced by Christ's New Testament (Jeremiah 31:31-34; Hebrews 8:6-13). Though the Old Testament is still to be used for our *"learning"* about all of the above revelations, it is not to be used as our religious law or authority (Romans 15:4; Matthew 28:18ff; II Corinthians 3:6-16; Galatians 5:3f; See my *Sabbatarian Concordance and Commentary* for a comprehensive study on the Two Covenants).

Before we move on to the New Testament, let's look at a few scriptural validations of Christ being the central focus of the Old Testament.

> *Ye searched the **scriptures** {OT}, because ye think that in them ye have eternal life; and these are **they which bear witness of me** ... For if ye believed **Moses**, ye would believe me; for **he wrote of me** (John 5:39, 46).*

> *Concerning which salvation the **prophets** sought and searched diligently, who **prophesied** of the grace that should come unto you: searching what time or manner of time the **Spirit of Christ** which was in them did point unto, when it testified beforehand the **sufferings of Christ**, and the glories that should follow them (I Peter 1:10-11).*

The New Testament

No one can successfully deny (though the RCC tries!) that the New Testament we have in our possession today contains the complete infallible truth that Christ promised, plenarily inspired, fully delivered/powerfully confirmed by the Apostles and providentially preserved through the ages. Thus Christ's New Testament is Christ's Only Covenant Choice for us. Hear Ye Him!

> *But the Comforter, even the **Holy Spirit**, whom the **Father** will send in **my name** {Jesus Christ}, he shall **teach you all things**, and bring to your remembrance all that I said unto you ... he shall **guide you into all the truth*** (John 14:26; 16:13).

> ***Every scripture inspired of God** {is inspired of God} is also **profitable** for teaching, for reproof, for correction, for instruction which is in righteousness: that the **man of God may be complete, furnished completely** unto every good work* (II Timothy 3:16-17).

In a nutshell, what we have in Christ's New Testament is the only authoritative, inspired, infallible, complete, all-sufficient and final revelation of God to man. Since the New Testament is all of this and more, there is absolutely no need or allowance for any later revelations, revisions, additions, subtractions, modifications, clarifications or amendments (cf., Revelation 22:18f). Therefore, all the other later Apocryphal Books, Gospels, Papal Revelations (Bulls, Dogmas, Encyclicals, Creeds, Catechisms, Comic Books), Covenants and "Bibles" (Book of Mormon, New World Bible, Koran, etc.), et al., are to be summarily dismissed and rejected as being conspired by men and not inspired by God. The RCC is not the depository or dispenser of God's Truth! Christ is!

Here are some of the essential truths that this Sovereign Soul would never have learned about the Creator, Creation, Jesus Christ, His Church, his Conquering Love, Heaven, etc., without God's Word as found in both the Old and New Testaments.

Without God's Word — I would not know my Creator's names, Triune Being or anything about the Who, What, When, Where, Why and How of His Creation. Yet now because of the Bible, and only the Bible, I have firsthand, **eyewitness** knowledge from the Creator about all these things. Consequently, I know more about my Creator and his Creation than I could have ever learned if I had sought these truths from all the secular scientific books ever written put together. Which books, by the way, were written by authors and "scientists" who were NOT THERE when any of the Creation occurred. I recently wrote a book, *The Supreme Scientist*, so I could personally honor my Creator and push his infallible scientific and historical Bible amongst his creation.

Without God's Word — I would not know He created me in his image with an everlasting soul, much less to be a "Sovereign Soul," as we just discussed in Chapter One. (And there are cultic perversions of the Bible, like the JW Bible, that seek to steal away man's soul by denying he ever had one!)

Without God's Word — I would not know about his Messianic plans for all sinners or angelic assistance for his saints (Hebrews 1:1f, 14).

Without God's Word — I would not know about Christ's virgin birth, miracle-ministry, vicarious death and victorious resurrection and ascension. (Apart from Jesus' New Testament, there's not a thimble-full of historical information about Christ's earthly life; and even that small amount was not inspired of God.)

Without God's Word — I would not know about his church or his authoritative teachings and simple pattern for continuing his church today (Matthew 16:18ff; 28:18-20). I would not know that those who do not build according to his word labor in vain (Psalms 127:1).

Without God's Word — I would not know about the heavenly rewards he has promised for my saved soul when I die, or for a glorious immortal body like Jesus' at the resurrection at the end of time (John 14:1f; I Corinthians 15:35-58; I John 3:2).

Without God's Word — I would not know about Christ's great *Love* for me ... yes ME! It has been said that the Bible is God's love letter to the world. A dearly departed Christian brother and friend of mine, Jack Exum — who was a lover of lost souls, preacher, missionary, author, and, yes, fierce golf competitor — included a great story in one of his many books on Soul Winning that illustrates this very point so poignantly and beautifully. So, in Jack's memory, and to illustrate Christ's great love story to us all in His word, I want to include some of that story for you now.

"WHOEVER FINDS THIS — I LOVE YOU"

THE STORY is told of an orphan child who had lived in some thirteen orphanages, throwing most of them into a state of confusion and leaving in his wake, harried housemothers and befuddled officials. They had tried every form of discipline. All had failed, so one by one they just passed him on to the next place with the hope that someone could reach him. After all, he was only eight years old. Some whipped him, others locked him in his room, while still others deprived him of all special privileges. No one seemed able to control him, much less impress him with better attitudes or improve him with better habits.

A special meeting was called to decide what was to be done with the boy. To the astonishment of the officials, they looked out the window and watched him reach through the fence and tack an envelope to a tree that bordered the road. 'Now is our chance to get him,' one said, 'for it is absolutely forbidden to communicate with the outside without an official censor.'

'He has broken the rule and all of us are witnesses to it,' another said gleefully. They rushed outside, surrounded him and one reached across the fence and snatched the envelope from its perch. 'Now we shall see what you are up to,' he said as he carelessly ripped open the letter. Suddenly his face turned pale. The note was then passed from one to the other until every head hung in genuine remorse and frightful shame. What did the note say? Why is it now framed in gold, hanging proudly inside the main entrance of this orphans home? Seven simple words scratched with crayon in bold red letters, WHOEVER FINDS THIS NOTE ... I LOVE YOU" (Jack Exum, How To Win Souls Today, pp. 132-134, 1970).

Isn't this what God did in giving us His Word? Didn't He, in effect, say — "Whoever finds My Bible love letters (John 3:16; 15:13; I John 4:10, 19), I love you?" And isn't "Whoever finds this cross, I love you" the real meaning of Christ's Cross? It was/is to me! How else can we interpret: **"For God so loved the world, that he gave {on the cross} his Only Begotten Son..."?**

Before moving beyond our discussion of God's love for us to our love for him, I want to make a point about what I had deduced from the scriptures long before I learned that it had already been specifically stated by "Saint" Augustine over 1500 years ago: **"That God loves each of us as if there were only one of us to love."** Indeed, the message of all the scriptures taken together is how God loves each person in the world as if there was only one to love. And sometimes when it seemed as if there was only one person in a given location that loved God — whether it was Job or

Elijah, the Samaritan lady at the well or the widow with the mite, Lazarus or the lady taken in adultery, or me or you — not only was the Omnipresent God there with each one of them, so is his LOVE available for all those who will accept his written invitation to love him in return (I John 4:10, 19). Another Exum saying was: *"I'm not lovable, I'm just loved!"* To which I must say: "Jack, you, your wife and family were loved by me and my family as if you all were our family! As they say in Hawaii, 'A hui hou' ... "till we meet again" ... with our Lord."

"Jack & Ann Exum"
(Circa 1970's)

So, dear reader, may I humbly suggest that from now on you might apply all the "God so loved the world" verses in the Bible to yourself personally by saying out loud: "For **God so loved me**, that he gave his only begotten son, that whosoever {includes "me"} believeth on him should not perish, but have eternal life." I know that I can apply Romans 5:8 to me when it says: "But **God commendeth his own love towards me**, in that, while **I was yet a sinner**, Christ died for **me!**" Of course, the **"me"** included in all these passages is not perfect, just forgiven! And was it not Jesus who said that those who are forgiven much loves much (cf. Luke 7:39-50)? And that greater emotional love applies to me — a "nothing" and nobody" amongst the world's chronic sinners — and His love constrains me to reciprocate his love by doing exactly what he requests and commands in his Word: to love him and keep his commandments and word just as he said, not just because he commanded me to do so, but because <u>His love</u> for me and <u>my love</u> for Him demand that I do so.

> ***If ye love me, ye will keep my commandments ... If a man loves me, he will keep my word:*** *and my Father will love him, and we will come unto him, and make our abode with him* (John 14:15, 23; II Corinthians 5:14).

SO, there you have **Christ's Choice of Covenants** as being *"my commands ... my word"* chosen for you and me right out of the Master's mouth. Soon after Jesus spoke these words about his commands and words, his New Testament was ratified via his death (Hebrews 9:15-17). Then, forty days after his resurrection and just before He ascended to his throne in heaven, He commissioned his Apostles to go into all the world and preach his New Testament Gospel and teachings to every nation and creature in the world. His "Great Commission" remains for us till this day:

> *But **ye** {Apostles} shall receive power, when the Holy Spirit is come upon you: and ye shall be **my witnesses** both in Jerusalem, and in all Judaea and Samaria, and unto the **uttermost part of the earth** ...* (Acts 1:8). *And Jesus came to them and spake unto them saying, **All authority** hath been given unto me **in heaven and on earth**. Go ye therefore, and **make disciples of all the nations**, baptizing them into the name of the Father and of the Son and of the Holy Spirit: **teaching them to observe all things whatsoever I commanded you**: and lo, I am with you always, even unto the **end of the world*** (Matthew 28:18-20; cf., Mark 16:15).... *And when he had said these things, as they were looking, he was **taken up; and a cloud received him out of their sight*** (Acts 1:9).

So we must conclude from Jesus' very own words while on earth, and from all the confirmations of the same thing from all of his Apostles, that Christ's gave us **all the truth** — infallibly written and miraculously confirmed by His Holy Spirit — we'll ever need to fulfill all of God's purposes for us. Which are: **(1)** To know God and His love for us, and to be known by Him and love Him in return (I Corinthians 8:2f; Galatians 4:9; I John 4:19. **(2)** To glorify God (I Corinthians 10:31). **(3)** To love our neighbors as ourselves. **(4)** To live eternally with God (John 20:31). We need no more than this! And all of this means we must be obedient to His New Testament law, which also means we must not advocate nor teach any other law for our neighbors to obey, if we are to respect Christ's loving Supremacy and Sovereignty and thereby allow Him to be *"the author and perfecter of our faith"* (Hebrews 12:2).

Thus, in keeping with that obedient faithfulness to Christ's word, I will not be adding any new laws from Christ, or facts about Christ, in this book. There will be no clarifications of His Word. How much clearer could Christ have made any of his laws: like his law on our physical marriage to the opposite sex he made for us; or our spiritual marriage to Him in the church he built for us (Matthew 16:18; 19:4-6; Ephesians 5:22-33)? The Lord did not give us any new laws or essential acts of obedience and worship in parables, puzzles or symbolic/figurative/apocalyptic words that are hard to understand. He used simple and common language (originally in Koine' Greek) and made his requirements plain. Some have difficulty understanding them because they don't agree with them. Others say they have difficulty understanding them because they quickly understood they didn't want to keep them!

There will also be no scriptural revisions, divisions, deletions, or personal interpretations based upon any personal claim on my part as to possessing any miraculous gifts or unique gifts of discernment, knowledge or interpretation. Just simple reading of the texts in context as they pertain to my chosen topical subject, original language definitions, and letting Christ's words speak for themselves (Ephesians 3:3-5). The scriptures and the original language lexicons are the tools of a preacher's trade. With these functional matters stated, let's get back to Jesus' words, including his smallest words, about His Word in John 14:15, 23.

Please notice that all of the loving words and reciprocating promises of Christ and God in the aforementioned "love/keep" texts in John 14:15, 23 were conditioned upon one of the smallest, yet strongest, words in the Bible, the ***If*** word: *"If ye love me, ye* *will keep my commandments... **If a man love me, he will keep my word.***" And, with Christ's love, grace and forgiveness ever before and behind us, they are not burdensome to keep (I John 5:3).

IF we are to be His loving "Sovereign Souls," we cannot do so by adding Moses' law and the Old Testament laws to Christ's New Testament. We are under *"the law of Christ"* and not the law of Moses or the Old Testament (see I Corinthians 9:20-21; II Corinthians 3:6-18; Hebrews 8:6-13; See my book, *Sabbatarian Concordance and Commentary*).

IF we are to love, honor, respect and obey Christ's commands and words as our sovereign authority, we may not accept, obey or teach any of the later unauthorized apocryphal "gospels" or church councils, creeds, catechisms, decrees, dogmas and doctrines. Nor are we authorized to accept any later so-called "holy" books or bibles like the Koran, Book of Mormon, et al., which have been delivered by alleged prophets and angels (cf. Galatians 1:8). They all not only contradict each other and the entire Bible, they also seek to contest and nullify Christ's claim that he would reveal *"ALL TRUTH"* in his last will and Testament right after his death. Besides the fact that none of these alleged prophets possessed any miraculous credentials like Jesus and his Apostles, they died and stayed dead, and didn't shed their blood for my sins or to ratify their new bibles (Hebrews 9:15-17)? They have nothing to offer!

Actually, those self-proclaimed prophets and inspired preachers who have claimed to speak for Jesus in the past, as well as today, failed to respect the fact that Jesus has already spoken for himself in person and through the twenty-seven books of his New Testament (Hebrews 1:2; 2:3f). Those who say they need to <u>clarify</u> what Jesus said are implying that Jesus didn't make things plain when he spoke and wrote about himself and his commands. They are doing the same thing the unbelieving Jewish leaders did when He was amongst them, who said: **"If thou art the Christ, tell us plainly."** To whom Jesus replied: **"I told you, and ye believe not"** (John 10:24)! The problem is not that Jesus didn't speak clearly when he was upon the earth, or didn't have his words written plainly in his New Testament after he left the earth, the problem is that many do not hear or read well, or believe what they read, or "feel" comfortable with it as it reads. Such is the case with all of the religious renegades who have sought to rewrite, revise, reverse and rule over Christ's Scriptures. They are the authors of the confusion they cause amongst their followers (I Cor. 14:33).

Those who say Jesus didn't speak for all ages to come, and his message needs updating, contradict his words — *"until the end of the world"* — in his Great Commission. And their <u>new updates</u> are nothing more than attempts by wolves to slip in the back door of Christ's flock/church and open <u>new doors</u> and <u>ways</u> — other than Christ the only door and way (John 10:7; 14:6) — for every type of sinner (practicing sodomites, polygamists, drunks, drug users and abortionists) and major religions to enter into their "Big Tent," Syncretistic, Polytheistic, Pantheistic and Paganistic version of Ecumenical Christianity. They are wolves in sheep's clothing!

To say we need human authority and/or modern miracles (especially their false "miracles") to confirm or reinforce Christ's Word today is to usurp Christ's divine and complete authority and undermine the Holy Spirit's complete work of delivering and miraculously confirming Christ's New Testament via the Apostles in the first century (John 20:30f; Hebrews 2:1-4; Jude 3).

On and on we could go with all the cultic and denominational leaders, creeds, manuals and doctrines that seek to share in, or usurp, Christ's total authority over us, or subtract or add to his word. We are sovereign only as long as we remain loyal to Christ's law and authority. We bow to no man, kiss no rings, call none our "Holy Father," and sit at the feet of no higher authority on earth today. If Christ's Authority is not ALL of our authority, it is none of our authority. Our Love for Christ is reflected in our lovingly keeping and repeating his word, laws and teachings as he gave them to us in his inspired New Testament.

So I am now going to show you some of the wonderful things that making that Choice accomplished in my life.

<u>I CHOSE CHRIST'S COVENANT</u>

I believe one of the best ways I can present all the ways that choosing to follow Christ's Covenant has blessed my life is by turning the word ***LOVE*** in John 14:15 into an Acronym. Thereby we'll see all the powerful "Sovereign Soul" attributes — <u>L</u>iberation, <u>O</u>bligation, <u>V</u>indication, <u>E</u>levation — our love for Christ's word will activate and accentuate in our lives.

L — Choosing Christ's Covenant is — **Liberating!**
O — Choosing Christ's Covenant is — **Obligating!**
V — Choosing Christ's Covenant is — **Vindicating!**
E — Choosing Christ's Covenant is — **Elevating/Eternal!**

-L-
Choosing Christ's Covenant is Liberating

Learning the truth that Christ gave me the unalienable right to choose his New Covenant/Testament truth as my sovereign authority and guide in all religious and moral matters was very liberating to me. Jesus did say to those Jews who believed in him: *"If ye shall abide in my word, then are ye truly my disciples: and* **ye shall know the truth, and the truth shall set you free** *... If therefore the Son shall make you free, ye shall be* **free indeed"** (John 8:31f, 36). And, indeed, I am free. In every way, I am free Indeed!

First, choosing Christ's Covenant was/is Self-Liberating ... meaning it freed me from myself! Though I was a rebel-rousing sinner who didn't want to listen to any mortal religious authority on that fateful night in 1963, when I was challenged by George Spurgin to check out Christ's rightful claim to having authority over me and my life, I didn't rebel or react to such as many others do by refusing to read what Jesus had to say about these matters. Rather, I read Jesus' inspired words in the Book of Acts that same night and accepted His authority over my life the next night! (As did my most sovereign wife!)

Personally, I was relieved that I had come to know on my own (by reading) that Jesus deserved my full attention, respect, devotion, service and, most of all, my love. So Jesus immediately became my only Master and Mentor in all aspects of life: religious, moral, social, and political. So it was not some subjective experience or mystical vision of Christ on that night that told me I was saved. It was the objective experience of obtaining knowledge of His Word, especially of Acts Two, that led me to do what Jesus said I had to do to be saved. It was as simple for me to do that as it was for the 3,000 who did it on the Day of Pentecost.

So no one but Jesus, via his word, had liberated me from myself that night. His word completely freed me from being my own source of truth about how I could live a better life than I was living, or if I should even try, or if there even was a better life than I was living. (I was having a good time and had more worldly friends then than ever since!) It freed me from my own fallibility, foibles, falsehoods, stubbornness, pride and perilous dependence upon my own ideas and instincts as to what was right and wrong. (I soon learned from Bible verses, like Jeremiah 10:23, that this was an impossible feat for any person to accomplish on his own.) I was freed from doing the same stupid destructive things over and over and expecting different results. (Einstein's alleged definition of "insanity.")

Best of all, Jesus' word freed me from my own religious ignorance about crucial and essential spiritual matters in my life: like my ignorance about all the moral sins and bad habits I needed to put away; and all the good things I needed to add to my life— including attending the Church of Christ's Choice, which I now knew had to be found in the New Testament Directory and not just in the Phone Book!

Before my Golf Trip I doubt if I would have remotely considered going way across the Island of Bermuda to attend the Brighton Hill Church of Christ ... that George wasn't attending at that time! And it goes without saying that I wouldn't have just up and decided I should return to the Methodist Church — which was listed in the phone book in Bermuda, which was the church where I was christened as a baby and was a member as a child? Which church I left when I was a young teenager. Nor would I have attended any of the other Protestant churches in Bermuda that I had also attended as a child with my relatives and going to VBS: including the Baptist Church and a Pentecostal Church, where I saw Oral Roberts supposedly heal Uncle Marvin, who died soon afterwards (See my *Now That's A Miracle* book)! And there's no way I would have ever considered going to the Roman Catholic Church which was located on the Kindley Air Force Base and spread throughout Bermuda. First, because I had never attended a RCC in my entire life. Second, none of my family or kin folk were Catholics. Third, my dad was anti-Catholic. Fourth, unlike now, I knew nothing about Catholicism or Catholics before that time.

Until, that is, George Spurgin sent me on the aforementioned "Golf Trip" to California. That Trip was, as they say, "A Real Game Changer!," in more ways than I could have imagined at that time.

For, ironically, one of the three golfers going with me on the Kindley AFB golf team to California was the Kindley Base Catholic Chaplin, "Father Mead." He looked and talked fast like Jan Murray from the "Dollar A Second" TV Game show circa 1950's. What intrigued me about the RCC, as was demonstrated by "Father" Mead during the trip, was how he was such a "fun guy." First he got more attention from the two female WAFs on the plane trip to California than the other worldly guys. Then he partied and drank like the rest of the golfers there ... and could, evidently, forgive himself in the morning! Now this was a "permissive" (now called "progressive") church worth considering for the old Jerry Neil III, who wouldn't have to change much of his sinful life to be actively involved. I mean the man was a "Priest!" (Actually, I had quit drinking booze a year before at Tech School in Texas, because I had experienced a lengthy drunken blackout after celebrating the news that my wife would be joining me in a week!)

Oh well, as it turned out, I didn't accept any church that wasn't specifically identified in Christ's New Testament — which included all the above late-arriving, biblically unmentioned and askew "churches" — because I had been added by Christ to his New Testament church that October night (19th) in 1963 (Acts 2:38-47; see Chapter Four, "Choosing Christ's Church"). I did, however, try to teach "Father" Mead about Christ and his New Testament Church at every opportunity I had throughout my last year in Bermuda. I did not succeed. Sigh.

<u>Seminal and Saving Point</u>: I still stand by my Choice of Christ's Covenant as my only Source and Authority of religious truth, and I will be forever grateful that His Choice to love ignorant sinners like me blessed me (as it will all others) to become the freedom-loving Sovereign Soul that only He and His Word can create.

Second, choosing Christ's authorized Covenant liberated me from all other earthly "authorities." When Jesus said he had ***"all authority in heaven and earth"*** as per our "unalienable God-given, Bible-Based Rights," that didn't leave any authority whatsoever — none, zero, zilch, nada — for anyone else. Thus there are no areas in life — including religion, morals, family, civil laws, etc. — over which the Lord doesn't exercise complete Lordship and authority. Therefore there is no person in any place or position that is above our Divine King of Kings, Lord and Governor when it comes to what we should/must say and do in our submission to him as Sovereign Souls. Whatever issue Christ has taken a "stand" on in Scripture, we must stand with him, always remembering "we're not the ones taking a stand...He Has and Is!"

For example, speaking of civil laws, though God told us to keep the laws and ordinances of the lands and governments wherein we dwell, you will notice that even those are under His divine oversight, and they must comport with his revelation about punishing *"evil doers"* and praising those who *"do well"* for society and His spiritual kingdom. Here are a few more texts that confirm this sovereign principle of God and each one of us.

> *Let **every soul** be in subjection to the **higher powers**: **for there is no power but of God;** and the powers that be are ordained of God. Therefore he that resisteth the power, withstandeth the power of God: and they that withstand shall receive to themselves judgment. For **rulers are not a terror to the good work, but to the evil**. And wouldest thou have no fear of the power? do that which is good, and thou shalt have praise from the same: for he {or "it" in mgn} is a **minister of God to thee for good**. But if thou do that which is evil, be afraid; for he beareth not the sword in vain: for he is a minister of God, an **avenger for wrath to him that doeth evil**. Wherefore **ye must needs be in subjection**, not only because of the wrath, but also for conscience' sake* (Romans 13:1-5).

> *I exhort therefore, first of all, that supplications, **prayers**, intercessions, thanksgivings, be made for all men; for **kings and all that are in high place**; that we may lead a tranquil and quiet life in **all godliness** and gravity. **This is good and acceptable in the sight of God our Saviour; who would have all men to be saved**, and come to the **knowledge of the truth**. For there is one God, **one mediator** also between God and men, himself man, **Christ Jesus*** (I Timothy 2:1-5).

And they {the religious rulers} *called them* {the Apostles}, *and* **charged them** **not to speak** *at all nor teach in the* **name of Jesus**. *But Peter and John answered and said unto them,* **Whether it is right in the sight of God** *to hearken unto* **you** *rather than unto* **God***, judge ye: for* **we cannot but speak the things which we saw and heard** (Acts 4:18-20).

After this "high and holier-than-thou" Sanhedrin injunction against the Apostles' preaching Christ, they did what was *"right in the sight of God"* and did the following: they went out and **preached** openly and with boldness (vv. 23-31); then they were **arrested again** and miraculously **released** by an angel of God who told them to go preach again (5:17-25); then they were **arrested again** and brought before the **religious council again** (5:26-27); and then the High Priest said this:

We strictly charged you *not to preach in this* **name** *{or authority}: and behold, you have filled Jerusalem with your teaching, and intend to bring this man's blood upon us.* {Which blood the Jews had earlier invited to be upon their heads, Matthew 27:25.} *But Peter and the apostles answered and said,* **We must obey God rather than men** (Acts 5:28f).

Putting all of these divine prohibitions and proscriptions together: **(1)** We conclude that our submission to our **religious or political leaders** is contingent upon their being in compliance with God's clear religious, moral, social, civil laws and commands. **(2)** We conclude that if any **civil law** conflicts with God's Word, it is not to be obeyed by mankind or Christians. **(3)** We also conclude that we must not obey any **religious law** that is contrary to God's word, regardless of whether it is being imposed by the "Church" or "State," or both together. To put it simply, our Christian walk and talk is based upon Christ's written authority. To support this scripturally, we may simply quote the following:

And **whatsoever** *you do, in* **word or deed***, do all in the* **name of the Lord Jesus***, giving thanks to God the Father through him* (Colossians 3:17).

To do something in Christ's **"name"** does not mean we are to simply say "in the name of Christ" every time we say or do something, like we often do at the close of a prayer. It means we must be able to show how all things we say and do were approved by him in his word, or have his authoritative signature.

Now this supreme authority of Christ's word will not be fully appreciated, respected or exalted by us if our allegiance to Him and His word is subject to being overruled by any other religious authority. We cannot fully surrender to Christ's will and authority if we willfully subject his Word to modification and nullification by any other person's religious opinion, regardless of his/her church's claims about his/her new visions, revelations, high religious office, authority or sainthood. Christ is our life, not any church-appointed surrogate or substitute (Colossians 3:4). As Christian citizens in Christ's kingdom, we are not under Kings; we are under the *"King of Kings."* We are not under earthly High Priests; we are under our only Heavenly High Priest. We don't bow to Saints; we bow to the Saint Maker. We don't bow to human creatures because they were all created equal with us. We must refuse to allow anyone to rob Christ of any glory, period!

Applying this Universally: Because of this manifest natural reality, most free rational human beings can easily understand and embrace the natural concept that all men were created equal, remain equal regardless of their material achievements, and thus stand as equal creatures before God and mankind. And as long as we humans maintain this individual dignity/sovereignty under God, and we don't surrender it to those who don't respect our God-given rights to live free from human tyranny and subjugation — be it political or religious, by Big Government or Big Religion — then, and only then, will Christ's Gospel of Peace and New Testament Truth produce the free and great churches, communities and countries that He intended it to create. He is not willing that any person should remain in the prisons of sin and perish (I Timothy 2:4; II Peter 3:9).

Applying this to Me: Now having said all of this, I cannot for the life of me commence to begin to understand why, in spite of this natural reality, that so many millions of equal human beings have accepted the narcissistic concept that some individual human beings are so superior to other equal human beings that they deserve to revered and served as if he/she was some sort of deity. Nor do I understand why any so-called "Christian" could ever so exalt himself above his fellow Christians and neighbors. I didn't understand this before I became a New Testament Christian, and I especially find such elitist and power-grabbing behavior repulsive since I became a Christian.

I have been a Bible teacher, Gospel preacher and author for most of my 72 years of life. Yet, I have never ever thought of myself as being anything more than an average man, Bible student (not a "Scholar") and simple "Christian" like every other true believer. I've never claimed to be a member of the "Clergy" or a superior saint or higher priest than any other Christian. (But I do claim to be an equal saint and priest with any other person on earth.) So pardon me if I don't accept, acquiesce, genuflect or put my body into awkward prostrate positions in the presence of such self-appointed Pompous Priests of Piety—regardless of their public popularity and millions of sheeple in their flocks! I don't claim to understand why so many people are so easily swayed to trade their God-given equality and individual sovereignty for mass subjugation to a few hundred pounds of human flesh (cf., II Corinthians 5:16). Yet I pray for their freedom and write this "2015 Thesis" for you to tack on their church doors!

When I personally encounter any person who seeks to "pull rank" on me due to his/her religious status or odd dress and accoutrement, I first take stock of myself as a Christian, set aside my own ego, and try to find out why this person has inflated his/her own ego to such a "holier-than-thou" status. Why have so many of the so-called "Christian Clergy" elevated themselves by fully utilizing their unscriptural elevating creeds, titles, robes, hats, backward collars, high chairs, bubblecars/popemobiles, etc., and, all the while, joyously accepting the power, pomp and praise all this bluster and bling brings to them? Why have they allowed themselves to become such objects of attention and devotion amongst, or should I say "above," their fellow church members?

And more importantly, why have they **totally** ignored Jesus' clear proscriptions against wearing elevating titles in Matthew 23:8-12? If Jesus commanded us not to wear or use ***"Rabbi, Father"*** as elevating religious titles, why do we find about every religious leader in most "churches" being identified, introduced and elevated by such titles? I mean, we not only find elderly people calling really young priests "Father," we also find them calling lowly human beings "Reverend"—a name used but once in scripture about God (Psalms 111:9). And, if that were not blasphemous enough, we find over a billion Catholics and even non-Christians calling one man in a robe, "The Most Holy Father!" For crying out loud, do Jesus' words mean anything to these people? **Who** do these Popes think they are? Better, yet **what** do they think they are? Jesus told his disciples they could simply call upon God the Father as *"our Father who art in heaven,"* and not "Our Most Holy Father." So these Pompous Popes invite people to constantly address/elevate them as being above God the Father!

Or even more to the point, **why** do they think they are so superior to others that they qualified for such lofty positions as an Apostle or Vicar of Christ in the first place? Since none of them were virgin born, worked miracles or possessed Jesus' heavenly words, what great thing did they do that any of their followers couldn't do? The Apostles didn't allow such personal elevations and divine devotion, and they could work miracles (Acts 10:25f; 14:15-18.) So why do our modern religious leaders do so, even if they do possess delusions of grandeur and claim to be "Apostles" just like the Twelve Apostles? What caused them to exalt themselves to such lofty positions? Did they just wake up one day and imagine that by some strange quirk of fate — by inheritance, location, luck, lotto, hook or crook — they're now the entire world's "Reincarnate Apostles, Representatives of Christ, Holy Fathers, Archbishops, and Popes?" Frankly, I know how Elvis became the "King of Rock and Roll" — he possessed great singing talent, sold a billion records, and proved that "50,000,000 ELVIS FANS CAN'T BE WRONG!" (*Elvis Gold Records, Volume-2*) — but for the life of me I don't know how a single one of those who have occupied the throne in the Vatican got there! WHAT DID THEY DO? What can they do that you and I can't do? NOTHING!

Please consider a little comparative analogy. Though I know Christ's New Testament only allows "Bishops/Elders/Shepherds" (all same office) to be over the local church, and that it nowhere hints there can be a Bishop or Pope over Christ's Universal church/flock, I can say without boasting that I am more qualified to be such than any Pope who's ever assumed such a lofty position because: **(1)** I know and accept the Lord's New Testament truth about "Bishops." **(2)** I qualify to be an "elder/bishop" in the Lord's church because I am a believer, married to one wife and have believing children (See leadership instructions in Chapter Four). **(3)** RCC "Bishops" don't scripturally qualify to be "bishops" in the Lord's local churches because they're not true believers, not married and don't have believing children. This is not what I say about them; this is what they say, and what the Lord's Word reveals about them and what they say.

A personal historical anecdote from this Sovereign Soul's memory might help illustrate this point. The first political one was shared with me by my old Bermuda friend, George Spurgin. After George left Bermuda and got out of the Air Force, he became a police officer in Dallas, Texas. Even there He was the best and most supportive friend my family and I have ever had to this day. He told me of an incident which occurred when he stopped an elected official for speeding. When he started to write the traffic ticket, the driver sought to stop him by saying: *"Do you know who I am?"* George then asked the guy to walk around his squad car. When he returned, George said: *"Just as I suspected, both of your feet remained on the ground, so you're going to get a ticket!"* In other words, the guy was just another guy like George, and unlike Jesus who could walk on water or glide through the air!

So no other human or angelic creature has a higher authority vested in his person or position than this "Sovereign Soul" possesses in the little New Testament he carries around in his shirt pocket. And, consequentially, no alleged higher authority has the right to ask me to violate my fidelity to Christ and his word (cf., Galatians 1:8). He's my Rabbi. He's my Lord and Master. I cannot serve two religious Teachers or Masters at once (Matthew 6:24). So it doesn't matter how large a religious or political position or organization a person in the Church or State touts, he/she has no authority in these matters where Christ's scriptural demands and directives exist. It doesn't matter how long their robes are — whether in the U.S. Supreme Court or RCC Councils — or how high their chairs are, they have no superior authority over me or you in the Highest & Holiest Court where we individual Christians must adjudicate before we act.

So, with this Supreme Bible Standard and Legal Standing ever before me, I couldn't care less what U. S. Supreme Court Jurors or

Presbyterian Bishops have to say about my refusal to accept "Gay Marriage." Jesus' Divine Decision in Matthew 19:3-9, Romans 1:26-32 and I Corinthians 6:9-11 trumps them all (see Introduction in my *Homosexuality And The Bible* book). Like David, who walked after God's heart, **"I esteem all thy precepts concerning all things to be right; And I hate every false way"** (Psalms 119:128). (Can we say anything bad about false ways, religions or churches, nowadays?) Therefore, I don't respect false teachings or teachers, and I won't stop preaching and writing against individuals in any culture, sect, cult or church, including in Christ's true church, who blatantly overstep their limited authority and seek to censure others from speaking Christ's whole truth to the whole world—so help me, God!

Applying this to You: Now let's apply some of the ways that Choosing Christ's Covenant will Liberate You.

It will free you from seeking the truth about any essential spiritual or physical issue — any salvation requirement, worship act, sexual act, family arrangement, social/cultural practice, acceptable foods and meats, gender benders, on and on — from any other religious or philosophical source. All you have to do is open Jesus' New Testament Handbook on living the good and acceptable physical/spiritual life before God, and then eat all meats, love your mate and family and enjoy all the good things He has legalized in His word and His world (cf. Mark 7:19; I Timothy 4:1-4). Since Jesus' word does not prohibit us from doing one good thing, can you imagine the regret that must be created in the lives of those who find out late in their cultic lives that they didn't have to forego marriage, having a family and eating all foods in order to be priests, saints and healthy happy Christians?

It will free you from bowing and bending to any human authority on earth or creature in heaven — regardless of whether that individual or entity claims to be equal to God, Christ's Vicar, inspired, infallible, angel or elder — when it comes to religious and moral matters that pertain to your obedience to God's word. Always kindly ask those who would seek to overrule your Bible beliefs on the basis of their religious or political <u>status</u> to present you with "Book, Chapter and Verse" in context in Christ's New Testament ... or to re-read His word and repent and obey it ... and be free like you.

It will free you from seeking any authority or approval of your beliefs and teachings on these issues upon which Christ has already ruled. He's not only my and your lawgiver and judge, He's also the world's lawgiver and judge (John 5:22, 27; 12:48; Romans 2:16).

–O–
Choosing Christ's Covenant is Obligating

*To whomsoever **much is given**, of him shall **much be required**: and to whom they commit much, of him will they ask more* (Luke 12:48b; see also Matthew 25:14-29).

There are many Bible texts like this one quoted and the one referenced, "The Parable of the Talents," that teach us that God expects us to receive His blessings with rejoicing and reciprocity in our hearts and hands. We are obligated to understand that our reception of individual physical or spiritual rewards from God in this life brings with them equal responsibilities to return to God more than just our own aggrandizement. This is especially true when it comes to individuals or nations being blessed with receiving His written truths in His word. Just as it did when God blessed Israel above all nations on the earth.

*He showeth his **word unto Jacob**. His statutes and his ordinances unto Israel. He hath not dealt so with any nation: And as for his ordinances, they have not known them. Praise ye Jehovah* (Psalms 147:19-20).

You only have I known *of all the families of the earth; therefore I will **visit upon you** all your iniquities* (Amos 3:2).

*What **advantage** then hath the **Jew?** or what is the **profit** of circumcision?* ***Much every way: first of all****, that they were* ***intrusted with the oracles of God*** (Romans 3:1-2).

The very fact that we have been blessed and entrusted with *"the oracles of God"* ("sayings/words of God") — as we have when we possess our own personal copy of Christ's New Testament, or even have access to such — is in itself a "pearl of great price" beyond any earthly treasure we could have ever received. It sure deserves more attention than just being a decoration on our coffee tables or dust collector on our library shelves. Just the personal possession of a Bible or New Testament demands our obligation to make better use of it than that.

As an aside, for any nation that has upon its currency, *"In God We Trust,"* to then ban the reading and use of God's only Bible in its public facilities and schools is an egregious insult to its Divine Author! To enthrone Charles Darwin above Jesus Christ is almost enough to make me rethink about there being some application of the very unpatriotic words of Jeremiah Wright: *"God &%#! America!"* Our God deserves more than this from you, America ... and that means from every single person who lives here!

AND THAT INCLUDES ME! And much more so. For I also know that Jesus' love for Me constrains/compels me — Yes, OBLIGATES ME — to love him in return and read and heed his word, even if He had not said I should in John 14:15 (cf., II Corinthians 5:14). I AM OBLIGATED BY LOVE! A favorite hymn of mine, "My Jesus I Love Thee," says this so poignantly I'll print a few verses here so you can sing it if you don't have access to a song book.

> *My Jesus, I love Thee, I know thou art mine, For Thee all the follies of sin I resign; My gracious Redeemer, my Saviour art Thou; If ever I loved Thee, My Jesus, 'tis now.*
>
> *I love Thee, because Thou hast first loved me, And purchased my pardon on Calvary's tree; I love Thee for wearing the thorns on Thy brow; If ever I loved Thee, my Jesus 'tis now* (W.R. Featherston, A.J. Gordon).

Love is a greater incentive than law, legalism or the fear of punishment will ever be when it comes to our stopping doing evil and starting doing good. That's why the **O**bligation that we Christians sustain is from the word *LOVE* and not from the word *"WOE,"* which word was used seven times by our Lord towards the hypocritical legalistic Jews: who had the scriptural talk but not the walk (Matthew 23:2f, 13-33).

We sustain the same loving **obligation** to learn, obey, study and teach what our Lord says is right as we do towards what he says is wrong. Neither side is an option. And as we'll see when we look at "Choosing Christ's Commission," it is our loving **obligation** towards our Lord's command to "love our neighbor as ourselves" and His desire to save all men that causes us to fulfill his Great Commission to share his teachings with all creatures (Matthew 28:18-20; I Timothy 2:4). It is that loving obligation that is behind this old evangelist's writing of this book and all books that I have written— to do the work of an evangelist just as Paul instructed the young evangelist, Timothy:

> ***I charge thee*** *{obligating me and you} in the sight of God, and of **Christ Jesus**, who shall judge the living and the dead, and by his appearing and kingdom:* ***preach the word****; be urgent **in season, out of season***, *reprove, rebuke, exhort, with all longsuffering and teaching. For the **time will come** {and still exists today} when **they will not endure the sound doctrine**; but, having itching ears, will heap to themselves teachers after their own lusts; and will turn away their ears from the truth, and turn aside unto fables. But be thou sober in all things, suffer hardship, do the **work of an evangelist**, fulfil thy ministry* (II Timothy 4:1-5).

There you go: if Timothy was obligated to know, practice and preach the truth regardless if it was the social, religious and political *"season"* or not, then the same goes for you and me. We must learn Christ's truth, live Christ's truth, and urgently enjoin everyone else to do likewise by engaging in the following: *"reprove"* them {convict them of their sins, John 16:8}; *"rebuke"* {censure or admonish} them if they will not do so; and *"exhort* {invite, invoke, implore, beseech) them to obey the *"word."*

We are obligated to convict ignorant or deceived sinners. Regardless if the world's culture, laws or leaders (political or religious) say their sinful behavior is normal, natural or "the right thing to do," we are obligated to convict them of their sins, plead with them to repent and be forgiven by the blood of Christ.

We are obligated to preach to them even if we know they will not listen. We are watchmen in the Lord's world of lost souls and are obligated to at least warn them so that God can say there was a preacher amongst them (Ezekiel 2:5; 3:17-19; 33:7-9). Jeremiah's success at getting sinners in his nation to repent after 23 years of preaching was so abysmal that he wanted to stop preaching and go on vacation to a "motel" (Jeremiah 25:3; 9:1f). But his passion for preaching God's word would not allow him to stop or shut up.

> *And if I say, I **will not make mention of him, nor speak anymore in his name**, then there is in **my heart** as it were a **burning fire** shut up in my bones, and I am weary with forbearing, and **I cannot contain*** (Ibid. 20:9).

Our obligation as preachers and teachers of Christ's word is to be Seed Sowers and not Soil Inspectors, who only want to sow seed on *"good ground"* that produces much lasting fruit, and not waste time sowing seed *"by the wayside ... on rocky ground ... amidst the thorns"* where it will not be productive (Luke 8:4-15). We are to sow the seed and allow God to give the increase (I Corinthians 3:6). If all our work ends up fruitless, we'll still be rewarded for faithfully doing the Lord's evangelistic work (Ibid. 3:14-15).

We are obligated to preach to them even if they hate us for doing so. Jesus was hated and killed for preaching the truth. And He warned us to expect persecution for preaching the same truths he preached (John 3:20; 15:18-19). So hatred for telling the truth is to be expected and disappointing on one hand; but the love you'll receive from those who accept it is much more rewarding (Ibid. 15:20; cf. Galatians 4:16). Let us never fall victim to the "Violence of Silence" when souls call for our help (Obadiah 10f).

We are obligated to defend the word when we see it attacked (Jude 3). We're all to be fearless outspoken biblical apologists! There have always been ignorant and/or arrogant people who for power, popularity or perversion seek to add to, subtract from or pervert the original language of the Apostolic Scriptures in their teachings and translations. And some of the greatest scandals being perpetrated in the name of "Christianity" since Christ are the denominational churches and cults they have created in their names. So we must speak against these Creators of Confusion.

> *But even if ye should suffer for righteousness sake, blessed are ye: and **fear not their fear**, neither be troubled; but sanctify in your hearts Christ as Lord: **being ready always to give answer** {apologia} to every man that asketh you a reason concerning the hope that is in you, yet with meekness and fear* (I Peter 3:14-15).

-V-
Choosing Christ's Covenant is Vindicating

Our Vindicator Speaks

*These things **I** {Jesus Christ} command you {Apostles}, that ye **love one another**. If the **world hateth you**, ye know it hath **hated me** before it hated you. If ye were of the world, the **world would love its own**: but because ye are not of the world, but I chose you out of the world, therefore the **world hateth you**. Remember the word that I said unto you. A servant is not greater than his Lord. If **they persecuted me**, they will also **persecute you;** if they **kept my word**, they will **keep yours also*** (John 15:17-20).

This revelation of Christ not only warns us about the pros and cons, costs and blessings of following him and his teachings, it also reveals our **need for his vindication**. So before I present some of the examples of how Choosing Christ's Covenant has vindicated me and my message from all personal hatred and false accusations, let's look at three things we Sovereign Souls need to do to physically, mentally and spiritually prepare us to survive and thrive through the struggles and successes of the Christian life.

We need to stay Focused upon our Loving Messenger (Hebrews 12:2). Please ever keep in mind that the Messenger speaking in the passage quoted above was the sinless, sweet-hearted and sinner-loving Son of God, as well as being the most honorable, most honest and most helpful human being who has ever walked upon this earth! And also remember that Jesus' Message was all about true agape love for God, the world, "*one another*" and our neighbor (John 3:16).

Yet it was this lovable Messenger who was so **"*hated*"** (*without a cause*) because of his loving Message and not because he was a bad Messenger. He was rejected by his own religious people, nation, priests, worldly friends, as well as by pagan people (the Romans) who didn't know him from Adam. He was **"persecuted"** like an intolerable menace and an enemy of mankind. He was hunted down like a common criminal and betrayed by one of his own disciples and most all of his religious leaders. He was then falsely accused, falsely indicted, falsely tried, falsely convicted and falsely crucified amongst two career criminals (one even railed upon him on the cross!). So always keep your eyes upon the Loving Christ at Calvary while you serve in his spiritual Army. As the old song *Onward Christian Soldiers* says, we are to keep this "Cross of Jesus going on before" us.

We need to stay Biblically Balanced. Please notice how our loving Messianic Messenger linked His positive message of brotherly *"love"* to both the world's negative response of *"hate"* and *"persecution"* and the positive response of those who accepted and *"kept my* {his} *word"* ... and would, therefore, accept and *"keep yours* {their) ... and **ours** *"also."*

The real physical and spiritual world is not all positive in its physical makeup or spiritual manifestations. Both science and the Bible confirm these opposing dichotomies (Isaiah 5:20). That's why we find positive and negative posts on our batteries, and why the Bible contains the history of both God and Satan, saints and sinners, love and hate, good and evil, true and false, and "Thou Shalt" and "Thou shalt not" commandments in both of its Testaments. (Eight out of ten of the Ten Commandments were negative "thou-shalt-not" commandments!)

Thus, expectedly this Biblical Balance of "love and hate, accept and reject" is also present in the biblical history of the Christian church and/or religion. **(1)** Everything our Lord said would happen to his **Apostles** when they preached his New Testament Message did in fact happen (Acts 2-5). Many people kept their word (Acts 2:41, 47; 4:4, 32; 5:14). But most of the same people who rejected Jesus' Message rejected theirs and hated and persecuted them (Acts 4:3-23; 5:17-40). **(2)** They then persecuted, indicted and killed an individual Christian, Stephen, based upon purely false accusations about his message (see Acts, Ch. 6-7). Many would believe because of this example, and many wouldn't. **(3)** They then, by the hands of Saul, falsely accused, indicted, persecuted and killed Christians everywhere they were found preaching Christ's word (Acts 8:1-4). Many believed, including Saul/Paul (Acts 8:4-8; 38f; 9:1ff; 10:48; 12:24). And many didn't (Acts 13:44-46; See John's Gospel for this same belief-disbelief result.)

And we Christians must fully expect the same thing will happen to us if we choose Christ's New Covenant as our only authority and preach it verbatim as did the inspired Apostles. Some will love us and keep the message; but the majority of people will not accept the message, and some of those will hate the message so much that they will seek to hurt the messenger. The truth is that the only way we can prevent the world's "hatred" of us and our message of love is to become "worldly" like Jesus said—as old Jerry Neil III proved back when he was "of the world" and loved by the world! If we do what Jesus did, we'll get what Jesus got!

Many modern churches, like old Jerry's old church affiliations and flirtations, have not scripturally upgraded their doctrines as Jerry did. Consequently, they have become even more "unbalanced churches" because they so desired to expand their audiences and worldly popularity that they only hired passive messengers, or preachers: who would push their positive "Big Tent, Inclusionary, Diversity" doctrines; and who would/will not allow any negative, exclusionary preachers or teachers to speak. Jesus Christ was exclusionary: it was either His "Way" to Heaven or the World's Broad Highway to Hell (Matthew 7:13f; John 14:6)! Sinners were told to *"Repent or perish"* ... turn or burn (Luke 13:3, 5)!

And as I will present, I have encountered a number of leaders in so-called "conservative churches," who have chosen to wander down this wider path, who have accused me of being a Bad Messenger with a Bad Message. The truth is they have turned the truth into a lie because they refuse to do all they do in word and deed *"in the name of Christ"* (Matthew 28:18; Colossians 3:17; See Supplemental Studies for **"President Barack Obama Indicts Christianity"** when he said at a prayer conference: *"people did terrible things in the name of Christ"*).

Considering all of this, plus the numerous New Testament texts warning about Christian persecution, if I had received no false accusations, attacks and indictments throughout my 54 years of being an outspoken Christian, evangelist and writer, I would seriously question myself as being a faithful messenger of Christ's New Testament. And as I will soon present in my **"Vindication,"** this very thing has happened to me over the past fifty years of my life as a Gospel Preacher ... and I consider myself blessed because of such (Matthew 5:11; 10:16f; Luke 6:26 and Acts 5:40-41)!

We need to stay the Course. We must not be distracted, deterred or detoured away from preaching and practicing Christ's complete Truth — positive and negative — or we'll will miss the joy of fruitfulness in Converting others as well as refining our faith through the fiery Conflict of being hated and persecuted for Christ's sake. *"Fighting the good fight and finishing the course"* requires both "fighting" for the faith and "keeping the faith" by sharing the positive and negative parts within its pages to friends and foes, in good times and bad times, until we get killed or die. No cross means no crown (Matthew 10:38; II Timothy 4:7-8)!

The Vindicated Speaks

To say I need **Vindicating** is to imply I have been accused and/or indicted by some person or authority for doing something that was legally/morally/religiously wrong or harmful to others. I already exposed how this sorry legal situation did exist during Jerry Neil Wright's teenage years when he was found guilty in courts of law and punished accordingly. Jerry was the bad guy being prosecuted by the good guys! But now we're talking about Gerald Wright's adult years being in need of vindication from indictments made by bad and biased people against a preacher and practitioner of Christ's New Testament laws and principles. Have they ever accused me of false, illegal or harmful teachings? YES! Have they ever proved, in debate or court, that I was guilty of said charges? NO! So right up front I can say my message has been vindicated in the academic halls and civil courts for over fifty years. Thank you, Jesus!

Now let's get back to presenting some of the false indictments I have already experienced, and that you can expect to experience (or already are) when you are a Sovereign Soul and Soldier for Christ (Ephesians 6:10ff). I will present them in order of seriousness and not chronologically. Keep in mind that I'm not presenting these to invite any praise as a hero or invoke any sympathy as a martyr, but to present the victorious and joyous vindications that can only come when we fight the good fight of faith. I will put some of the verbal and physical attacks that have been lodged against me in public forums, newspapers and in person into three categories: Verbal Insults, Libelous Statements and Physical Attacks.

Verbal Insults — include constantly referring to me as *"Gerald Wrong,"* or as an *"old-fashioned, ignorant, Bible-thumper"* for appealing to Moses' Creation Account, or Jesus' marriage restriction to *"male and female"* in Matthew 19:4f, or Paul's condemnation of homosexual behavior in Romans 1:26ff ... and even his salvation of homosexuals in I Corinthians 6:9-11. (You can't win with some people!) I don't believe I ever read a letter supporting my letters, calling me "Gerald Right." So as we'll see in a minute, I changed my pen name to *"Kele Dikaiosune"* to say such myself! Actually, only those who know they can't win the debate on the biblical or scientific facts have to resort to such juvenile ad hominem tactics.

Libelous Statements — include their attempted character assassinations of labelling me in public print as *"a homophobe, bigot, misogynist, etc."* I didn't dignify these slurs with any rebuttals because: **(1)** The newspapers won't print them. **(2)** The Lord's vindication of his Old and New Testaments has vaccinated me against reacting to such, much less over-reacting. For I know that: *"He that correcteth a scoffer getting to himself reviling"* (Proverbs 9:7; cf., Matthew 7:6). Or to put it metaphorically: "If you fight with a porcupine or skunk, you'll get stuck or come out stinking!" **(3)** I know, and sometimes tell the hostile opposition in person, that the Lord is the one to blame or bless for the words in his New Testament, as well as the one to credit for my **vindication** for quoting them! He inspired it all, authorized it all and told me to quote him — *"in his name"* — on it all!

A local "transsexual" was allowed to publish a letter to the editor accusing "Gerald Wright" of being a possible suspect in a brutal machete attack on his life in his home. He has never fully recovered from that murderous attempt. And the newspaper never retracted or apologized for that libelous attack on my character!

The *"hatemonger"* accusation became so serious over time due to pro-gay propaganda, alleged pro-gay support and the media and legal progressions of this evil agenda, that I ended up being systematically banned from submitting letters to most of the newspapers in Hawaii: including *The Honolulu Advertiser, West Hawaii Today, Hawaii-Tribune Herald* and *The Big Island*

Journal. Two of the publishers put this censorship in writing. The Big Island Journal put this in a block ad with bold letters on their front page: ***"Write us a letter!*** *We'll be happy to publish it.* ***Exception:*** *Gerald Wright."* (All "Ban-Gerald" letters are on File.)

Because of this personal media bias, I became so intent on getting around this selective and bigoted censorship, and getting the conservative Christian message out to the Hawaiian people, especially during the State's vote on the "Same-sex Marriage Amendment," that I began to write Op Ed letters under several nom de plumes: like "Jerry Neil III" (yes, a better Jerry Neil III!); "Keli Dikaiosune" ("Keli" is Hawaiian for Jerry, and "Dikaiosune" is Greek for <u>Righ</u>teousness); and "Frances Meredith" (which is my wife's middle name and her maiden last name). Eventually, these new-named writers were also banned, proving again that it was the conservative Christian message that liberal publishers, editors and readers didn't like and not just the messenger!

Physical Attacks — One pro-gay counsellor, who lived in one of the hundred rental properties I maintained for a local property manager (in my secular business, 'Jerry's Renovations & Repair'), became enraged when I mentioned I had written a book on homosexuality (*Homosexuality And The Bible*). He insulted me and then, unbeknownst to me, called the police on me. I left before the police arrived and wasn't allowed to return and finish the job. This anti-Christian, alleged "gay friendly" sentiment has cost me untold thousands of dollars in my Real Estate and Construction businesses. A local roofing company refused to sell me shingles for my own house because my published views on homosexuality and same-sex marriage were not "gay friendly!"

Before I move on to more serious physical threats, I'd like to touch upon the charge that I am not ***"Gay friendly."*** And besides this narrow specific charge, I've been told a number of times that *"Nobody accepts your narrow views here ... you have no friends here and should leave!"* (This is in spite of the fact that over 69% of Hawaii's voters voted against Same-sex marriage!) Though I haven't changed my views or left Hawaii (yet), I actually preached a sermon entitled "Why I have no friends!" I opened the lesson with this comedic joke by Rodney Dangerfield: *"I get no respect. I'm telling you, I get no respect. I told my psychiatrist that everyone hates me. He said I was being ridiculous—everyone* *hasn't met you yet!"* (Most people who hate Christian writers haven't met them, haven't read their letters carefully and haven't read their books at all!)

Seriously now, it is true that I have no "gay friends" as so many well-meaning people, politicians and preachers now claim to have. (Which I actually had when I was a "hell-raising" teenage playboy and not a "hell-fire" preacher against drinking and deviancies!) The reason I don't have any "Gay Friends" as a Christian preacher is not because I treat people who claim to be "Gay" with any less love and kindness than I treat any other group of people that claims to be enslaved in any other type of sinful behavior — like "Alcoholics, Drug Addicts, Sex Addicts" — even if they don't know they're claiming to be <u>wilfully sinning</u> in their pursuit of our declining culture's latest "Drug or Deviancy Du jour."

I have no "Gay Friends" because: **(1)** I refuse to insult our God and Creator by saying His attempt to create a pure heterosexual male/female human species was/is flawed. **(2)** I refuse to injure a human being by stereotyping him/her into accepting he/she is "different" and not suited for having a natural marital-sexual life and biological family. **(3)** I refuse to accept the homosexual premise and agenda that any person is "born Gay," and is not just a heterosexual male/female involved in sinful sexual acts. **(4)** I preach forgiveness of homosexual sins in Christ and ask them to believe, repent and become "<u>ex-gays</u>," as Paul said they could become in I Corinthians 3:6-9. The most loving and excellent prefix to add to our human or cultural identity is to introduce ourselves as: a "**Christian**-person/Jew/American," and not by our sexual proclivities and/or "Orientations." **(5)** I do have many <u>ex-gay</u> friends! Ask America's most famous "Ex-Gay," Stephen Bennett, who has carried my homosexual book in Bookstore on his website (SBMinistries.org) for about seventeen years. **(6)** I also have thousands of friends who know, have read, and believe and accept my "Bible-friendly" views on all moral and religious issues! And I, unlike Elijah, who had to be reminded that he was not alone, believe I have thousands of friends I don't know about (cf. I Kings 19:10-18). **(7)** As we'll see later, all of my Bible views are "gay friendly." None hurt them, and all help them. And if they do not allow God's loving truth to make me their enemy, they will learn that "I am their best friend" (Galatians 4:16).

Lastly, as far as **physical attacks**, I've been personally confronted and threatened with bodily harm a number of times. And I have actually been assaulted and even arrested for standing for Christ's Old Ways in his Word. Again, there are no "woe is me" tears and pleas for pity intended here. As they say, "If you can't take the heat, get out of the kitchen (or pulpit)." If you can't take being a "Sovereign Soul," then be a "Squeamish Soul," do as they say, and "sit down and shut up!" I choose the former because I understand that people and nations (like in Israel and Judah) often refuse to follow the "Old Ways of God."

Thus saith Jehovah, **Stand ye in the ways** *and see, and ask for the* **old paths***, where is the* **good way***; and walk therein, and ye shall find rest for your souls: and they said,* **We will not walk therein** *(Jeremiah 6:16).*

Christ's Vindication Accepted

Now that I've revealed my need for divine vindication in this sinful world, let's apply it to Christ's Message and Messengers.

Christ Vindicated his Message — When the Jewish leaders questioned Christ's authority to speak for God, he vindicated himself and his message by pointing to his good deeds, inspired words and miraculous works via the Holy Spirit (John 14:11; 15:24). He thereby vindicated all of his commands related to what's right and wrong scripturally, morally, socially ("The Golden Rule"), non-coercive conviction and conversion plans for sinners, and His church pattern for membership, worship, evangelism, Christian living, etc. Jesus promised to give all the truth any person would ever need to live a godly life and receive eternal life (John 16:30; 20:31; II Timothy 3:16f; II Peter 1:3). That's enough for this Sovereign Soul!

Christ Vindicated his Messengers — Christ left nothing to chance when it came to getting his truths to the world. He, via his Holy Spirit, inspired his Apostles, validated their message with miracles, and thus vindicated everything they said and delivered to us in writing in Christ's New Testament (Mark 16:20; Hebrews 2:1-4). Which is still our New Testament today.

Thus the Vindicated person of Christ vindicated all of His truths during his ministry and in perpetuity through his Apostles and New

Testament writers. He did not leave a single essential issue open to further or later interpretations, updates, revisions, amendments or addendums. Thus "The Buck Starts and Stops with Jesus' New Testament!" We need to Read it, Repeat it, and Remind people to take up their disagreements and anger over any of it with its author: Jesus Christ! Blame him for His words if you dare.

And that is the only Validation that I need today to authorize and vindicate every word and deed that I have done that is in keeping with his Word and is Christ-like (or "Christian"). And, as no one could point to anything harmful done by Jesus and his Message, so they cannot point to anything harmful done by my Christian message—especially the points they have protested the most. For they helped people, didn't hurt them, and thereby vindicated my message, and this messenger, by their results. Here are some of the results.

* Not a single baby has been murdered in the womb because of my biblical anti-abortion views. The Lord knows how many were spared because of my book on abortion, *A Mother's Son*. My hands are clean. But the hands of those who falsely accuse me of hating women and taking away their right to control their own bodies are full of innocent baby blood. (Especially since babies in the womb have God-given rights over their "own bodies!")

* Not a single son, daughter, mother, father has ever been convicted of drunk driving, or been maimed, crippled or slaughtered by a drunk driver because they or any person followed my biblical anti-alcohol views. The Lord knows how many have been spared because of my book on booze, *"Sobering Questions."* My hands are clean. But the hands of those who promote the recreational use of ethyl alcohol are full of blood.

* Not a single sexual sinner — regardless of his/her sexual disorientation — has ever spent his/her life alone without a suitable "helpmeet" or biological family, or chosen to die prematurely by suicide or a slow death from Hepatitis or AIDS because of my New Testament anti-sodomy message. Or should I call "homosexuality" what both Jesus and his brother, Jude, called it: *"extreme fornication"* (Jude 7)? The Lord knows how many struggling sexual souls have been spared physical suffering and received spiritual salvation by my book, *Homosexuality and the Bible."* But the hands of those who consent to this deadly behavior

are as full of blood as those who were/are thereby encouraged by their consent to practice it (Romans 1:32).

Physical Vindication: Gerald Wright's use of the Great Physician's (Jesus) health, safety and well-being manual (the New Testament) is blameless and fully vindicated according to the world's most used medical oath: "First do no harm." My message has caused: no broken hearts, no broken bones, no bad livers, no bashed brains, no butchered babies, no busted marriages, no broken homes and no tombstones. But it has prevented such suffering and sorrow — and this I know from personal experience and testimony — and produced much sweet fruit (Matthew 7:16).

<u>Caveat: Physical Vindication is often bittersweet</u>**.** For much of the vindication that I have actually experienced in my life has not been an occasion wherein I wanted to shout "Victory in Jesus!" Nor was it even an opportunity to tell the victim of my vindication: "See, I told you so!" Rather, most all vindications have brought a burden of sympathy and sorrow upon my heart for the suffering and dying sinners who didn't heed my message, as well as for their loved ones left behind with doubts and fears about the goodness of God: "Why would a good God take my son, daughter, like this?" A few very real and very sad examples will suffice.

I recall my last funeral when I was a preacher in Florida. A young teenager, who didn't listen to my personal warning about smoking marijuana, got high on pot and hit a concrete house going over a 100 mph in a Plymouth "Demon" car. I watched him lie in a coma for almost two months before he was declared legally dead.

I also remember trying to stay the execution of a murderer, John Spenkelink, in Florida's "Old Sparky" electric chair. I had hoped to share the good news about Christ's dying for his sins before he died in and because of his sins. Sadly, my request was denied.

I wish the newspaper in Hawaii, that had no problem publishing the "transsexual's" charge that I had something to do with an attack on his life, would have published the cold-hard fact that if he would not have had the surgery and displayed it to young kids he would never have suffered the attack in the first place!

I recently was behind a drunk driver who killed another young teenager — whom I had known since he was a small child — in a head on collision near my home in Hawaii. Another stark reminder of how painfully pertinent my book on booze really is!

I also painfully recall praying for a young "Gay" man dying from AIDS (effectively meaning "**A**nother **I**nfected **D**ying **S**odomite") in our Hospital here. I'll let these kinds of deeds and dreads for and over the plight of all sinners prove that my heart's desire is always to help and save sinners ... as well as to serve as proof that my **message**, like my mentor's (Jesus), has always been vindicated as being "Good News" (Gospel) for all the world! It is Sovereign above all others in truth and love for sinners.

Spiritual Vindication: Not a single sinner who has ever heard me teaching or preaching, or read any of my letters, articles or books, has ever gone to hell because of what he/she heard or read pertaining to his/her belief in the true God, Creator and Savior of the Bible. But I know I have made their way to heaven scripturally clear (John 14:6; Acts 4:12). I just did it again!

Now I know many people fault preachers for telling people there is a hell and/or that unbelieving and unforgiven sinners are not going to heaven. Well, aside from the fact that Jesus Christ did preach all the above facts (Matthew 7:13-23; 10:28), and thus we should do likewise, the reality is that our preaching either side of this issue will not accomplish either result in their lives. For even the most negative, passionate and persuasive "hell-fire and brimstone" Gospel preacher cannot send even the most sinful, unbelieving, non-Christian person to hell. Only God can do that. Just as the most positive, powerful, "heaven-is-for-all-good people" humanistic preacher cannot send the most charitable, conscientious, unbelieving, non-Christian person to heaven. Only God/Christ can do that (John 5:22-29; 12:48). But neither of these shortcomings on our part absolves us from the responsibility to warn every person that there are only two options in the Afterlife: it's either hell or heaven; and not annihilation, or an unconscious Nirvana, Purgatory or even 72 virgins who will each become incredibly older each passing century in some physical forever-afterlife ... that Jesus totally repudiated (Matthew 22:30).

Which brings us to the next "Elevating" aspect of our study on how our L-O-V-E for Christ will lead us to learn all of His New Testament, obey his commands and teach his whole truth, and nothing but his truth, so help us God.

-E-
Choosing Christ's Covenant is Elevating

We could add many other beneficial words to represent the "E" in our "LOVE" of Christ and His Word besides "Elevating." A few that come to mind would be "Empowering, Energizing" and most of all, "Enthusing," which means "in God" (from "en theos"), or "God in, inspired by God, possessed by God." And it is true that having the Words and Love of God in you creates higher aspirations and enthusiasm than anything on earth can. *"Unless there is within us that which is above us, we will succumb to that which surrounds us and sink to that which is beneath us!"* Oh well, since all of these are "Elevating," I will just deal with all such "exalting" words and concepts within that term. Let's get started!

Christ delivered unto us in his New Testament more truth about both heaven (and hell) than can be found in the entire Old Testament and all other "religious" books combined. He tells us that He is the only way and truth to eternal life in heaven (John 14:1-6). He tells us how to know if you're on the wide road to hell or the narrow way to heaven. And He tells us sinners exactly how to get to heaven from the highest place of self-righteousness to the lowest gutter or prison cell of the worst sinner's life, even if near death and falling into the fiery abyss (cf., Jude 23). From Matthew to Revelation, the theme and thrust of Christ's New Testament is Salvation from sin, Victory in life and over death, and receiving a Crown of Righteousness and Life in heaven (I Corinthians 15:1-3, 54-58; II Timothy 4:7-8; Revelation 2:10; 22:17).

Apart from Christ's New Testament, there's no way we could discover or know anything of substance about Christ as our Savior and Judge or about any of these crucially essential spiritual realities. We can't know he's the Way or the personification of Truth if we don't know his written truths in his Word. We can't become like Christ by reading secular or extra-biblical books. We can't think as Christ thought and possess his heavenly *"mind"* set until we read his logical and heavenly thinking (Philippians 2:5; 4:7). We can't talk as he talked, or walk as he walked, until we read how he talked and how and where he walked in his own inspired history. We can't walk on his higher and holy ground if we will not meet him there in his scriptures. We can get to heaven from anywhere on the earth or in outer space (as astronauts, or inhabitants on the moon); but we can't get to heaven without his scriptural roadmap.

Thus our main point, purpose and privilege as preachers is to motivate and move all people to seek to rise above this mundane world of hedonistic living that leads to hell and go to heaven by reading the roadmap to each place. We want to convict people of their sins so they will be convinced and compelled to convert to Christ and face Him as their Savior when they die. We don't desire to simply convict them so they will be without excuse when they face Christ as their Judge (John 15:8; 5:24). That's why we're called Evangelists (Good-News Preachers) in the New Testament and not "Watchmen" as in the Old Testament. (Though, as per warning people about hell, we're still obligated to fulfill that obligation.) So that's why I want to close this chapter with all the higher, uplifting, ***Elevating*** aspects and benefits we're blessed with when we **LOVE** Christ and his Word.

Our Heavenly Message. We begin our journey as Christian "Sovereign Souls" by accepting a *higher calling* via a message that came to us directly from the God-man from heaven (see Philippians 2:5ff; 3:12-14). There's no way we could have ever known about the true God of heaven and his desire to save us apart from his divine revelation in the Bible (See *The Supreme Scientist,* 'Natural Theology,' pp. 92-94, for more discussion on this subject). All the divinely inspired scriptures came from our God in heaven (II Timothy 3:16; I Peter 1:11; II Peter 1:21). They reveal to us how God personally visited this planet in anthropomorphic (humanlike) manifestations in the Garden of Eden and other events, and finally coming *"in the likeness of sinful flesh...being made in the likeness of men"* as the Incarnate Son of God (Romans 8:3; Philippians 2:7; John 1:1,14; Hebrews 2:14). And as this God-man, this divine heavenly Messenger delivered unto us things from heaven and not from the earth (John 8:23; 14:1f). The writer of the book of Hebrews began and continued his letter by exulting in and extolling both the heavenly Messenger and His ***"Better"*** heavenly New Testament Message:

> *God, having of old time spoken unto the fathers in the prophets by divers portions and in divers manners, hath at the end of these days* **spoken unto us in his Son**, *whom he appointed heir of all things, through whom also he made the worlds ... But now hath he obtained a ministry the* **more excellent**, *by so much as he is also the mediator of a* **better covenant**, *which hath been enacted upon* **better promises** (Hebrews 1:1-2; 8:6).

Everything we Christians know about Christ and all heavenly matters is a blessing from God that lifts our lives and spirits as high as possible while we walk as pilgrims upon this earth. Listen to what Paul says about this heavenly phenomenon and its elevating impact upon our lives.

> **Blessed be the God and Father** *of our Lord Jesus Christ, who hath* **blessed us** *with* **every spiritual blessing** *in the* **heavenly places in Christ** (Ephesians 1:3).

The more knowledge of God's word that we possess about heavenly persons (Father, Son, Holy Spirit, angels, departed human spirits) and spiritual things redounds to more heavenly persons and spirituals things becoming a part of our thoughts and communication to others. The more we possess the heavenly the more the heavenly possesses us. So much so that where ever we are becomes a *"heavenly place."* We become more and more heavenly, and less worldly, as a human being. (Which explains why mundane-minded people might perceive you to be an "alien!") The more we partake of God's *"divine nature,"* the more we will reflect the Divine Image with which Adam was created. Let's quote Peter on this heavenly transformation.

> *Grace to you and peace be multiplied in the* **knowledge** *of our God and of Jesus our Lord; seeing that his* **divine power** *hath granted unto us all things that pertain unto life and godliness, through the* **knowledge** *of him that called us by his own glory and virtue;* **whereby** *he hath granted unto us his precious and exceeding* **great promises***; that through these ye may partake of the* **divine nature***, having escaped from the corruption that is in the world by lust* (II Peter 1:2-4).

Just knowing that our God has spoken to us, visited us, lived amongst us, and best of all, loves us and wants us to be like him and live with Him eternally in heaven, is supremely Elevating in and of itself! It's also Edifying and Eternal! Makes me sing the old hymn: "Love lifted me" (by James Rowe, Howard E. Smith).

I was sinking deep in sin, Far from the peaceful shore, Very deeply stained within, Sinking to rise no more; But the Master of the sea Heard my despairing cry, From the waters lifted me, Now safe am I. Love lifted me! Love lifted me! When nothing else could help, **Love lift-ed me!**

Well, since we could write a book on any one of the high and holy things God has in store for us, let's close this very elevating point and chapter by supplying a short list of some of the many elevating things that we Christians already know and enjoy because we "Sovereign Souls" chose the most elevating book, Christ's New Testament, as our only Covenant between us and God and heaven.

* When we arose from our New Testament New Birth of water and Spirit, we abandoned our old Rejected life of slavery to sin and accepted our new Elected life of freedom from sin and sainthood (John 3:3-5; 8:31f; Romans 6:1-4; 8:33; I Corinthians 1:2). That's Elevating!

* From that birth forward we "Saved Souls" no longer lived and walked amongst the spiritually dead in a dark sinful world, but amongst the spiritually resurrected and enlightened ones in the radiant and guiding light of God's Word, imputed holiness, and divine fellowship in his heavenly kingdom/church (Acts 2:38-47; Ephesians 1:3-14; 2:1-6; Colossians 1:1-14; I John 1:1-7). We climbed out of the Valley of Sin and the world's gutters up to the Road to and Mountain tops of Glory in a single day! That's so Elevating we need to quote *"the author and perfecter of our faith"* for more praise about our new heavenly habitation:

But ye are come unto **Mount Zion**, *and unto the* **city of the living God**, *the* **heavenly Jerusalem**, *and to innumerable* **hosts of angels**, *to the general assembly and* **church of the firstborn** *who are* **enrolled in heaven**, *and to* **God** *the judge of all, and to the* **spirits of just men made perfect**, *and to*

Jesus the mediator of a new covenant*, and to the blood that speaketh better than that of Abel* (Hebrews 12:2, 22-24).

Hallelujah! Can you grasp the personal spiritual promotion we experienced the day we chose to obey Christ's word and be added to his church (Acts 2:38-47)? Speaking for myself, sometimes it seems like it was just yesterday when I was wasting my young life in Roanoke, Virginia — the "Star City of the South" (has a giant Neon Star on top of Mill Mountain) — running around with our local version of the infamous "Hell's Angels" motorcycle gang. And then, a new day came and I learned (from passages like the one quoted above) that as a Christian I was on top of *"Mount Zion,"* a citizen of *"the city of the living God, the heavenly Jerusalem,"* and surrounded by *"innumerable hosts of angels"* (Hebrews 1:14; II Kings 6:17; Revelation 5:11). ("Heaven's Angels" are much higher and better than "Hell's Angels!"). And besides all this swift transition, I found myself in constant fellowship with the *"Living God and judge of all ... Jesus the mediator of the New Covenant* (that I had in my pocket) ... *church of the firstborn* {first Christians} ... *spirits of just men made perfect* {all the believing departed spirits before Christ}. All of these spiritual promotions, and more to come, flood my mind every time I recall the Elevating, Exciting and even Entertaining Words that I found when I chose to read and accept Christ's New Covenant and become a Christian and His "Saved/Sovereign Soul."

* **But there's more elevation on earth as well.** For in Christ's universal church, and spiritual kingdom, we find we have been given many exalted names, positions and promises. This I know because the Bible tells me so.

— For Christ's word says every Christian's name is written in heaven before he dies (Revelation 13:8; 17:8). Actually, our omniscient God knew us before the foundation of the world and our birth (Ephesians 1:3f; cf., Psalms 139:13; Jeremiah 1:5).

— Every Christian is a Priest in the Higher Priesthood of Melchizedek and under a Higher High Priest than Melchizedek, Jesus Christ (Hebrews 7-8; I Peter 2:5; Revelation 5:10).

— Every Christian has direct access to Heaven's Holy of Holies, Throne of God and Father through Christ our mediator: *"For there is one God,* **one mediator also between God and men,** *him-*

self man, **Christ Jesus** (I Timothy 2:5). People often fail to distinguish between an "Intercessor," who stands by our side before God, and a "Mediator" who stands between us and God. We can have as many intercessors as we choose or who want to go <u>with</u> us before God's throne (like prayer partners), but we only have one mediator that stands *"<u>between</u>"* us and God, ***"Christ Jesus."*** This text assures us that as surely as there is only one God who we "Sovereign Souls" must believe and obey, there is only one mediator — himself being a *"man"* (human being} and anointed king (*"Christ"*) — that we must go through in order to present our case and petitions to God.

Thus every Christian can confess his sins, pray and present his petitions — no matter how small or great our sins or requests happen to be — unto our King and Savior God, wherever and whenever he/she desires, without having to seek out, make an appointment, or submit to any human mediator to plead our case or present our greatest petitions. One suggestion, remember the words of the old hymn — "Come, My Soul, Thy Suit Prepare" — by the author of "Amazing Grace," John Newton. Here are a few lyrics:

> *Come, my soul, thy suit prepare: Jesus loves to answer prayer; Himself has bid thee pray, Therefore will not say thee nay; Therefore will not say thee nay.*
>
> *Thou are coming to a King,* **Large petitions** *with thee bring; For His grace and power are such, None can ever ask too much; None can ever ask too much.*

Thus We "Sovereign Souls" are also "Self-Sufficient Souls" when it comes to our individual spiritual needs and service before God. We are not dependent upon any higher human office or mediator on earth when it comes to our communication with God, or worship of God, through Christ—because there are no higher human beings than each and every one of us. This is very liberating and elevating! And we are not through with our earthly elevations yet. Let's go higher!

— Every Christian is a ***"called to be a saint"*** while he is alive, and is equally sinless, blameless and holy with all other living "saints." This is because Christ's blood continually cleanses every sinner's sins and imputes his righteousness and sanctification unto all forgiven sinners' account, <u>equally</u> (I Corinthians 1:2). Why?

How? Let's see:

Why? *"that no flesh should glory before God"* (I Cor. 1:29).
How? *"But of him are **ye in Christ**, who was made unto us wisdom from God, and **righteousness and sanctification**, and redemption: that, according as it is written, He that glorieth, let him **glory in the Lord"*** (I Cor. 1:30-31; cf. Romans 4:3-8; II Corinthians 5:21; I John 3:7).

This means no Christian's "Sainthood" is in any way lower than any other Christian's "Sainthood" because, as our initial cleansing from sin was a "free gift" from God, so our continuous cleansing/sanctification from sin is also a free gift from God (Romans 6:23; I John 1:7; I Thessalonians 4:3-8). Sanctification, or "Sainthood," is not a legalistic promotion of a few "Do-Gooders," by a few higher church "Officials," taking place within a Meritocracy. Also, as anyone can easily see from Christ's clear declarations on this matter of "Sainthood," it is endowed by Christ upon all faithful Christians daily. It is not a Special Elevated Status, determined by a self-appointed group of superior "Priests," who allot it to a Select few of departed Christians who allegedly accomplished greater humanitarian or alleged miraculous works. Each and every faithful Christian is a "Sovereign Saint!"

— Every Christian is an equal *"fellow-citizen"* in Christ's Kingdom (Ephesians 2:19). Every Christian is endowed with equal New Testament authority status with all other religious "authorities" who also claim Christ's New Testament as their sole authority, and above all those who claim any other religion's non-biblical or extra-biblical authority.

— Every Christian has Christ for his Advocate (attorney), who uses his blood to pay for their propitiation (I John 2:1f). Plus every Christian has the Holy Spirit dwelling in him/her as his/her Intercessor and assurance that God knows our hearts better than we do (John 14:16f; Acts 2:38; Romans 8:26f; I John 3:19-21)! All of this is Elevating and Enabling! This is what "Sovereign Souls" become when they choose Christ and His New Testament as their sole authority and access into God's heaven. This shows how there's so much more about being a "Sovereign Soul" than just calling yourself one.

— Every Christian, like the Apostle Paul, should be using all of these aforementioned blessings that come with loving Christ and obeying his word to press on to the most excellent way and **highest ground** he can achieve with God's grace and to His glory. Let's close this Chapter with the uplifting words of Paul and then a few verses from an old hymn.

> *Yea verily, and **I count all things to be loss for the excellency of the knowledge of Christ Jesus my Lord**: for whom I suffered the loss of all things, and do count them but refuse, that I may gain Christ, and be found in him, not having a righteousness of mine own, even that which is of the law, but that which is through faith in Christ, the righteousness which is from God by faith: that I may know him, and the power of his resurrection, and the fellowship of his sufferings, becoming conformed unto his death; if by any means I may attain unto the resurrection from the dead. Not that I have already obtained, or am already made **perfect**: but **I press on**, if so be that I may lay hold on that for which also I was laid hold on by Christ Jesus. Brethren, I count not myself yet to have laid hold; but **one thing I do**, **forgetting** the things which are behind, and **stretching forward** to the things which are before, **I press on toward the goal unto the prize of the high calling of God in Christ Jesus*** (Philippians 3:8-14).

Higher Ground

> *I'm pressing on the upward way, New heights I'm gaining ev'ry day; Still praying as I onward bound, 'Lord, plant my feet on **higher ground**.'*
>
> *I want to scale the utmost height, And catch a gleam of glory bright; But still I'll pray till heav'n I've found, 'Lord, lead me on to **higher ground**.'*

Chorus: *Lord, lift me up and let me stand, By faith, on heaven's table land; A higher plane than I have found, Lord, plant my feet on **higher ground*** (Johnson Oatman, Jr., Chas. H. Garbial).

CHAPTER THREE
Sovereign Souls Choose Christ's Cross

CHRIST'S CHOICE

Our Heavenly Father, through his Son and Holy Spirit, created his first earthly children, Adam and Eve, in his own image as free-will, sinless adult individuals, under His laws regulating their lives in the Garden of Eden (Genesis 1:26 thru 2:25). Yet they chose to surrender their Sovereign Souls, Free Will and "Freedom of Choice" to Satan and break God's only prohibitive law (2:17). Due to their sin of rebellion, they died spiritually and thereby severed themselves from his physical blessing of everlasting physical life and his spiritual fellowship in the Garden of Eden (Genesis 3). Aren't you glad this historical biblical narrative didn't end there? Let's proceed with expectation and gratitude in our hearts.

Though our Heavenly Father could have, justifiably, abandoned Adam and Eve, and all their offspring (who lived long enough to sin by breaking any of God's new laws governing their lives outside the Garden) to live out their physical lives without any way to renew any spiritual relationship with God on earth or any objective expectation for a heavenly reward after they died, Jehovah God did the opposite. He — being their loving Father who desired their fellowship — had pity upon their lowly bodies of dust (Psalms 103:10-14) and left them, their progeny and the world with a ray of hope by revealing that He had already provided a way for their victory over Satan, salvation from sin and eternal fellowship with Him through Eve's *"seed"* (Genesis 3:15, 20; cf., 12:1-3). This Hope became History in the birth of Christ and his death at Calvary (Galatians 3:16-19; I Peter 1:17-21).

All these loving plans we know because our God wanted His Bible to tell us so! How our loving God, Creator and Savior chose to suffer and die to save every sinner who seeks his salvation is in and of itself "The Greatest Love Story Ever Told!" Especially since He had other justifiable options he could have pursued.

Physically Speaking

God could have saved millions (or billions) of Adam and Eve's extended world family from untimely physical deaths by allowing them to die of old age <u>in their sins</u> rather than by bringing physical judgments against them by a universal curse of decay, destruction and death upon all things physical, a worldwide flood, fire from heaven (Sodom) and conquering armies. But, that wouldn't have saved any sinners amongst them so they could be with Him in heaven after they died.

Spiritually Speaking

He could have saved the souls of all sinless children who died before the age of accountability without dying for them (Isaiah 7:14ff; Jonah 4:11; See *The Supreme Scientist*, "The Supreme Salvation Standard," pp. 260, 275-288.) But that wouldn't have saved a single accountable sinner then or thereafter.

He could have saved the souls of all innocent unaccountable adults — those who never possessed mental rationality — without dying for them. But that wouldn't have saved a single sinner then or thereafter, either.

He could have allowed everyone from Adam till the end of the world to try to keep his holy laws perfectly, never become a lost sinner, and go to heaven when they die. But that wouldn't have saved a single sinner from Adam till the end of the world. And He, in his omniscience, knew this before He created man, and from history ever since Adam. **(1)** For if the perfect man, Adam, didn't keep one law perfectly, no man would keep all of His laws perfectly. **(2)** If God's showcase people, Israel, wouldn't, or couldn't, keep his perfect legal-religious law system perfectly as required in that law (Deuteronomy 27:26; Galatians 3:10), He knew that man wouldn't be able to earn his way out of one sin, much less his way to heaven by perfectly keeping His law or any law (Ezekiel 18:20; Romans 3:9, 19-23). The Pharisaical Jews, who tried and taught this legalistic salvation system, only committed another sin: teaching the false and cursed doctrine of faithless legalism (Galatians 1:6-9; 2:16; 5:1-6). **(3)** And He knew the bloody sacrifices of animals — which He had required for ceremonial cleansing of the flesh and to serve as a type of Christ's bloody sacrifice — would not take away a single sin (Psalms 51:4,

14-17; Hebrews 9:11 thru 10:22).

So Christ knew man needed a Savior from his first sin, as well as from his inability to save himself from his sins thereafter by perfect law-keeping. So Christ chose to make the Supreme Sacrifice and offer his body upon the Cross in our place and his blood for all of our sins of omission and commission. And, thereby, He gave us his *"perfect law of liberty"* that forgives imperfect humans (James 1:25; 2:10-12; Romans 3:24-31; 8:1-4); instead of another perfect legal law like the Old Testament — a *"ministration of death"* — that killed them for their sins (II Corinthians 3:7; Romans 7:9-12)! All of this is good news!

Furthermore, the good news of the Gospel is good news for all sinners because Christ chose to sacrifice himself and shed his blood for the worst sinners and not just for those who might appear to be blameless or claim to be "self-righteous" (Matthew 19:16-22; Philippians 3:6). He knew one sin would make a person a sinner, and "a sinner indeed is a sinner in need." Thus he shed his blood ***"once for all"*** sinners for all time (Hebrews 7:27f; 10:10-14).

Consider how Christ told the boastful "self-righteous" Jewish leaders that the despised *"Publicans"* (tax collectors) and dejected *"harlots"* would enter into the kingdom of God before they would (Matthew 21:31-32). Actually, the surrounding parables before and after this divine verdict tell us that the self-righteous Jews wouldn't enter into the kingdom at all! This tells us how level the "Sinful Playing Field" of the living is! But there's more.

It has been said that the ground is level at the gravesites in a Cemetery since all men die, regardless of their power or prosperity, and they can't buy their way out of it or take anything with them (Hebrews 9:27; Job 1:21). That's why there are no pockets in a shroud! In like manner, I believe the Bible teaches that the spiritual ground is level at Calvary. For we all stand at the foot of Christ's cross as equal sinners — *"Just as I am without one plea"* — with no special seats or standing-room only privileges. Jesus said: *"**if I be lifted up from the earth** {on the cross}, I will draw **all men unto myself**"* (John 12:32). ***"All men"*** includes all sinners because all sinners are equally lost and equally in need of the forgiveness that only Christ's blood on the cross can purchase from God for us.

Though Jesus' old rugged cross was/is on a hill faraway from most of humanity back then and now, for those who were there to witness and hear all the cruel actions and heavenly spectacles that took place during our Lord's crucifixion, it was the highest plateau on the face of the earth. I say "plateau" because it was spiritually level at the foot of Jesus' cross. Indeed! For how much more could a **"Sinner's Equality Status"** be demonstrated for us than Jesus' telling the thief beside him that he would be with Him in his spiritual kingdom in heaven on that day ... while his greatest religious and political leaders and enemies who put them on their crosses — the Jewish Priests and Roman Powers — were shut out and, as far as history reports, never became Christian citizens in his kingdom! (Except for the Centurion, who confessed Jesus' divine Sonship and, according to tradition, became a Christian.)

Furthermore, even Jesus' loving mother, disciple and friends at the foot of his cross, did not receive any more assuring words and attention from Jesus during this most telling period when he was a dying man uttering his "last words." Such was not a time for Jesus to waste words or lie about his identity. He knew his hour had come! He knew that, without his death, Mary, John and his friends were as lost in sin as the thief. This also was a time for him to come clean and confess his own sins and shortcomings ... if he indeed had any. So this is yet more proof that Jesus was the sinless Son of God. "Dead or dying men don't tell tales!"

Point Made: Jesus Christ made his Choice of Crucifixion in eternity and revealed it through his prophets: that He would be *lifted up* on a torture stake *amongst transgressors*, where he would suffer unto the point of death, then give up his spirit and die. He deliberately chose this slower execution method rather than by other swift methods like hanging, stoning or by the sword.

> *And as **Moses lifted up the serpent** in the wilderness, even so must **the Son of man be lifted up**; that whosoever believeth may in him have eternal life ... And I, if **I be lifted up from the earth**, will draw all men unto myself. But this he said, signifying by what **manner of death** he should die* (John 3:14f; 12:32f).
>
> *And they made **his grave** {the dying process} **with the wicked**, and with a rich man in his death {Joseph of Arimathaea's tomb} ... he poured out his soul unto death, and was **numbered with the transgressors** {between two*

criminals on the cross}: *yet he bare the **sin of many*** {those below the cross and in the world}, *and made **intercession for the transgressors*** {for his executioners and the penitent thief on the cross}... (Isaiah 53:9,12b; cf. Matthew 27:57f; Luke 23:32-43; see Psalms 22:7-18). THE CROSS WAS CHRIST'S LOVING CHOICE FOR US!

In keeping with our previous Choice of Christ's New Testament as our sole source of truth about Christ, as delivered by his Apostles, we find that all the Apostles preached the **Crucified Christ as being the fulfillment of:**
— All the Old Testament prophecies (like Psalms 22 and Isaiah 53) about his death, burial, resurrection and ascension to his heavenly throne over his world-wide kingdom (Acts 2:22-36; 3:18-26; Romans 1:1-4; See my *Killing Jesus,* pp. 42-50).
— All the legal requirements of the Old Law pertaining to man's complete and continuous justification from sin (Romans 8:1-11).
— The shedding of sinless human blood for the ratification of his New Testament and its offer of forgiveness of sins (Hebrews 8:6-13; 9:11-28; 10:1-22).
— Providing the priceless blood that purchased His Church (Acts 20:28; I Corinthians 6:20: I Peter 1:18-20; Revelation 5:9f).
— Putting the power to save sinners in the Gospel (Romans 1:16).
— The only human Sacrifice they ever glorified (Galatians 6:14).
— The complete and confirmed Gospel of Faith, Hope, Love, Peace, Grace, Justification, Redemption, Reconciliation and Salvation they witnessed and preached unto all nations (Mark 16:15; I Corinthians 15:1-11). Christ alone had the *"Words of Life,"* and may I add, "The Wood of Life" in the "Old Rugged Cross." Apart from Him, I can do nothing ... and I am nothing (John 6:68; 15:5).

> *Being therefore **justified by faith**, we have our **peace** with God through our Lord Jesus Christ; through whom also we have had our access by faith into this **grace** wherein we stand; and we rejoice in **hope** of the glory of God. And not only so, but we also rejoice in our tribulations: knowing that tribulation worketh steadfastness; and stedfastness, approvedness; and approvedness, hope: and hope putteth not to shame; because the **love of God** hath been shed*

abroad in our hearts through the Holy Spirit which was given unto us. For while we were yet weak, in due season **Christ died for the ungodly** {that included me!). *For scarcely for a righteous man will one die: for peradventure for the good man some one would even dare to die.* **But God commendeth his own love toward us, in that, while we were yet sinners, Christ died for us.** *Much more then, being now* **justified by his blood**, *shall we be* **saved** *from the wrath of God through him. For if, while we were* **enemies**, *we were* **reconciled** *to God through the* **death** *of his Son, much more, being reconciled, shall we be* **saved by his life**; *and not only so, but we also rejoice in God through our* **Lord Jesus Christ**, *through whom we have now received the* **reconciliation** (Romans 5:1-11).

It is this Apostolic Gospel Faith which we all have been commanded to accept, preach and defend (Jude 3). I have accepted Christ's Supreme Sacrifice and Saving Faith because...

CHRIST'S CROSS WAS MY CHOICE

Now that we have established beyond all debate that Christ's death upon the Cross was his own personal, planned, and even prosecuted choice to save His fallen children from sin and eternal judgment, we can be assured beyond all doubt that the only choice we sinners have been given to be saved from our sins is <u>Christ's Cross</u>. If there were other options or "ways" to heaven from which to choose, Jesus would have told us so. It's really that simple. He could have said there were other ways, options and choices when it comes to having our sins forgiven. Yet He not only didn't hint at there being other options, He specifically and emphatically said He was the only option, as did his Apostles (John 14:6; Acts 4:12).

Personally, I can tell you this with certainty, there has never been any doubt in my mind over my decision to accept Christ's Cross and all it stands for — His beaten body bearing my sins and the stripes I deserved upon the tree; His wounds shedding innocent blood to pay for this guilty person's sins, His undying love for this unlovable sinner and lost sheep — as the one and only Supreme Sacrifice from the Only Savior and Shepherd that I would ever need or accept (John 15:13; I Peter 2:21-25). I thank God daily for giving me the opportunity to make **Christ's Choice My Choice** over fifty years ago. What a blessed privilege! What Powers His Cross has brought into the life of this Sovereign Soul!

Christ's Cross Powers

In order to fully appreciate how much Christ's cross empowers us to be Sovereign Souls in this world, we need to repeat again how much He accomplished for us at Calvary. Briefly, here's what he did for us. **(1)** He defeated and demoted our greatest enemy, Satan. He crushed his head, meaning he took away his spiritual power over us (Genesis 3:15; Matthew 12:24-29; Luke 10:18; John 12:31f; Romans 16:20). **(2)** His shed blood was for the forgiveness of all the sins of the faithful since Adam, including ours since the beginning of our sinful lives to our conversion (Romans 3:24-26; Hebrews 9:15). **(3)** His shed blood forgives all of our sins after we become Christians (I John 1:3-7). **(4)** His overcoming death via his resurrection took away Satan's greatest physical weapon against us, the fear of death (Hebrews 2:14).

Considering all of this, we might call Christ's New Testament our "Declaration of Independence" from Satan and all of his minions who are aligned against our freedom (John 8:32-36). For, just as accepting the truth that "all men are created equal" with "certain unalienable rights" endowed by their "Creator," as upheld in America's 'Declaration of Independence,' made every human being who accepted that compact sovereign above all human powers that seek to impose their Godless "wrongs" upon them, so does accepting Christ's Cross and its unalienable rights, as per his New Testament Declaration of Independence, empower all Sovereign Christians over and above all their physical and spiritual adversaries.

Yet our Christian Declaration of Independence is based upon more than the sons of men writing their biblical beliefs upon paper with pen and ink; ours were written in blood upon Calvary by the Son of Almighty God! Our Declaration of Independence frees us from all of our physical and spiritual enemies and heals us from all their wounds, even when fatal! Our Cross Power is supremely superior because the Person on the Cross was the most Supreme

Person of Power who ever lived amongst us! Please passionately consider Him and His Cross Powers again.

+ There's Savior Power in the Cross! There's Personal Sovereign Power in Christ's Cross for each one of us because there was a "Personal Savior" upon his Cross. There was Savior Power on his cross because Jesus was the most powerful person in human history, who overcame every spiritual and physical enemy in his life before, during and after his crucifixion: including Satan, demons, sinful temptations, hunger, assassination attempts, fear, pain, beatings, humiliations, crucifixion, and estrangement from God. Then our Conquering Savior administered the death stroke upon old Scratch's (Satan's) head by shouting *"It is finished"* right before He exercised his divine prerogative and sovereignty over Satan by taking charge of his physical death-march and giving up his human spirit upon his command. Below is a blend of two Gospel Accounts:

> *When Jesus therefore had received the vinegar, he said, **it is finished**: and he bowed his head ... And, Jesus, crying with a loud voice, said, Father, into thy hands **I commend my spirit**: and having said this, **he gave up the ghost/spirit** (John 19:30; Luke 23:46; see also John 10:18 for Jesus' claim of having the power to "lay down...and take up his life").*

"It is finished" is from the Greek word, "Tetelestai," which is not a desperate cry of defeat. Jesus did not say *"I am finished."* He said *"It is finished."* It is a shout of victory because He had finished/reached his goal of completing his work of redemption by offering up his sinless body as our sacrifice. Satan may have thought he had won the battle when Christ breathed his last breath. But our Lord kept his word and won the war when He was raised from the dead and, thereby, took away Satan's number one fear-factor when it comes to keeping sinners in bondage to him and sin: *"the fear of death"* (Hebrews 2:14-15)! Satan was finished!

All this *"Savior Power"* becomes our Savior Power and our Sovereign Power when we understand He didn't do this for his benefit; he did this For Us? To save us! To give us similar power over Satan, sin and all of our spiritual adversaries that would otherwise upset us (Hebrews 12:1-2).

+ There's Saving Power in Christ's Cross. There's Saving Power in the Cross for us because there's Saving Power in Christ's blood. As the old hymn goes:

> *Would you be free from your burden of sin? There's* ***pow'r in the blood****, pow'r in the blood; Would you oér evil a victory win? There's wonderful power in the blood.*
> Chorus: *There is pow'r, pow'r, wonder working-pow'r In the blood of the Lamb; There is pow'r, pow'r, wonder-working pow'r In the precious blood of the Lamb* (*There is Power in the Blood*, L. E. Jones).

Our Great Physician's drops and streaks of blood upon Calvary's tree did in six hours what thousands of gallons of spilled animal blood over 1500 years in Israel couldn't do: forgive one sin (See Psalms 51:2-3,16f; Hebrews 10:4). There's divine forgiving power in His blood!

Our Great Physician did with his blood — cleansed and cured a person's sinful soul and cleared his guilty conscience — what all the world's greatest physicians have been unable to do with their powerful medicines and machines (lasers, Xrays, microscopes), that can detect, cure and destroy all sorts of cancers and horrible diseases. (Just as Christ alone created life and raised the dead!) They can't even cleanse a single guilty or terrified person's conscience without a lobotomy or drugging him/her into such a stupor that he doesn't know who he is, much less who Christ was.

Yet, a single baptismal bath in Christ's blood has already cleansed some of the worst sinners in the world, from John's baptism until now, including the Christian-killer, Saul of Tarsus (Acts 22:16; See "John's Baptism" in my *There Has Always Been One Baptism* book)! Just as He cleansed this sinner! There is power, power, wonder-working power in the blood of the "*Lamb of God, that taketh away the sin of the world* "... and me (John 1:29)!

+ There's Sanctifying Power in Christ's Cross. There is not only the *"wonder-working"* saving power of forgiveness that comes when we first secure the benefits of choosing Christ and his Cross as our Savior and Solution to sin, it is also the "Sanctifying Power" that keeps "Saved Souls" saved, safe and separate from their sins (I John 1:3-7). We can't remain "Saved Sovereign Souls" in this world apart from Christ and his Cross. It, and it alone, raises us above this sinful world. Calvary is the top of the highest spiritual mountain for us. Free at last! Free at last! Thank God Almighty, Free at Last! (Not just from physical slavery, re: Martin Luther King, but from spiritual slavery!)

+ There's Sovereign Power in Christ's Cross. The previous "Savior, Saving and Sanctifying Powers" that we found in Christ and his cross are the powers that make it possible for any and all sinners to become and remain the power-filled "Sovereign Souls" God wants us all to be. Without these perpetual sin-forgiving powers, we sinners wouldn't have been able to escape our enslavement to Satan's power over us in the first place, nor remain free if we had.

But since we do possess these powers in the "Powerful Gospel" that we received, accepted and obeyed (Romans 1:16), let us seize upon every opportunity to exercise our God-given Sovereignty to live as sin-free men, carry Christ's cross, diligently preach His Gospel, valiantly defend His Gospel and deliver it to all people, equally (Matthew 28:18-20; Jude 3).

God has already endowed us with the following **"Sovereign Cross Rights"** to enable us to overcome all obstacles and enemies that we will encounter in our Service to Him and His Cause!

Our Sovereign Cross Rights

We Cross-Choosing, Blood-Bathed, Blood-Bought Christians have *Sovereign Cross Rights* that no creature, power, person or event (including death) can take away from us. They make us more than conquerors and "Sovereign Souls" in every way!

> *What then shall we say to these things? If **God is for us**, who is against us? He that **spared not his own Son**, but delivered him up for us all, how shall he not also **with him freely give us all things**? Who shall lay anything to the charge of **God's elect**?* {Like Satan did to Job 1:6-12; 2:1-6.} *It is God that justifieth; **who is he that condemneth?** It is **Christ Jesus that died, yea rather, that was raised from the dead**, who is at the right hand of God, who also maketh intercession for*

us. {Who also delivered us from all "condemnation," 8:1-4.} ***Who shall separate us from the love of Christ?*** *shall tribulation, or anguish, or persecution, or famine, or nakedness, or peril, or sword? Even as it is written, For thy sake we are killed all the day long; We were accounted as sheep for the slaughter.* ***Nay, in all these things we are more than conquerors through him that loved us.*** *For I am persuaded, that neither death, nor life, nor angels, nor principalities, nor things present, nor things to come, nor powers, nor height, nor depth, nor any other creature, shall be* ***able to separate us from the love of God, which is in Christ Jesus our Lord*** (Romans 8:31-39).

Oh death, where is they victory? *O death, where is thy sting? The sting of death is sin; and the power of sin is the law: but thanks be to God, who giveth us the* ***victory through our Lord Jesus Christ*** (I Corinthians 15:55-57).

We have Access Rights. We have only one mediator and High Priest, Jesus Christ, between us and our access to God's heavenly throne, holy of holies and altar (I Timothy 2:5; Hebrews 2:17; 3:1; 8:1f; 9:11f). And He has provided Christians, from their spiritual rebirth to their faithful physical death, individual access to the benefits of his shed blood: his sin-mediation, arbitration and propitiation/sin payment (I John 2:1f). And that right of access cannot be denied or infringed upon by any regal or religious person or power on earth, or angel in heaven, for that matter (Galatians 1:8).

No king is above our King of Kings. No kingdom is higher than the Kingdom/Church of which we are all equal members. No High Priest is above our High Priest. No mediator is above our Mediator (I Timothy 2:5). No self-appointed or church-anointed pope, priest or saint is above any other Christian priest or saint (I Peter 2:5: Revelation 5:10). In fact, if any of these kings, priests or saints are not Christians or members of Christ's church as per His New Testament requirements, then they have no access whatsoever to Christ's blood or God's throne and altar ... much less any superior access that we Christians need, or must acquire, to become or remain fully forgiven of our sins and faithful members of His Church.

Christ is the only mediator and legal advocate we'll ever need to plead our case before the judgment seat of God and pay the necessary propitiatory blood-penalty for our confessed, or unknown, sins. The Holy Spirit, who knows our hearts' intent better than we do, is also our Intercessor (Romans 8:26-30; see I John 3:20). Though we can have as many human intercessors on earth that choose to pray with and for us, we don't have, nor do we need, any higher human mediator or intercessor in heaven or on earth to fully present our petitions or settle our case before God our Judge (I John 2:1f). One Sovereign Christian Soul can accomplish more in his/her closet than a thousand so-called "Superior Saints" can accomplish in their coffins or cathedrals!

We have Baptismal Rights. Christ actually endowed all responsible sovereign souls, or sinners, with baptismal rights. No priest, church or doctrine can deprive any of God's sovereign souls of their right to access Christ's sin-forgiving blood in baptism by restricting the accomplishment of the act to "ordained" ministers, priests, or to so-called holy places and water. Nor can they deprive any of Christ's baptized believers of their right to baptize others for forgiveness of their sins.

Since every baptized, blood-washed sinner represents another victory for Christ over Satan, Satan uses many false teachers, preachers, and deceptive doctrines to prevent people from being baptized or from being baptized scripturally. I will list a few now, and discuss them more fully in the next chapter, "Sovereign Souls Choose Christ's Church." Some of the unscriptural anti-baptism teachings and practices we will expose, along with some churches which have partnered with Satan in falsely teaching and practicing them are: Infant Baptism, Water-free Baptisms, Blood-free Baptisms, Belief-free Baptisms (e.g., "Baptism Of Desire").

We have Continual Blood-Cleansing Rights. All of Christ's baptized brethren became and remain "Saints" because they were promised total past forgiveness and continual present and future forgiveness and sanctification as long as they continue to seek perfection by walking in the light of Christ's word and cleansing of his shed blood. Their stumbles and sins are not imputed to their account as long as they keep their faith and maintain their resolve to try to walk more like Christ every day (Romans 4:6-8; I John

1:7-10). No Christian can walk perfectly like Christ, but all Christians can be perfected by Christ as he walks. Christianity is a daily walk towards the goal of perfection by growing in the grace, knowledge and forgiveness of Christ; not talk about our personal walk of perfection apart from Christ's forgiveness (Philippians 3:9-12). We seek perfection; but leave the "perfecting" to Christ. All Christians have a blood-bought right to receive this perfection as a gracious gift that they could not possibly merit or purchase. *Grace for grace ... from faith unto faith* (John 1:16; Romans 1:17).

This means all Christians will stumble, but none have to fall! All Christian will be tempted to sin, but none beyond their ability to escape (I Corinthians 10:13). (But their ability to know all their sinful practices and ways of escape is not perfect.) All faithful Christians suffer some sort of persecution and get knocked around and down, but none have to be knocked out of Christ's blood-bought and "bathed" church (II Corinthians 4:8f; II Timothy 3:12). All Christians have some sort of cross to carry for Christ, and some will even die on a Cross like Christ, but none who live faithfully until they die will die in their sins or lose their souls (Matthew 10:38; 16:24; Revelation 2:10).

So just as Satan's *"wages of sin"* keep on indebting an unbelieving sinner and killing his soul until he dies, so God's blood-bought *"free gift of eternal life in Christ Jesus our Lord"* is "the gift that keeps on giving" (Romans 6:23). It keeps on erasing our sin debt ... crediting our sin-account forward ... keeping our record and conscience clean ... removing our condemnation by being our justification, righteousness, peace, rest and joy ... purchasing our freedom, our hell-fire insurance (ahem!), our earthly church membership and spiritual mansions in heaven. Obviously, we have received abundantly many more blessings than we deserved or could have imagined (Ephesians 3:20f)!

All of these blood-bought blessings are fully (to all sinners), freely (w/o charge) and forever offered and backed by the full faith and credit of Christ's heavenly Blood-Bank, High Priesthood and Divine Guarantee.

> *But **Christ** having come a **high priest** of the good things to come, through the greater and more perfect tabernacle, not made with hands, that is to say, not of this creation, nor yet*

*through the blood of goats and calves, but through **his own blood**, entered in **once for all** into the holy place, having obtained eternal redemption. For if the blood of goats and bulls, and the ashes of a heifer sprinkling them that have been defiled, sanctified unto the cleanness of the flesh: how much more shall the **blood of Christ**, who through the/his eternal Spirit offered himself without blemish unto God, **cleanse your conscience** from dead works to serve the living God. And for this cause **he is the mediator of a new covenant**, that a death having taken place for the redemption of the transgressions that were under the first covenant, they that have been **called** may receive the promise of **eternal inheritance*** (Hebrews 9:11-15)

*....then hath he said, Lo, I am come to do thy will. He taketh away the first {OT Covenant}, that he may establish the second {NT Covenant}. By which will we have been **sanctified** through the offering of the **body of Jesus Christ once for all.** And every priest indeed standeth day by day ministering and offering oftentimes the same sacrifices that can never take away sins; but he, when he had offered **one sacrifice for sins for ever**, sat down on the right hand of God; henceforth expecting till his enemies be made the footstool of his feet. **For by one offering he hath perfected for ever them that are sanctified*** (Ibid. 10:9-14)

Because all of Christ's New Testament blood-bought blessings were given *"once for all"* people for all time, they are not open to being rationed, regulated or refused by any higher human religious authority or church/organization due to any of their extra-biblical ecclesiastical rules, restrictions and rituals. Since they didn't do anything to provide these blessings, they don't get to decide how to dispense them. Our Blood-Bought Rights are in our Bible's 'Bill of Rights.' They not only support our freedom of religion in Christ; they also support our freedom from all false religions that would seek to infringe upon our Christian Rights to "Free Salvation." Christ's blood-stained truth hath set us free from Satan and religious dictators (Matthew 20:25-28; John 8:36)!

We have Communion Rights. The major Communion Texts are Matthew 26:17-29; Mark 14:12-25; Luke 22:7-20; John 13:1-

30; Acts 20:7; I Corinthians 10:16; 11:23-30. These texts tell us that Jesus partook of his final earthly Passover on the night he was betrayed and delivered up to be crucified. Jesus said he ***"desired"*** to partake of it with them (Luke 22:15)! It is significant that Jehovah (Jesus Incarnate) gave the Jews the 'Passover' as a Memorial to remind them of their deliverance from the destroying angel by putting lamb's blood on the lintel and two sides of their doors (Exodus 12:21ff). On that first Passover night, Jehovah executed judgment upon all of Egypt's false gods, religions, rulers, priests, and even beasts (Ibid. v. 12). All of Egypt's false gods and leaders had enslaved God's chosen people for over four hundred years. God's bloody judgment that night led to their <u>physical freedom</u> from Egyptian slavery.

So it was entirely fitting that Jesus would institute his Lord's Supper during this Passover Observance. For He, as the Lamb of God, was soon to become our "Passover" by judging the supreme false god, Satan, and freeing his people from <u>spiritual slavery</u> to sin during that same Passover Week (I Corinthians 5:7). This He would accomplish by sacrificing himself and using his own blood to protect us from God's judgment.

When you take all these communion texts together, you'll learn much more about the significance of our **"Communion Rights."**

(1) <u>You'll learn about our "Citizen Rights"</u> in Christ's Kingdom/Church. For Jesus told his Apostles that He would not partake of it again *"until the kingdom of God shall come"* (Luke 22:18). He also said He would not take it again *"until that day when I drink it new with you in my Father's kingdom"* (Matthew 26:29). Then we're told that we, as the Apostles, have communion (or fellowship) with Christ in our partaking of it in his blood-bought *"church"* (I Corinthians 10:16; see Matthew 16:18f for Jesus' use of the words *"kingdom"* and *"church"* interchangeably).

(2) <u>The two elements</u> are unleavened bread and fruit of the vine (usually grape juice). The bread represented his body that was about to be sacrificed in our stead. The fruit of the vine represented his blood of the New Covenant, which was poured out for the remission of our sins. There is no biblical authority for using fermented (leavened) wine in the Lord's Supper. If the Lord had wanted us to drink an intoxicant any time, especially in his

Communion, He could/would have said so. He doesn't ever say fermented wine is to be used for any ceremonial or recreational purpose (see my *Sobering Questions* book). Besides this lack of scriptural authority and harmony with the Passover ingredients, there are legal, religious, moral and health problems involved in dispensing alcohol to Christians or the public without regard for their age, beliefs and health that may be jeopardized by such reckless drug dealing. (The same goes for those cultic "Christian" groups that use marijuana as a sacrament.) The two authorized elements do not have to be blessed or miraculously changed to Christ's real flesh and blood by some higher priestly power or miraculous act. They don't become Christ's flesh and blood; they symbolize Christ's flesh and blood, just as in John 6:53. The charge of "cannibalism" against early Christians was false! Nor is one element, like the fruit of the vine, to be restricted to just the server of the supper.

(3) The Day of Communion is *"the first day of the week,"* also called *"the Lord's"* (Acts 20:7; Revelation 1:10). The text is "generic" as far as the specific time of the day it is to be partaken. (More on "generic" commands later.) That means we have no right to say it is wrong to partake of it any time during the day. The early church partook of the communion after the Resurrection time on Sunday morning because to partake of it earlier would have been before Jesus proved his death was "good news" about his deity and death for us by that resurrection (Romans 1:4). It was never partaken on the "seventh day of the week," the "Sabbath," or upon special manmade holidays that fell upon other days than Sunday (see my *Sabbatarian Concordance and Commentary*). We should desire and plan on meeting with the Lord at his table because He has said he had a *"desire"* to partake of it the first time with his Apostles before he died, and that He would be with them, as with all of those thereafter, who choose to commune with him there (Luke 22:15; Matthew 26:29; I Corinthians 10:16).

(4) The Communion is to be partaken in a "worthy manner" (I Cor. 11:27). We are to remember Christ's death as we partake of his body and blood because it was his death that made our freedom from sin and hope of resurrection possible. We owe Him our full attention and praise as we partake of His spiritual Memorial Feast. Our thoughts are not to be upon the attendants at the table, or who deserves or doesn't deserve to partake of it, or when will we get to eat the real physical food in the old church "Agape Feast," or our new "Pot Luck Meals."

To partake of communion in an *"unworthy manner"* is to partake of it to satisfy physical hunger or ritualistic and legalistic requirements. It does not refer to the sinfulness of an unworthy Christian who has sinned during the past week since his last communion. No Christian would ever be able to partake of communion if he/she could only partake it after living a sin-free week. It is Christ's death and blood that makes all Christians worthy of sitting with him at His table, not their own sinless lives.

We meet with the Lord at his table because He's there and He deserves to be there, not because we deserve to be there. In fact, it is our daily need for forgiveness by His atoning blood that should compel us to meet with Him at his table and **thank him** for his grace, mercy and forgiveness during the past week. When Jesus cleansed the ten lepers, and only one returned to thank him for his mercy, His question, *"where are the nine?,"* shows he expects us to be forever grateful for his physical and spiritual blessings (Luke 17:12-19). The old Communion Hymn expresses our Savior's sentiment so well:

I gave my life for thee, My precious blood I shed, That thou might'st ransomed be, and quickened from the dead; I gave, I gave My life for thee, What hast thou giv'n to me? I gave, I gave my life for thee, What hast thou giv'n for me? (Frances R. Havergal, P.P. Bliss).

Please abide a little personal candor from this old Christian. If fellowshipping with Jesus in His Communion isn't the reason I'm there to partake of it, then I can find no reason to be there at all. Or if I attend a church that does not honor Christ's word and keep his Communion as He instructed, on every first day of the week, I won't be attending that church a second time. I'd rather travel a hundred miles to attend a small scriptural church (like Philadelphia) where Jesus is present in His Communion than to cross the street to attend a large liberal church (like Laodicea) where Jesus has never arrived or has left the auditorium. (Just like I left the coliseum in Lubbock, Texas on May 31, 1976, when they announced that "Elvis had left the auditorium!") "If Christ isn't there, it doesn't matter where there is! If Christ is here, it doesn't matter where here is!"

(5) <u>Communion is by Invitation Only</u>. We must never forget that we Christians get to commune with our Creator, Lord, Savior, King, High Priest and Best Friend on earth because He **invited** us to do so. It's as if the Lord said: "That's right, Gerald, I'm inviting you to meet with your best friend (John 15:13f), in Sweet Communion every first day of the week!" This is why partaking of Communion is not presented as a command in scripture; it is presented as a blessed privilege that we should **desire** to do as *"often"* as He chooses, just as Jesus **desired** when he instituted it. (If you have to be commanded to attend a person's funeral or memorial service, you didn't really love that person!)

So it is all of these precious things that we need to remember when making our decision to partake of Communion. We need to remember that since Christ has promised to be there, **He deserves and expects us to be there.** This divine expectation is multiplied exponentially when we consider that Christ invited us to be there even if it requires us to sacrifice our time, profit, pleasure, worldly pursuits and appointments to be there (Luke 16:16-24). If He's there, for whom would I be elsewhere? If He's there for communion, for what event, short of a loved one's funeral, would I be somewhere else? If He's always going to be there, or anywhere I choose to partake communion with him (including in my home), why would I ever plan on being anywhere else? Because our Communion with Christ is a God-Given Invite, we Sovereign Christian Souls must consider it as our God-Given Right and Blessing to meet there and commune with Him.

(6) <u>This Communion Right</u> is not to be misused or abused. The Lord's Communion is NOT to be used as "sacrament" of merit for our forgiveness, or refused as a form of punishment for our sins. Even if a Christian has fallen away and been disfellowshipped, there is no Bible injunction against his beginning his restoration by partaking of the very emblems that represent Christ's sacrifice for his sins (II Peter 1:9). We need to remember that we have a right to sit at Christ's table with Him because of His Invitation and not anyone else's. If any church refuses to allow you to partake of Christ's Communion with them, do it by yourself at home: you will never dine alone! (Many churches, who disallow those who are non-members or disfellowshipped to partake of Communion in their assemblies, do not deny them the right to pray, sing and donate money in their assemblies. Think about it!)

We have Restoration Rights. Christ made the restoration of an erring Christian a matter of spiritual personal sorrow and penitence and not a physical ecclesiastical process (compare I Corinthians 5:1-13 with II Corinthians 2:5-11). Therefore, no erring brother may be required by any religious ordinance or doctrine to do any extra-biblical, ritualistic acts — like counting beads, saying "Three Hail Mary Prayers," citing rosaries — or engaging in any acts of *"severity to the body"* in penance for his sins (Colossians 2:20-23). If Christ didn't require such before we became Christians — when we were laden with years/decades of unforgiven sins and were not His brothers & sisters — then surely He doesn't require such of his erring brethren and sisters who have returned from their wayward pursuits (see Hebrews 2:11-12). What does our Shepherd say:

About His straying sheep? According to His words in Luke 15:3-7, a straying sheep is to be lovingly and diligently sought for and led back to the fold ... not whipped or driven back to the fold. We must remember that our Good Shepherd laid down his life for his sheep (John 10:11-18). They are His sheep, not ours!

About His Prodigal Son? According to His words in Luke 15:11-32, the Son who separated himself from his Father's love and family was welcomed back with opened arms and continued blessings because of his change of heart (which is the definition of the word "repent") ... not with a list of reparations and repercussions inflicted by the superior self-righteous son. (This is yet another reason why we should not call any man on earth our "Father" in the sense of spiritual reverence or Sonship!)

About His Church's Public Sinners? According to His words in I Cor. 5:1-11 and II Cor. 2:5-11, the church fornicator — who had been coddled, cajoled and even encouraged to continue in his sin by weak Christians, rather than being rebuked and withdrawn from by the members of the church (for their protection as well as the church's image) — was still to be received upon his true repentance ... and not after imposing additional unauthorized church punishments. These non-biblical and unChristian acts only assist Satan by allowing him to use Christ's church to prevent a struggling saint from availing himself of his immediate rightful return (or *"seventy seven returns"*) to Christ — whom he really left (not just the church assembly) — and his cleansing blood (Matthew 18:21-22).

When we see one of our blood-bought brothers and sisters being drawn back into the world and straying from the fold, we need to remember that "There but for the grace of God go I." And we need to lovingly and seriously convict them of their sin, rebuke and reprove them, encourage them to repent, give them time to repent, and offer to lift them up ... not kick them while they're down. If our Holy God offered "time to repent" to the wicked fornicators and idolaters in the church of Thyatira, our fellow Christians deserve likewise from us blood-washed saints (Revelation 2:21; 7:13-14). Struggling and fallen sinners don't need to be put through more physical suffering for their sins; their sins already do that. They violated Christ's laws, not ours. They considered Christ's blood for nought, not ours. Their first need is Christ's forgiveness, not just ours. If Christ is willing to use his blood to forgive their sins without anything more than a simple "forgive me Lord" request, that's His business, not ours. It cost Him his life, not ours. He's the Savior, not you or I or the church. We need to protect the "Restoration Rights" of our brethren equally with the "Salvation Rights" of the lost ... because we might need them ourselves! We all need and cherish all of **Christ's Blood Rights!**

Freedom isn't Free!

Of course, all of these Christian Blood Rights sound almost too good be true. It sounds so easy for us. I mean, who wouldn't want all these rights, freedoms and "free gifts" from God? And, indeed, physically speaking, God made it very easy for us to accept and keep his free gifts without physical, legalistic or monetary costs. He had to because His gifts (like forgiveness) were so priceless that no one would ever be able to merit or pay for a single one of them. Even if a person kept everyone of God's laws after he had broken just one of them, he would only be doing his duty and not earning any forgiveness for his past or future infractions (Luke 17:10). Even if every sinner shed his own blood for his sins, he wouldn't be paying <u>for</u> his sins, he would be paying <u>because</u> of his sins. Because of this, our God didn't demand that we shed a drop of our blood for our past sins. Nor did he require that we shed any of our blood to remain forgiven. God's Blood-Gifts have to remain "Free" regardless of what we do after accepting them.

So it is easy to talk about all of our Christian Rights and Freedoms. It's also easy to open God's word and prove to others that they're our Religious Rights. Just as it's easy to read the American Bill of Rights, and do the same thing! I've done both ... without any cost! Freedom <u>of</u> religion, and, yes, even freedom <u>from</u> religion, is God's Gift of Freedom to all mankind!

But .... that doesn't mean there's no cost to be incurred by us for accepting, rejecting and sharing God's blood-gifts with others. For like all other God-given rights and righteous freedoms, this freedom isn't free! Just because Christ's gift of salvation from sin isn't "For Sale," and you don't have to physically pay for it upon your acceptance, doesn't mean it's free for anyone to take without meeting Christ's preconditions of ownership. Just because you are free to reject it and continue sinning without incurring any immediate physical judgment from God doesn't mean you won't regret it later in life or after you die (Ecclesiastes 8:11-13; Hebrews 9:27). As they say, "There's a Payday Someday!" Just because it's ours to freely share doesn't mean there's no cost to us for sharing it.

For, you see, my dear reader, we Christians can't possess or publically display such a powerful right and freedom in a sinful world ruled by Satan and his wicked human servants without any costs to bear. Proof of that can be found by looking at the great costs that were required and paid by those who provided the freedoms and "free gifts" that we sometimes take for granted.

Proof: It cost Jesus his life to earn this freedom for us. As the old hymn, "Jesus Paid It All," so powerfully proclaims:

> Verse 3: *For noth-ing good have I, Where-by Thy grace to claim—I'll wash my garments white In the blood of Calvary's lamb. Jesus paid it all, All to him I owe; Sin had left a crimson stain, He washed it white as snow* (Mrs. H.M. Hall & John T. Grape).

Proof: It cost the Apostles their physical freedoms and lives to deliver it to us. We must remember that Satan killed most of Christ's greatest cross-carrying freedom-fighters, who put sharing their blood-bought freedom from sin above their own physical freedom to live (II Corinthians 4:7-12; 11:23-33). Satan enslaved and killed their bodies, but he could not kill their souls (Matthew 10:28). Rather, he freed their souls by killing them:

> *For I am already being **offered**, and the time of my **departure** {exodus} is come. I have **fought the good fight**. I have **finished the course**, I have **kept the faith** {and shared it}: henceforth, there is laid up for me the **crown of righteousness**, which the Lord, the righteous judge, shall give to me in that day; and not to me only, but also to **all them** {us} that have loved his appearing* (II Timothy 4:6-8; cf., Philippians 1:21-23).

Now these blood-drenched Apostles didn't sacrifice their lives to deliver Christ's blood-bought individual freedoms so we could turn around and surrender our intelligence and sovereignty to a bunch of wolves in sheep's clothing who want to lead Christ's sheep to sectarian slaughter. They didn't deliver Christ's inspired truths to any self-appointed "clergy," made up of pious men in robes upon lofty podiums in elaborate cathedrals, demanding that people come and bow before them for their sacraments and sermonizations. They gave them to the "people" (Greek "laos," English "laity"), who would go house to house, into the market places, highways and byways, to proclaim the freedom of Christ to the unwashed masses. The Lord Jesus, who rode into town on a donkey, built his church — His "called out people" ("Ekklesia)" — upon himself and *"without walls;"* not upon a man residing within walls of a fortress and riding around in a chariot, limousine or "Popemobile" (Matthew 21:1-11; Zechariah 2:4).

Proof: It cost countless thousands of Christians their lifestyles and life's blood to preach Christ and him crucified all over the world (see Acts 8:1-4).

Proving to Us: Satan is still active in our world. We Christian "Sovereign Souls" and Soldiers are his primary targets. We are armed for spiritual warfare against him and all of his spiritual and physical allies who seek to keep us from continuing to fulfill Christ's Great Commission to preach the Gospel of light to every sinner in his world of darkness (Ephesians 6:11-18; II Corinthians 4:3-6; 10:3-6).

The Apostle Paul warned all Christians during his day and afterwards about Satan's constant assault on Christians via his many spiritual allies, human helpers and wicked devices:

> *But the Spirit saith expressly, that in later times* {not "end times"} *some shall **fall away from the faith**, giving heed to **seducing spirits** and **doctrines of demons**, through the hypocrisy of **men that speak lies**, branded in their own conscience as with a hot iron....*(I Timothy 4:1-3).

> *But I will tarry at Ephesus until Pentecost; for a **great door and effectual is opened** unto me, and there are **many adversaries**"* (I Corinthians 16:8-9).

> *But to whom ye forgive anything, I forgive also: for what I also have forgiven, if I have forgiven anything, for your sakes have I forgiven it in the presence of Christ; that no advantage may gained over us by **Satan**: **for we are not ignorant of his devices*** (II Corinthians 2:10-11).

The Apostle John listed three of Satan's most effective ***"devices"*** — or maybe I should say "human vices" or "Achilles heels" — in his warnings against apostasy:

> *For all that is in the world, the **lust of the flesh** and the **lust of the eyes** and the **vain glory of life**, is not of the Father, but of the world* (I John 2:15).

Which three devices were used very effectively against Adam and Eve in the Garden of Eden in Genesis 3:6.

> *And when the woman saw the tree was **good for food*** {lust of the flesh}, *and that it was a **delight to the eyes*** {lust of the eyes}; *and that the tree was to be **desired to make one wise*** {the vain glory of life}, *she did eat ... and he did eat ...* and you know the rest of the story has been repeated ever since!

Finally, the Apostle Peter warned First Century Christians about the need for constant vigilance against our Number One Enemy, Satan: *"Be sober, be watchful: your **adversary the devil**, as a roaring lion, walketh about, seeking whom he may devour"* (I Peter 5:8). Since nothing has changed in this sinful world since then, we have also been forewarned that Satan has his sights set upon us, including you, my fellow Christian soldier! "Semper Fi!"

Thus, Satan has many helpers and allies in his army. He has many sinful devices (including the "Three Devices" we just discussed) and seducing spirits with demonic doctrines, which are perpetrated upon unsuspecting humanity by hypocritical, lying preachers, teachers and churches. Satan uses all these human helpers and hellacious devices to keep sinners enslaved in sin ... or to keep sinners from knowing they are sinners ...... or to keep them from knowing how to be saved from sin ... or to recapture them after they have been saved from sin (Revelation 2:20; I Timothy 4:1-3; I Peter 2:11; II Peter 2:1-22). (Note: We will learn more about Satan's use of Demonic Doctrines in our next chapter on "Choosing Christ's Church.")

So, what shall we say about our Free Gifts and Gospel of Salvation? The Christ who provided them, and the Ones who delivered them to us in Christ's New Testament, paid dearly for them. Even so shall we have to continue to pay whatever physical price it takes to fight the good fight if we are to keep the faith till our final departure from this war-torn world. We need to pray for all Christians who are engaged in these costly struggles and deadly battles. We also need to pray for all men in high and helpful positions — politicians, rulers, soldiers — whom God uses to keep our world peaceful enough for us to continue to share His freedom-giving gospel (I Timothy 2:1-4). For these, and all others, who fight in any war to further God's desire to save all men, I offer this short prayer request: "Rule Righteously" (Proverbs 14:34; Romans 13:1-7). I also want to offer a verse from a past popular and patriotic song, entitled *"Some Gave All,"* for all fallen soldiers who gave and give their lives to protect religious freedom for all:

All gave some, some gave all. Some stood through for the red white and blue – and some had to fall. And if you think of me, think of all your liberties...and recall, some gave all (Billy Ray Cyrus, singer and author, with Cindy Cyrus).

CHAPTER FOUR
Sovereign Souls Choose Christ's Church

CHRIST'S CHOICE

The Modern Denominational World's First Church Choice is *"Your Choice."* I know this is so because *"Attend the Church of Your Choice"* is the most respected and revered quote in today's ecumenical "Christian" world of hundreds of denominational churches with different names, organizations, founders, prophets, creeds and "Bibles." Their Second Choice is: *"One church is as good as another."* Their Third Choice is: *"All churches" are above Christian Criticism."* Their Fourth Choice is: *"No church is worth arguing about."* (For, you see, they don't "argue religion and Politics!")

The main problem I have found with all of these go-along-to-get-along "Christian" profundities is that I haven't been able to find a single one of them ever coming out of Christ's mouth or his Apostles' pens in the entire New Testament. I haven't been able to find any New Testament text or teaching that remotely says: "Attend the Church of Your Choice, Their Choice, My Choice" or "Everybody's Choice." I can't even find one "Attend Saint Peter's Church ... Saint Paul's Church ... Saint Mary's Church" or "Peter, Paul & Mary's Church" in the entire New Testament. Can you imagine that?

Maybe the reason I haven't been able to find any of these different church affiliations in the New Testament — nor any of the modern names like "The Baptist Church, Methodist Church, Mormon Church, Lutheran Church, Roman Catholic Church," et al. — is because Christ never authorized any churches to separate themselves apart from, or above, other churches by naming or identifying themselves by any of these kinds of persons, places or doctrines. And since Christ hasn't updated or amended his Unabridged New Testament Church Directory since He fully and finally revealed it in the First Century, maybe that's why I can't find any mention of, authorization for, or need for any of these manmade churches today. Wasn't His Church-brand good enough?

But, now, let me tell you what I have found in Christ's "Church-Manual"— His New Testament. I have found Christ praying that all of his disciples would be united in his teachings (John 17:21-23). I have found, right out of the mouth of the Lord Jesus Christ himself, *"I will build My Church"* (Matthew 16:18). And I believe I am well within biblical application boundaries to say that if you would have asked Jesus Christ if you could attend the *"church of your choice,"* that he would have said something like this: *"No, you need to attend THE CHURCH OF MY CHOICE!"*

I have also found the Apostle Paul preaching that same "unity" within Christ's *"one body/church, faith"* before he roundly condemned some who were seeking to divide Christians by identifying themselves by the **name** of their favorite Apostle or preacher (Ephesians 1:22f; 4:3-6; I Corinthians 1:10-13). I have also found churches being stigmatized and condemned by their sinful and unscriptural behavior, like in Revelation 2-3, but not promoted as such as if it was a unique and good thing. You know, like how we now have so-called "Christian Churches," like the Metropolitan Community Church, proudly promoting themselves as being "Gay Churches" (see my *Homosexuality and the Bible*)! Of course, we Christians still aren't supposed to say anything bad about another person's bad religious beliefs, behaviors or church. Believe that at your own risk!

Oh well, I digress. Let us proceed with Christ's Church Choice and see why HIS CHOICE is the ONLY CHOICE any Sovereign Soul should consider in his attempt to please the Sovereign Christ.

Christ's Church/Kingdom was Planned in Eternity

Christ's New Spiritual Church/Kingdom was planned in eternity as a vital component in his *"eternal purpose"* and scheme of redemption (Ephesians 1:3-11; 3:5-11). (The word "kingdom" emphasizes the rule of Christ, the word "church" refers to the people of Christ.) If you read these verses, you will see that His church members today were also foreknown before the foundation of the world. This proves the church was not an afterthought of Jesus — an interim arrangement and temporary substitution for any alleged physical kingdom to come — which Jesus was forced to set up because he had been rejected as being the king of the Jews. **First,** because such a stupendous oversight would prove Jesus was not the Omniscient God he claimed to be. It makes Christ's will subservient to man's actions and destroys his sovereignty thereby. We Sovereign Souls reject such a wimpy defeatist belief. **Second**, because the Jewish population wanted to make him king (John 6:15). **Third**, because Jesus made it clear that his new kingdom would not be a worldly physical kingdom that you could see ... but a spiritual kingdom within us (Luke 17:20-21; John 3:3-5; 18:36). His word also makes it clear that Jesus cannot be a Royal High Priest on earth (Hebrews 7:11-17; 8:1-4). **Fourth**, because the many prophecies about Jesus' birth (born to be a king!), life, death, New Covenant, Divine Royal Priesthood (which requires Jesus to be a King at the same time he is a Priest), worldwide kingdom/church of all races of people, until the end of time (not just over Jews in Israel for a thousand years), repudiate this narrow, ethnocentric, nationalistic view in its entirety. **Fifth**, the fact that Christ's Kingdom and reign as king upon his throne can be found numerous times in the past and present tense throughout the New Testament proves it had come right after his Ascension (Acts 2:29-36; I Corinthians 15:24f; Colossians 1:13; Hebrews 1:8f; 12:28; Revelation 1:9; 5:10). How can Jesus be called the "Christ" (anointed Messiah and King) and "King of Kings" if He is not yet a king over any kingdom? **Sixth,** the present church-kingdom of Christ on earth cannot be removed or destroyed to make way for a new earthly kingdom (Hebrews 12:28). **Seventh,** this spiritual kingdom is to be delivered up to God at Christ's *"coming,"* at *"the end,"* and not changed into a physical one to last for a thousand years (I Corinthians 15:23-26).

Christ's Church/Kingdom of Prophecy

Though the New Testament name, "Jesus Christ," and appellative, "Church of Christ," cannot be found in the Old Testament, the identity of Jehovah, the pre-Incarnate Christ, as the new King, High Priest, Branch, Shepherd of his New Testament people (Jews and Gentiles), worldwide spiritual kingdom of Israel (without walls and boundaries) are too abundant to include in this book. So here are just a few prophetic texts fulfilled **in** Christ's new kingdom/church: **Genesis 12:1-3** in Luke 1:55,73; Galatians 3:8-29; Isaiah 2:2-4; 9:6-7; 46:9. **Joel 2:38** in Acts 2:15-47; 3:18-26; 15:14-18. **Jeremiah 31:31-34** in Hebrews 8:7-13; 10:16f). **Daniel 2:31-44; 9:2, 27** in Luke 2:-25-32; 21:20-22).

Christ's Church/Kingdom Promised

Before Jesus died, He promised he would build his church after he died (Matthew 16:16-19). He also promised in this premier church text that the *"gates of hades* {the unseen realm of the disembodied spirits} *would not prevail against it."* That means Jesus promised he would return from the grave to build his church, and not just have his Apostles build his church in his absence. How could Scripture be more clear and complete in telling us of Jesus' divinely planned, prophetically promised and powerfully executed spirit-departure, bodily death, burial, spirit-reentry, bodily resurrection, ascension, coronation and church-building all packaged in one sentence from the Master's mouth?! He also promised his coming kingdom in a similar bold and prophetic statement to a head of the Jews, Nicodemus, and Governor of the State, Pilate (John 3:3-5; 18:33-37). With such a Supreme Sovereign King and Savior, how could we ever bow to any other mere human church founder or leader? This Sovereign Soul doesn't bow to any man, woman or angel!

Christ's Church/Kingdom Preached

The Lord's promise to give Peter the *"keys of the kingdom"* in Matthew 16:19 was a prophetic appointment of Peter being the first Apostle to preach the arrival, or opening, of Christ's new church/kingdom. Scriptural proof of the fulfillment of this promise can be found in Acts 2:14-47. On the Day of Pentecost, Peter was empowered by the Holy Spirit to preach the first gospel message, which resulted in three thousand Jews being added by the Lord to his church/kingdom. So, in this historical and symbolic sense, Peter used Christ's revealed entrance instructions — *"keys"* — to unlock the door into Christ's church. All the Apostles preached the same Gospel which offered entrance into Christ's Church, or Kingdom (I Corinthians 15:1-8). And they were responsible for people of all nations becoming members of Christ's church ... not **their** churches (Ibid. 1:10-17; Galatians 1:6-12)!

So Peter's being given the *"keys of the kingdom"* has nothing, whatsoever, to do with Peter being appointed to a higher office than the other Apostles. It is not equivalent to Peter being made into the foundation, head or door of the church, as some churches teach. Those "top positions" belong to Christ (John 10:7-9; I Corinthians 3:12). Nor do Jesus' words to Peter in John 21:15-17 — *"Feed/tend my lambs/sheep"* — mean He was made the "Chief Shepherd." Peter, himself, said that position belonged to no one but Jesus Christ (I Peter 2:25; 5:4).

Notice, the "keys" were Christ's "keys," not Peter's. It was Christ's church/kingdom, not Peter's. Christ was the door, not Peter (John 10:7-9). Christ opened the door, not Peter. Christ allows or disallows entry (Acts 2:47; Revelation 3:7f,). If a person does not obey the Gospel, Christ will not add that person, or allow that person to enter into His church or kingdom (John 3:5). (Just as He locked all others outside the Ark when he locked Noah inside the Ark!) If a preacher does not use the same "Keys" that Peter used in Acts 2:36-47, none of those who follow his/her entry instructions will gain entry into Christ's church. This is serious business! This is why we simply must insist on being Sovereign Preachers who rely totally on Christ's sovereign word in our preaching. The Key to effective Gospel Preaching is to "Preach the word," or the "key words," or the "word keys" (II Timothy 4:2)!

Christ's Church/Kingdom Structure

Founder: The Founder and Builder of the Church of Christ is Christ (Matthew 16:18). Any other founder/builder is totally unqualified, incapable and unacceptable. (For more study on this text and other alleged founders/builders see Supplemental Studies).

Foundation: Christ is also the Foundation of the His Church (Matt. 16:18). He is the foundation preached by the prophets and apostles, and upon which they built by preaching his word and instructions for each stone to be added to his holy temple (I Corinthians 3:11; Ephesians 2:20-22: I Peter 2:4f). He's also the

"Cornerstone," which is a part of the foundation and is the stone from which all the straight lines and angles (the laws and principles) of the entire building are set (Isaiah 28:16).

Head/King: The Founder of the Church is the *"Head"* of the Church/Body (Ephesians 1:22; Colossians 1:18). You can't have two heads on His body! You can't serve two masters (Him and the Pope!). He is also the *"King"* of His Kingdom. (You can't have a "King" if you have no "Kingdom!") His church members are also called *"citizens of His Kingdom"* (Ephesians 2:19). You can't enter a kingdom, receive a kingdom, or be a citizen of a kingdom that has not come (John 3:5; Colossians 1:13). So the Kingdom the prophets foretold was, and still is, here (Acts 3:24-26)!

Church Body/House/Temple: Christ's church is not a physical building, temple, institution or organization. It is a living, breathing Body/Organism made up of living stones. Its members are called "Christians, churches of God/Christ, members of his Body, His brethren, saints, children of God, household of God, priests and living stones in his spiritual temple, on top of Mount Zion in the heavenly city of Jerusalem; the Israel of God" (Acts 11:26; I Corinthians 1:2; 12:12-20; Galatians 6:16; Hebrews 2:11f; 3:4ff; 11:10; 12:22f; I Peter 2:5). The Lord's true church is not totally identified by any one of these appellatives/names being over its door; but by being what every one of these descriptive terms requires. We may call the Lord's church anything that it is! For example, it is not called "The Lord's Church" in the New Testament, but it is ok to call it such because it is the Lord's church! It is not called "Peter's Church" in the New Testament, and not ok to call it such because it never was Peter's church!

Considering all of this, what sovereign soul would exchange his membership in Christ's worldwide church and spiritual kingdom for one physical church built by a man? Such is not only vanity (Psalms 127:1); such is also to forfeit salvation. For Christ has promised to *"save his church/body/bride"* at the end of time, and no other (Ephesians 5:22-32).

Christ's Church Pattern

Just as our Creator gave Adam and Eve instructions as to how to maintain their perpetual physical existence and spiritual relationship with God in the Garden of Eden ... just as our Physical Savior gave Noah specific instructions as to how build the Ark and save mankind ... just as our Holy God gave Moses instructions on how to build the Ark of the Covenant and the Tabernacle (Exodus 25:40; Hebrews 8:5)... and Solomon the Temple ... so our Lord and Savior gave his Apostles specific instructions as to how to assist Him in continuing the building of his spiritual kingdom/church.

He did this by giving them a New Testament **"Pattern"** (from Greek "Tupos" – die, form, mold, model) as to how His church could be exactly duplicated, even in small details, until the day He delivered it up to God at the end of time. Surely, if we can duplicate countless physical things (from automobiles to houses) and institutions from human blueprints, models, documents, instructions and Patterns, we can duplicate the Lord's Church by simply following his original instructions and words rather than the latest fads, fashions, fellowships and ways of thinking.

In carrying out this Plan and Pattern, we must make sure we follow what the Lord told us to do and not do what he didn't tell us not to do. This is one of the main reasons there is so much division and chaos in Christianity today. The biblical philosophy of many churches is that they can do anything that the Lord didn't specifically prohibit, rather than they must only do what He specifically authorized. For example, the Lord only told us what to use in Communion (*"fruit of the vine and bread"*); but He didn't tell us not to use "water" as Mormons, fermented wine as RCC, marijuana as Coptic Churches and Roger Christie's THC Ministry and Church in Hawaii, or any of the other possible unmentioned combinations: meatloaf and whiskey, popcorn and Pepsi! If your only Church Affirmatives are Negatives, you have no case for being Christ's Church or before the throne of Christ!

To the extent that churches conform to the Lord's Pattern for His Church, is the extent of their being His church. If they fail to meet his Pattern as per Initial Church Membership (as we'll present first), then they will not be members of the Lord's Church regardless of how many other parts of the Pattern they follow. If any church fails to follow any of the key parts of the Pattern, then that church will be an erring church of the Lord subject to being judged by the Lord as He sees fit. Let's cite the texts that assure us of these Pattern Facts; then some that warn against deviating from

Christ's Church Pattern; then we'll go into all the "Divine Details" found in that Pattern.

> *I beseech you therefore, be ye **imitators of me**. For this cause have I sent unto you **Timothy**, who is my beloved and faithful child in the Lord, who shall put you in remembrance of **my ways which are in Christ**, even as **I teach everywhere in every church*** (I Corinthians 4:16f).

> *Hold the **pattern of sound words** which thou hast heard from me, in faith and love which is in Christ Jesus.... And the **things which thou hast heard** from me among many witnesses, the **same commit** thou to **faithful men**, who shall be **able to teach others also*** (II Timothy 1:13; 2:2).

> *The elder {John} unto the **elect lady** {the elect church/bride of Christ} and her **children** {members}, whom I love in **truth**; and not I only, but also all they that know the truth; for the **truth's sake** which abideth in us, and it shall be with us **for ever**: Grace, mercy, peace shall be with us, from God the Father, and from Jesus Christ, the Son of the Father, in truth and love. **I rejoice** greatly that **I have found certain of thy children walking in truth**, even as we received commandment from the Father* (II John 1-4).

1. <u>Christ's Instructions on church membership</u>. Christ's 120 disciples and 12 Apostles were the first members of Christ's first church that officially began on the Day of Pentecost (Acts 1:13 thru 2:47). These disciples and the Twelve Apostles had already been immersed in John's Baptism for the forgiveness of their past sins and were <u>added</u> by Christ to his New spiritual kingdom/church when He ascended to the throne (cf. Mark 1:4f). These are the first members of Christ's newly built church — the *"church/ekklesia"* ("the called out ones"), the *"them"* — to whom the three thousand new converts were <u>added</u> on The Day of Pentecost (Acts 2:41,47). These new converts were <u>added</u> to the Lord's Church by the Lord after they had believed and accepted that Christ was the Son of God, their new anointed King over spiritual Israel, who was sitting on God's throne in heaven, repented of their sins, and were baptized for the forgiveness of their sins. They were then given the indwelling *"gift of the Holy Spirit,"* as a seal of their divine sonship and guarantee of their resurrection (Acts 2:38f; Romans 8:11; Galatians 3:26 thru 4:6; Ephesians 1:13-14).

Notice: you do not "join" Christ's Church; He adds you to it upon your sincere and faithful obedience to his membership instructions. They're Christ's simple instructions, not mine or any other church's entrance requirements. Christ only adds people to His Church of His Choice and not to any other church, or choice, regardless of its claims or size. He never added a single soul to any false church, even if that church called itself "The Church of Christ/God/Holy Spirit" or "Universal Church." And He never accepted, or will accept, any false church as His Church.

Many modern manmade "churches" have more requirements than Christ gave here in Acts 2:38-47 in order to become a member of their church! For example, read what you must believe in order to be considered a member in the Roman Catholic Church:

> *"The Faithful, the **Members of the Church**, are those who are baptized and who **acknowledge the Pope to be the Vicar** of Christ on earth and the visible **head of the church."** ...* which includes ***"devotion to Mary**, the Mother of God"* (Penny Catechism 72, "Who are the Members of the Church?").

Besides the fact that there was no such church as the "Roman Catholic Church" in existence from the First through the Fourth Centuries, Bible believers must reject their baptism of infants, mode of baptism (sprinkling or pouring), the Pope as the Vicar of Christ and Head of the church on earth, and the notion that we in any way worship Mary or call her something the Bible never calls her, "the Mother of God." But I digress.

Christ also taught us how to disfellowship (not the same as RCC "excommunication") an erring member of His church, and told us He would remove the candlestick of any church that left Him and His teachings (I Corinthians 5:1-13; Revelation 2:4f). If other churches were acceptable, Christ would have told us so. Yet, instead of doing that, He told us there was only **One Head of One Body**—Christ over His One Church (Ephesians 1:22f; 4:4).

All new members of Christ's church immediately become "Priests" and "Saints" (sanctified ones), and all were called

"Christians" after the Lord had them *"called"* such in Antioch (Acts 11:26; 26:28; I Peter 4:16). For ***"priests"*** see I Peter 2:5,9; Revelation 1:6; 5:10. For ***"saints"*** see Romans 1:7; I Corinthians 1:2; 14:33; Ephesians 1:1; Philippians 1:1; Colossians 1:2,4,12,26; etc. There are no Higher Priests and no Special or Super Saints mentioned in the New Testament.

Speaking personally, I'm as high of a Christian, Priest and Saint as there is. And so are you if you're a Christian. As a Christian saint and priest, I can offer my own spiritual sacrifices and commune with God directly in and through Christ (Hebrews 13:15). As the old Country singer, George Jones, once said: "I don't need no rocking chair," I say: "I don't need no high chair; I don't need no dead saint to help me in prayer; I don't need no priest's confession booth to help me reach the Man upstairs; I don't need no rocking chair!" I'm a Sovereign Saint!

2. <u>Christ's Instructions on Church Leaders/Offices</u>. Christ didn't leave any important work, leadership or office in his Church-Kingdom open to uninspired human standards and qualifications. Many people are surprised to find out how our Lord revealed so many detailed instructions on every position of service in his kingdom: from the highest (Apostles) to the lowest church-dependent widow (See Ephesians 4:11). Actually, as the Lord's exaltation of the "Widow's mite" illustrated, there are no low positions in the Lord's church! As one of the Old Temple doorkeepers said, *"I had rather be a doorkeeper in the house of my God, Than to dwell in the tents of wickedness"* (Psalms 84:10).

Head of the Church — Christ was, is, and always will be the Only Head and Highest Leader of His Church and King over his kingdom (Ephesians 1:22; 4:15; 5:23). If God viewed Israel's choosing to have an earthly king as a rejection of Him as being their King, how much more is any church's choosing to have an earthly head and king a rejection of having the Omnipresent Christ as their head and king (I Samuel 8:4-7). He was born to be our king (John 18:37). And He died, was resurrected and ascended to his throne to prove He would always be our only king (Acts 2:22-36). And He will reign as king until he delivers up His kingdom to God (I Corinthians 15:24f). He is the *"only Potentate, the King of kings, and Lord of lords"* (I Timothy 6:15; Revelation 17:14)!

Therefore, the anointed Christ/King needed no Successor because He is always with and over his church (Matthew 28:20). That's why you will not find a single syllable in His entire New Testament about Christ needing an earthly Successor, Substitute or "Vicar" to act in His place. Since no human could qualify, He appointed his Holy Spirit to deliver his New Testament to His church and to indwell every new member of his church as their Paraclete/Comforter (John 14:16-17, 26; 16:7; Acts 2:4ff, 38).

This means that every person, priest or pope who has ever claimed to be any sort of substitute, or "Vicar" of Christ (from Latin "Vicarius Christi"), has usurped not only Christ, but also the Holy Spirit who is with us and in us. We cannot be the Sovereign Souls God recreated us to be in His Church by doing anything under any authority or name other than that approved by *"the Father, Son and Holy Spirit"* (Matthew 28:19). Christ didn't set us free from slavery to Satan and sin so we could be subservient to mere men and their sectarian authority and doctrines. And any church that doesn't comply with all of Christ's essential instructions and requirements does not compare with it, complete it or continue it. It just contradicts it and confuses the masses.

Apostles — There are two kinds of "Apostles" mentioned in Christ's New Testament. (The Greek word *Apostolos* simply means "one sent forth, a messenger, delegate.") There were those who were sent out by churches or went with another Apostle, like Barnabas (Acts 14:14), who did not have to meet the same qualifications as the Twelve Apostles: who were all equal *"Ambassadors"* for Christ (II Corinthians 5:20). They were appointed as such when they were sent out to represent Him and repeat His words. Yet such is a work they had to do, not a rank.

Paul made it clear that an Ambassador of/for Christ is a person who acts in behalf of Christ, not in place of Christ. The Greek word Paul was inspired to use here for *"ambassador"* ("Presbeuo") means "a senior person, elder, who acts as a responsible mouthpiece for Christ. One who does not utter his thoughts, offers, promises and demands, only those of his ruler or king." And not a one of Christ's Apostles ever exalted himself above the other Apostles as a "Chief Ambassador/Apostle," and not a one of them ever dared to exalt himself as being "Christ's Vicar." Let's read Paul's full quote in II Corinthians 5:20 and reinforce his understanding of the equality of all the Apostles as Ambassadors:

> *We are **ambassadors** therefore **on behalf of Christ**, as though God were entreating by us: **we beseech** you **on behalf of Christ**, be ye reconciled to God.*

This verse clearly shows that the Apostolic Ambassadors knew they were speaking *"on behalf of Christ"* and not in the "place of Christ." It also show they didn't lord themselves over the lowly heathen sinners by asking them to bow to them. Rather they humbly begged (*"beseech"*) them to be reconciled to God.

It is of extreme importance, in these days of **false apostles**, which is nothing new (II Corinthians 11:13), to study and strictly apply Christ's required qualifications for any replacement of any Apostle. **(1)** They all had to be living during the Ministry of Christ and had to have seen the Resurrected Christ (Acts 1:21-26). **(2)** The Apostles themselves chose the only Apostolic Successor (of Judas) who was ever to be replaced in order to fulfill David's prophecy and to maintain the number of Twelve Apostles (cf., Psalms 69:25; 109:8). And it is important to note that the Eleven Apostles chose Matthias, by casting Divinely directed lots (cf., Proverbs 16:33). **(3)** All of Christ's Apostles worked miracles to confirm their apostleship (Hebrews 2:3f). Paul was chosen directly by the Lord as the last, untimely-born, Apostle to the Gentiles (Acts 9:1-16; 26:16; I Corinthians 9:1; 15:5-8). And his Apostleship was confirmed by his miracle-working powers and later endorsements by the other Apostles. For Paul's miracles, see Acts 13:11f; 14:8-10, 19f; 16:25f; 20:9-12; 28:3-6. For Peter's endorsement of Paul, see II Peter 3:15f. **(4)** Christ gave no other lower qualifications for any later successors of the Apostles because His Twelve Apostles (from Acts onward) would continue to rule in His spiritual kingdom via their inspired New Testament Gospels and Epistles (Luke 22:29-30).

So there are no living Apostles or Apostolic Successors on earth today as some churches (RCC, LDS, Anglican, Churches of Apostles) claim to possess BECAUSE none of their modern "Apostles" meet any of the required qualifications we just listed above. **(1)** Their Apostles were not alive during Christ's ministry, nor saw him after his resurrection. **(2)** They were not predicted or appointed by the Lord's Original Apostles. **(3)** They can't work miracles to confirm any thing they teach. **(4)** Their churches use their alleged "Apostles" to contradict what the Original Apostles wrote. Thus all modern Apostles are false apostles! We'll deal with the false RCC doctrine of Apostolic Succession for its Archbishops and Pope in the Supplemental Studies Section.

Prophets — include those inspired fore-tellers of the future during the first century like John the Baptist (Luke 7:26-28), or those forth-tellers, or "Preachers" (Kerux/Kerusso), like Luke (Luke 1:1-4; Romans 10:14). Paul claimed to be an Apostle, Preacher and Teacher (I Timothy 2:7). There were also true female prophetesses like Anna (Luke 2:36; also Acts 21:9). Jezebel was a false "Prophetess" (Revelation 2:20). Jesus and his Apostles all warned about false prophets (Matthew 7:15; 24:11; Acts 13:6; I John 4:1). There was no need for any inspired, foretelling prophets after the completion of Christ's New Testament. Those who claim to be such today lack all the miraculous and inspiration credentials of our Lord's Prophets and are patently false ... as are all the modern churches that claim to be founded by, or built upon, such false prophets and their "revelations" and "bibles" (See my book, *Now That's A Miracle!*).

Elders — are also called "servants, shepherds, pastors, overseers, bishops, presbyters" (Acts 20:28). They represent the highest spiritual *"office"* the Lord installed in his church. Physical and spiritual maturity was/is required. Elders are called "Elders" because they are older in years and in the faith. They are not young men or new converts (e.g., as young Mormon "elders"). Their required family qualifications are found in I Timothy 3:1-7. Only a married man with a faithful wife and believing children may be an elder. (The Lord also included "Marriage Instructions" for everyone in his New Testament, Matthew 19:3-9; I Corinthians 7:1-17.) Speaking personally, I meet all of these qualifications for being an elder or bishop. The Roman Catholic Bishops, Archbishops and Chief Bishop (Pope) do not meet any of them. Their "King has no clothes!" So I am more qualified to be the highest religious leader in the Lord's true church than any of them!

The first elders were selected by the Apostles, and then by the evangelists and members of the church (Acts 14:23; Titus 1:5). A church may not have qualified elders, yet still fully function by following Christ's word. Elders may be physically compensated for their service, and they may be rebuked for their sins and/or departures from Christ's word and deemed disqualified from office by the members (I Timothy 5:17-22).

The Apostle Peter, who was an elder, listed a number of the spiritual leadership requirements elders must possess and utilize in guiding and teaching their congregations.

> *The **elders** therefore among you I exhort, who am a **fellow-elder**... **Tend the flock** of God which is **among you**, exercising the **oversight**, not of constraint, but willingly, according to the will of God; nor yet for filthy lucre, but of a ready mind; **neither as lording it over the charge allotted to you**, but making yourselves **ensamples** to the flock* (I Peter 5:1-3).

Notice, elders are to *"tend the flock of God which is **among you**"*— in their local congregation. Elders don't take their local eldership with them when they go to another congregation, where they may not know the members, nor will the members *"know"* them (I Thessalonians 5:12). Since each of the *"churches of Christ"* is autonomous, there is no earthly head or headquarters over the Lord's church, or "Archbishops" over more than one local church (Romans 16:16). The fact that they are called *"shepherds"* who *"feed the flock/church"* doesn't make them Chief Shepherds or Vicars of Christ (I Peter 5:4; see Supplemental Studies).

Elders are *"servants"* who lead by example, not by *"lording it over the flock."* They must be *"apt to teach"* the Lord's word, and guide and rule the congregation according to Christ's word and not by their superior claims of inspiration or authority (Matthew 20:25-27; Hebrews 13:17; I Peter 5:1-3). None of these inspired Elder-Bishop qualifications demand that any Christian surrender his Sovereignty to Christ's authoritative word to a fellow human being. We are told to *"submit"* to their leadership, not surrender to their lordship! We have one Lord in Authority.

Deacons — This is also called an "office" in the New Testament, and refers to the male, faithful Christian "servants," aka., "ministers," in the church that attended to the physical needs of the church. The first deacons were appointed in Acts 6:1-6. Their specific physical and spiritual qualifications are listed in I Timothy 3:8-13. Female servants in the church were not included as a distinct office within these specific qualifications.

Evangelists — are to be qualified to do the *"work of an evangelist"* who teaches and preaches the Lord's word ably and accurately (II Timothy 4:5). There's only one way the Lord Jesus provided for those in the early church to be able to do that:

> *Give diligence {or **study**, KJV} to show thyself **approved** unto God, a **workman** that needeth not to be ashamed, **handling aright the word of truth*** (II Timothy 2:15; also 3:16ff; more on this text later).

Of course, as far as being heralds of the Gospel, the "Good News," every member is to be an evangelist and give an answer for the hope that lies within us (I Peter 3:15). My beloved and dearly departed evangelist and friend, Jack Exum, put it very simply: he said he always tried to put in a good word for Jesus every day at every opportunity. It can be as simple as handing out a card, or saying "Jesus died for sinners like me ... Jesus is my best friend," or as Jack would say, "I'm not lovable, I'm just loved" (by Jesus).

Teachers — Though some Christians are not qualified to be teachers due to immaturity, all Christians should study God's word and grow in the knowledge of Christ until they can teach others (Hebrews 5:12a). Though there are gifted "five talent" Christians who are able to be Bible teachers in groups, Bible classes and Schools (Romans 12:7), that does not mean they replace the need for less talented Christians to teach the essential and basic Christian commands, tenants and principles to the non-Christian individuals they alone will meet (Matthew 25:14ff; I Corinthians 12:28). Of course, some are so misinformed or wilfully biased and ignorant that they shouldn't be teachers until they repent and grow up (Hebrews 5:12b-14; James 3:1). And, as there are false Apostles, there are false teachers (II Timothy 4:3; II Peter 2:1).

Enrolled Widows — are those widows in the church that can serve in the work fulltime, and be paid by the church (I Timothy 5:5-16). They must be at least sixty years old and have already been involved in all the works of compassion and charity.

Though I have presented all of these church leadership details to show how our Lord organized his church completely, and left no position of power open that would invite human invention and elevation of themselves so they could Lord it over His people

(Matthew 20:25-28), I have also presented them to show how those churches who elevate their leaders to positions higher than Elders and Apostles do so without even the detailed scriptural qualifications of an enrolled widow! So please remember all of these details when you read about the installation and replacement of the "undocumented" Pope in the Supplemental Studies Section.

3. Christ's Worship Instructions. Just as God did not leave true worship to Him in the Old Testament to the whims and feelings of man, so Christ did not leave true worship to God (Father, Son, Holy Spirit) to the whims and feelings of man in His New Testament. He said Christians are to worship in *"spirit"* and in *"truth,"* meaning sincerely from the heart and intelligently from the mind as per God's revealed worship instructions (John 4:24; see I Samuel 12:24).

Christ and his Apostles condemned worship acts and rituals outside of God's word (Matthew 15:3-9; Colossians 2:20-23). Though there are only five basic acts of worship in the church — preaching/sharing the word, praying, singing, giving of our means and the Lord's Supper — our bodies and lives are to be offered to God as our *"spiritual service/worship"* (Romans 12:1-2). Christ even gave specific instructions regarding the practice of temporary miraculous gifts, like "speaking in tongues" and "prophesying" (I Corinthians 14:13f, 27-33; 13:3-13). When Christ said he would give his Apostles *"all truth,"* that included all the truth about our religious lives and acts as well as all the other aspects pertaining to his kingdom and church. Consider this text:

> *Grace to you and peace be multiplied in the **knowledge** of God and of Jesus our Lord; seeing that his divine power hath granted unto us **all things that pertain unto life and godliness** {religious piety}, through the **knowledge of him that called us** by his own glory and virtue* (II Peter 1:2-3).

I CHOSE CHRIST'S CHURCH CHOICE

Why did I choose Christ's church after I was scripturally baptized as a 21 year old adult in Bermuda in 1963? Well, biblically speaking, I actually didn't choose His church, it (or He) chose me! I didn't go through any church installation or induction process after I was baptized. I just had to accept by faith that the Lord added me to His universal church just as he added all those newly baptized adults I read about in Acts 2:38-47. I only had to accept a few essential truths at that time: that I believed Christ was the Son of God and my Savior; that I needed to repent of my past sins and change my ways; that I had confessed that belief; that my sins would be washed away by Christ's blood by being buried with Him in baptism; and that Christ would add me to his church after I, in faith, accepted and fulfilled those requirements. I was confident that Christ had added me to the His "Right Church," and not to any other person's "wrong church."

Of course, I didn't know all the details about Christ's true church the night I was baptized; I had only heard the full Gospel the night before! (Those three thousand Jewish converts on Pentecost, who were added to Christ's church, knew less about His church than I knew!) At that point in my life, I thought all churches were basically the same, and that "one church was as good as another." As I stated earlier, I was church-hopping from an early age up to that point in my life and never even thought about whether I was in the right church or not! In spite of my biblical ignorance, denominational ideas and biases, I soon learned otherwise when I read, for the first time in my life, all of Christ's Church Details in His New Testament.

It was during this personal enlightenment period that I made my choice to only accept Christ's revealed church details whether I formerly believed in them or not. I also decided to measure any church that I had attended in the past, or would attend in the future, by Christ's scriptural standards. I decided I could not delegate such a serious responsibility to other uninspired and often biblically illiterate men and women. I mean, I had already learned that my first childhood preacher and church (Reverend Star of The Methodist Church) and my last adult priest/friend and his church (Father Meade of the RCC) could not be trusted to tell me what was in Christ's Church Manual instead of their Methodist and Catholic Church Manuals. So I concluded that I would also need to learn more about false churches that claim to be Christ's church, as well as more about Christ's true church. (Hear me now, believe me later, learning everything you need to know about Christ's ancient true church in the Bible is a far easier task than learning about all the strange things you'll be challenged to understand and refute in modern mainstream churches and cults!)

I soon learned that faulty and false churches should be expected today because they were present in the days of the Apostles in the first century: like in Corinth and Asia Minor (I Corinthians 5:1ff; Galatians 1-6; Revelation 2-3). During the days of the Apostles, there were churches that did not believe in the deity of Jesus Christ (I John 2:18f; cf. John 8:24-59 for Jesus' condemnation of this belief). Today, there are churches that still preach the same thing (Iglesia ni Cristo, JW's, LDS). They are manifestly false! And I have preached and written against them for decades (see *The Perversions and Prejudices of the NWT*).

In the days of the Apostles, there were also churches that embraced all sorts of biblically condemned pagan and moral evils (I Corinthians 5:1ff; Revelation 2-3). And today there are churches that embrace even worse moral evils than pagan prostitution, and even invite all who practice those evils to join them, and even marry them. And I have called such churches "false churches" from public and political podiums, pulpits and in print (see *Homosexuality and the Bible,* Newspaper Articles, pp. 232-248).

I believe all churches should invite all sexual sinners to come to their services, repent and become "ex-sexual sinners," just like all drunks, thieves, whores, and Jerry Neil III, were invited to become ex-sinners. Just like Stephen Bennett, head of SBMinistries, is a well-known "ex-homosexual." Just like the Apostle Paul called all these types of sinners in Corinth — including those guilty of fornication, idolatry, drunkenness, sodomy — ex-sinners: ***"Such were some of you: but ye were washed..."*** (I Corinthians 6:9-11).

So if "one church was not as good as another" during the days of the Apostles, why would any Christian think "one church is as good as another" today? All churches are not created equally today unless they were/are created by the Creator of the Church!

Some may ask why Christ allowed all these false preachers and teachers to corrupt his church and capture and condemn unsuspecting souls therein. This same question could be asked about why did God allow Satan to be on earth to tempt, convert and condemn Adam and Eve. Because He created humans as freewill beings, not puppets, to live upon the earth amongst other freewill human beings. And he also created His church to be on the earth and amongst sinners—in order to save sinners (I Corinthians 5:10). It was not created to be a physical community where saved sinners could retreat from contact and communication with all the sinners and sinful influences in the world. Nor was it created to be a physical, unattractive monastery on top of some isolated mountain to separate and shield them from the sinful world's assaults. Rather, it was created to be an attractive, bright, spiritual city without walls on a hill that would draw all sinful men unto it, and into it (Matthew 5:14; Zechariah 2:4). And our Heavenly Father, Christ (Chief Shepherd, Commander in Chief) and Holy Spirit (Comforter, Helper, Intercessor) expect each and every member of their Divine Family, Flock, Church, and Calvary to spiritually prepare and arm themselves to guard their own souls from sin, defend the faith, and feed, protect and rescue the faithful ... and, *"having done all to stand, Stand therefore ..."* (Ephesians 6:13f)!

I also soon learned that one of the most controversial things any Christian can say is that he is a member of ***"The Lord's True Church."*** In fact, such a claim is usually countered by an immediate rebuke like this: *"So you're saying **your church** is the **true church, the right church**, and all the other churches are false and wrong. Oh really! That just shows you are in the **wrong church**, for Christ told us not to **judge** people by their religion (Matthew 7:1)!"* There are many ways to counter this subjective, sinister sophistry that seeks to stifle freedom of all religious speech, stop Christ's true sovereign souls and evangelists from seeking the lost in false churches, and keep those trapped in those false churches from ever seeing the light of the truth.

First, we can teach them the truth about the text which they erroneously interpret and apply about judging another person's church (Matthew 7:1). The truth of this text is Jesus was indicting the religious *"hypocrites"* (verse 5) amongst the false teachers and leaders of his day — the scribes, Pharisees and Sadducees — about their inability to judge people righteously. He was not issuing a command forbidding Christians to render any scriptural judgment about serious religious matters. In fact, Jesus told the multitudes in his day, and us via his written word, to *"judge righteous judgment"* (John 7:24). Personally, I know I'm not being hypocritical when I say I'm in the "Right Church." I would be if I said I was in the "Wright Church." (Like other less knowledgeable founders of modern churches have done by naming their new churches after themselves!) But I never say "My church is right." I always say "Christ's New Testament Church" was/is right: which church can still be duplicated today by simply complying with all of Christ's instructions as per his New Testament *"Pattern"* for all true *"churches of Christ."* How can any of this be wrong?

If they say it's our attitude or bold confidence that is offensive, maybe we should ask them if they'd be less upset over such if we said we were in the Lord's false church? Or if we said we were happy not having a clue as to whether our church was true or false, or of Christ or of Satan? Is ignorance really bliss? Is it good when we're more emotionally pleased with the blind leading the blind than with Christ leading us by the hand via His scriptures to where He wants us to go to church? You be the judge!

Second, we can show them many scriptures where Jesus told us to make judgments about which church is right or wrong, true or false. He told us to do this every time He and his Prophets and Apostles told us to beware of the false apostles, prophets and teachers that would divide his church and draw away disciples after them by their great words of vanity (Acts 20:29f; II Peter 2:18f; also II John 8-11; III John 9f; Jude 17-22). He told us to be of the *"same judgment"* in his church, especially when it comes to dealing with people who seek to create *"divisions/schisms"* and splits within His true church, or differing denominations apart from His church—that still claim to be His church (I Corinthians 1:10).

Third, we can point out how every Catholic, Denominational and Cultic church claims to be Christ's true church, or the "Right Church." I have personally heard or read all of these churches claiming to be Christ's true church, especially the RCC, Mormon Church and JW Church/Kingdom. I have heard them insist that, "My/Our Church is right," in countless discussions and debates. But I have never heard one of them say "I am in the Wrong Church!" I've also, now get this, never heard one of them say he/she believed all other churches were right. But I have heard all of these churches — including members of ecumenical churches who insist "they don't believe in judging other churches" — saying other churches are wrong, especially the church that Gerald Wright attends! I lie not!

On the other hand, this old Christian never says all churches that call themselves — "The Church of Christ, Church of God, The Christian Church" — are true and right churches. I know some who are not, and the Lord knows all who are not (John 10:14; II Timothy 2:19; Revelation 2:2, 9, 13, 19; 3:1, 8, 15)!

Fourth, we can ask them how they know their church is right and others are wrong. This will get us to where we need to be on this issue. **(a)** We can get them out of the spitting contest over who is going to win the argument over which church is right or wrong (often both sides are wrong!). **(b)** We can get them into looking at how people of all religious beliefs may easily know which church is undeniably the Lord's Right Church as outlined in his New Testament. **(c)** And we can get them to see how all churches that don't match that model are to some degree wrong and not the Right Church. (All the members of the Lord's First True Church were not perfect in their lives and doctrine, nor are they today.)

If the religious people with whom you're trying to have an orderly conversation about Christ's church answer this question correctly by saying — "we must prove which church is right or wrong by Christ's New Testament teachings and pattern" — you can use this opportunity to study all the important facets and teachings in order of importance: from the foundation up, and from becoming a member up. You might ask them, after looking at each one of the Lord's simple instructions on any subject (salvation acts, worship acts, office requirements, etc.), what they find to be unacceptable just as He's written it for us all to understand alike.

If their answer is by any other way than by Christ's New Testament teachings and pattern, use that as an opportunity to ask them to compare their church's history, teachings and manuals with Christ's New Testament history and teachings about His Church. If they're willing to do this, you will need to study the history and doctrines of their church first, or you may fail in your attempt to show the fallacies within their Bible Versions and interpretations, or you may even fall prey to their pseudo Bible versions, clever interpretations, boastful claims and seductive teachings. The Lord's Successful Sovereign Soldier must be ready, willing, able and scripturally armed in his/her quest for souls (Ephesians 6:10ff).

Dear Reader, I know, after all of these negative charges against

other churches, you might want to ask me this: ***"Gerald, how do you expect to get people in these false churches to listen to you or read any of your books if you condemn their churches like this?"***
* Well, I know from fifty years of experience that such is difficult, but not impossible. I know Jesus and his Apostles spent much of their time pointing out the false teachings in the much divided and scripturally detoured Jewish religion and first century churches. I know I won't get any of those in false churches to invite me to come into their churches and homes to preach against their false views and practices. So I write books in hope of reaching some.
* I know that these false churches prevent millions of often naïve or biblically uneducated men and women from ever knowing the truth and, consequently, leave them to face the Lord yet in their sins. I know it is not enough just to preach to atheists, pagans and the saved ("the choir"), but also to those who are lost while they think they are saved in false "Christian" churches. I know it is not enough for a good religious neighbor to stand on the other side and ignore that his religious neighbors are being led like so many sheep to the slaughter by phony preachers and pathological pied pipers to perdition, like Jim Jones and David Koresh (Obadiah 11).
* I know it is not enough to preach about all the attractive benefits of being in the Lord's true church, but also about all the attractive allurements of the false churches that often times seduce weaker brethren away from Christ and into bed with Jezebel (Revelation 2:20; II Peter 2:18f).
* I know that I, as a Gospel Preacher and Watchman, must warn all people about false religions, churches and teachings, or be held accountable if they fall prey to them. I also know I must try to convict them of the doctrinal and moral sins that they have been brainwashed to accept (John 16:8). And I know that the best way to convict any person who's in a church that isn't true to Christ's word is to ask them to personally present clear words and teachings in Christ's New Testament that support his/her church's teachings. If I must prove my church is true to the faith, so must every other person prove his/her church is true to the faith before I will say it is true or tell anyone else to go to it or stay in it. It is not my fault if a person can't find specific words to support his/her church's New Testament origin: like "The Baptist Church, The Methodist Church, The Roman Catholic Church, The Mormon

Church," et al. It is not my fault that I can find my beliefs in the New Testament, or they can't find specific New Testament words to support their church's teachings: like infant baptism, sabbath-keeping, forbidding marriage and meats, using wine or pot for the Lord's Supper, popes and pianos. If Christ didn't care about His church's teachings, as do they, He could have put generic words saying so in His New Testament: like "My Church is to be like a Cafeteria; It can offer anything on its menu that suits your taste!"

If any church's teachings are fully supported in Christ's New Testament, they and I can simply confirm them together and be in full fellowship. If any church's teachings are not fully supported in Christ's New Testament, their beliefs need to be marked as being without Christ's Authority and false, just like Peter and Paul did when they confronted false churches and teachings. In fact, we can use the very Apostolic arguments against the falsehoods in their day to repudiate and condemn similar falsehoods in our day. Modern doctrinal errors are like moral sins, they're just new ways to violate one of Jesus' old commands or teachings. For example, the old "Docetism" is found in many modern cults that teach Christ was not God in the flesh. And the old "Gnosticism" is found in many liberal churches that downplay sins in the flesh as having any effect on the status of a person's spirit.

* I also know that you won't get anyone to even consider leaving his/her family/favorite church if he/she doesn't believe it is bad for him/her, and that Christ's New Testament church is right and better for him/her. And this is especially true in today's modern New Age and Big Tent — *"anything goes, come as you are, stay as you are"* — Churches. Many of these "Big Temples of Titillation" are full of "tuned out and turned on" throngs who sing *"We're here for the party"* (ala., Gretchen Wilson) and not for the Prince of Purity. They not only don't promote pure Christianity and living, they put it down and label those who do as being "old fashioned" and "out-of-touch" with the modern world. They not only don't condemn evil, they promote it.

And though they claim this is what "New Age Churches" should do, they further show their biblical ignorance because they are nothing more than reincarnations of the worst of the worst in the old sinful, sin-filled churches of ancient Corinth and Thyatira (I Corinthians 5:1f; Revelation 2:18-23). Like them, they're "Puffed up" and "Out and Proud" of all their *"deep things of Satan."* Like them, they don't convict people of their sins with Christ's words; they seduce them into extreme fornication by flaunting all their free sex, flowing booze and idolatry (II Peter 2:18f). Like those older sinners in Israel, they sin with cheer instead of fear and are beyond blushing over the most disgusting and destructive behaviors (Jeremiah 6:15). Everything that was/is good (like God-ordained heterosexual marriage) is called bad, and everything that was/is bad (like "Same-sex marriage") is called good (Isaiah 5:20). It is this old error and evil that we're asking them to leave. And it is all of the old tried and true truths of Christ's New Testament and the good Christian life in Christ's true church — which is always new and never grows old or out of date — that we're asking them to accept (I Peter 3:10-12). (I know if we don't do it, who will?)

What makes this defection from Christ's New Testament Church even worse is how all the shame and blame against Christ's true church and Christianity in general has arisen from the very people who were blessed to have had the word of God to direct their steps in their nations, churches and homes for centuries. It is in these blessed countries and churches where all these evil practices are being preached from their pulpits, published in their books, paraded up and down their/our streets and projected in living color into their/our living rooms via all of our modern visual media. Well, Christ deserves better than this from all the peoples and nations He has blessed with His Bible in abundance (Amos 3:2). And Christ's Church deserves better than this because Christ's Church is Better than this. In point of New Testament fact, Christ's Church is the BEST CHURCH ON EARTH ... which is better than all manmade churches put together when it comes to living a full and joyful life on earth, and going to live with Him in heaven when we die, or when He comes to receive His Church.

Christ's Church is the Best Church

Christ's Church is Best because Everything Christ said or did was always The Best! So why would anyone think His Church wouldn't be the best? Or that any other puny person's church would be remotely comparable, much less improved?

Christ's Church is Best because It is the Oldest Church. It is the oldest Church/Kingdom of promise, prophecy and preaching (see earlier). It is the First Church of Christ, established in Jerusalem on the Day of Pentecost in A.D. 33. Any church founded later or anywhere else than this is not Christ's Church. Period! Some things get better with age, and the church is one of them. Why? Because it gets more saved members every passing day/year and closer to being saved in the end! It was the first church, and it will be the last church standing (I Corinthians 15:24; Hebrews 12:28). Just like it's Builder is the *"First and Last"* in every good thing that has been done on this planet, including creating it as a perfect physical habitation for us (Revelation 1:17; Isaiah 45:18).

Christ's Church is Best because It is the Original Church. The Original Church is best because it is the Only Church Christ Built via his Apostles. The Apostles built according to all of Christ's inspired specifications and qualifications. They left their written specifications as a "Pattern" for us to literally follow to the letter (I Corinthians 4:17; II Timothy 1:13). They left no room for later modifications, alterations or replacements by unqualified biblical amateurs or uninspired imposters. Master Builder Paul left the following admonition for all who build upon that Original Church:

> *According to the grace of God which was given unto me, as a **wise masterbuilder** I laid a foundation {which is Christ}; and **another buildeth** thereon.* ***But let each man take heed how he buildeth thereon*** (I Corinthians 3:10).

The Original Church will be replicated every time the New Testament Pattern of that Church is followed. Proof of that is the fact that it is still here! And all Sovereign Souls insist on nothing less than the Best. And I, a physical home builder and church builder, have noticed that all the later or "New Model" churches were not built according to the Original Pattern by their biblically illiterate founders/builders/leaders. Though the leaders of these modern churches were/are quite able to bloviate and pontificate about being the true church, they are totally inept to authenticate the existence of any of their churches by citing a single verse/code in Christ's New Testament Church Blueprint and Manual.

Christ's Church is Best because It had/has the Best Builder. For Christ is the One who built the Universe. He also built the Kingdom of Israel. Which kingdom was corrupted and divided by lying leaders and ignorant citizens who changed God's moral and religious laws (Hosea 4:6; 5:11; Matthew 15:7-9; 19:3-9). We must always insist on the "Built by Christ Church" label (Matthew 16:18)! If the sign over the church door has any other person's name on it, that's a good sign and signal that the church isn't His! And if it isn't His, it isn't the best! It's not even good, it's bad!

Christ's Church is Best because It has the Best Foundation. We Sovereign Church Members/Builders accept no one but Jehovah God as the Founder and Foundation of the True Church. And that's exactly what we received in Jesus Christ: *"Immanuel/The Rock"* (Matthew 16:18f; I Corinthians 3:11; 10:4; See "Jesus is Jehovah Texts" in Supplemental Studies). Only God can build "Divine Institutions." To those who claim to be in churches built upon human foundations, claims and doctrines, rather than upon the Will of God, I say: "On Christ the solid rock I stand, all other churches are built on sinking sand" (Matthew 7:21-29; See "Jesus Is The Rock" and foundation of His Church, and "Peter was not the first Pope" in Supplemental Studies).

Christ's Church is Best because It has the Best Building. Only God can build "Divine Temples" (Psalms 127:1). Only God can save our souls and add us as *"living stones"* into His *"spiritual house, church, temple"* (Acts 2:36-47; I Peter 2:5). Men may build colossal church buildings, crystal cathedrals, temples and audiences, but they can't add the first stone into Christ's Greatest Church. That's His Job! And so far, He's done it perfectly.

Note: There is no New Testament requirement for a "church building." Early Christians preached in, taught in, studied in and worshipped in synagogues, prisons, schools, houses, open stadiums, catacombs, etc. (Acts 16:25; 17:17, 22; 19:19; 20:20; 24:11f; Romans 16:5; I Corinthians 16:29; Colossians 4:15; Philemon 2). What we learn from this variety is: <u>where</u> or <u>in what</u> Christians assemble is as generic and open to all options, including church-owned buildings, as <u>how</u> or <u>on what</u> are we to "go {travel} into all the world" as per Matthew 28:19.

Christ's Church is Best because It has the Best Book. Christ's Church has only One Book — Christ's New Testament — that contains every single law, teaching and principle that they need to study, learn and obey. Though Christians are encouraged to study and learn from the Old Testament, they are not required to know or obey a single law, keep a single holy day, or engage in a single sacrifice or worship rite found within its pages (Romans 15:4; Galatians 4:10; 5:3f).

Thus, Christians can learn the entire history of the Lord's True Church, as well as all of its membership, moral and office requirements, acceptable worship acts, approved good works, and such like within a week's reading time. And we're not talking about a single subject that requires a college degree to understand. Even the *"hard things"* of Paul can be understood by those who aren't biblically ignorant, or interested in making the scriptures fit their preconceived ideas, or twisting them into supporting their unscriptural practices and agendas (II Peter 3:16). We all can read and understand the literal texts of required truths alike, or the Lord and his Apostles would not have said so and demanded such (John 8:32; 17:19-23; I Corinthians 1:10-13; Ephesians 3:3-5). Since we have all been told to *"grow in the grace and knowledge of our Lord,"* it is obvious that we are ever to be students of the word and never settled "scholars" of the word, and are always subjecting our conclusions to any necessary corrections we discover in our continued mining of Christ's scriptural treasures. That's why I, as other students of the word, are continually revising our written works with each reprint! (And you are invited to submit any errors you uncover in this book, or any of my books, to my website.)

The Lord's Book is Best. So the Lord's members and preachers should be the Best as long as they remain true to His Book. In like manner, the Lord's Church will always be the Lord's true church and the "Best Church" as long as it remains faithful to using His Book as the final authority in all matters of life and religion.

Now let's look at yet another reason why other manmade churches are not the Best Churches to attend, must less belong to. Most Denominational and Cultic Churches, including the RCC, base many of their doctrines, teachings, priestly dress and worship practices upon Old Testament laws and rituals. This is one reason why we find all the elevating distinctive garb worn by their priests and preachers. This is why we find all the priestly rituals, meat restrictions, sex restrictions (celibacy), purification rites, keeping of the Old Sabbath, and all the old Pharisaical ostentatious displays of their religious piety in their churches. Christ made it clear that he would **fulfill** and then **abrogate or abolish** all the Old Testament laws and sacrificial requirements (Matthew 5:17f; Luke 21:22; 24:44; Acts 3:24; II Corinthians 3:6-16; Colossians 2:14; Hebrews 7-9).

These outdated OT rules, ranks and restrictions alone are reason enough for any freedom and equality-loving Sovereign Soul to choose Christ's New Testament Church over any church that seeks to bind any of the OT requirements upon them. And when you factor in all the uninspired extra-biblical books and "bibles" of these churches — like the Apocryphal books and catechisms of the RCC, the Book of Mormon, Doctrine and Covenants, et al — you're comparing their confusion with God's clarity, night with day (II Corinthians 3:7-18). Why would anyone want to be a member or priest in a church that denies any of the good things that Christ has created for our physical/spiritual sustenance and security: like all meats, marriage, family, travel on any day, blood transfusions, and such like? Not to mention all the bad things some of these pseudo churches subject their members to: like withholding so-called "sacraments" from them, refusing to release their loved ones from their pseudo "purgatory," treating them like second-class "saints" and "priests" (calling them the "laity" under their "clergy"), saying their unbaptized babies are sinners, bowing to mere human beings, engaging in polygamy, embracing same-sex marriage, even drinking booze and smoking pot! If you find yourself in such a church that teaches such doctrines of demons, and has thereby made a Deal with the Devil rather than an Alliance with the Almighty, run away from it for your very life! You can't love the truth God loves if you don't hate the falsehoods He hates (Psalms 119:128).

When the author of the letter to the Hebrews (Christian Jews) said Christ's New Covenant was *"better,"* he meant it. The Old Testament law is called *"a yoke of bondage"* and an *"administration of death"* (Galatians 5:1ff; II Corinthians 3:7). Christ's New Covenant/Testament is called *"a law of liberty, freedom"* and *"life"* (James 1:25; John 8:32; Romans 8:1). Christ's

New Testament Church offers the "good life" that can only be had by following Christ's principles, laws, commands and example (I Peter 3:10-12). Need I say more? "If thy faith is weak, why choose the harder side?"

Christ's Church is Best because It has the Best Membership. As far as initially becoming a full-fledged, heavenly-enrolled member, brother/sister, saint and priest in the Lord's Church, there is no entry fee whatsoever, no Bible IQ test to pass, no lengthy entry exam, criminal background check, gender exclusion, sexual orientation test, drug test, or need for any distinguished church officer to sponsor you or vouch for your sincerity or sanity. Proof of that is the entry of 3,000 Jews being added to the Lord's True Church membership on one day, and without any such pre-qualifications check (Acts 2:36-47). How can this be? Is this the case in all churches of Christ? Yes, and if not, it is not a true church of Christ. And after I show you why, I will show you, yet again, why all churches that don't offer this are not the Lord's Church and not the Best Church.

First, because the sole proprietor/owner and door keeper of the Lord's Church is the Omniscient Christ who already knows everything about you, including all your thoughts, intentions and the number of hairs on your head (John 2:25; 6:64; Hebrews 4:12; Matthew 10:30). So there's no chance of any insincere, insane or sadistic person slipping in the front or back door of the Lord's church. (As I used to slip in the exit doors of two of the movie theaters in Roanoke, Virginia! I told you I was a lying, cheating thief!) Nor does any person accidently fall into the church. Membership is an easily identified <u>action</u> by the Lord's members, and an easily identified <u>attitude</u> by the Lord Jesus Christ. *"The Lord knoweth them that are his"* (II Timothy 2:19; John 10:14; also Matthew 7:16). Christ makes you a member, not anyone else!

Second, because you are still a sinner before you become a member of the Lord's church, and as such you do not deserve to be in the Lord's Church on your own merit, nor are you remotely qualified or worthy of being an instant "saint" and "priest" in direct communication with God! (Shoot, most people can't even speak to any of their lowest political officials, much less their Senators or President!) So, the Lord offers you all of His Church

Amenities free of charge because no person on earth could/can afford to buy a single day's worth of any one of them! Full Membership is free, and you don't have to pay a dime or shed a drop of your blood to become a fully forgiven, blood-bought Saint!

Third, because every prospective church member must express his/her willingness to repent of all of his past sins and present sinful actions or lifestyles before he is baptized for the forgiveness of his past sins. Though only God can know any person's heart and sincerity in repentance, and only God can actually know if the person was added to his spiritual church upon his/her obedience, anyone in the church can see if the person continues in his/her past sinful life or progressively changes his/her life: *"By their fruits"* you can know them (Matthew 7:16). Members who openly remain worldly and sinful will be removed from faithful status.

Christ's Church is Best because It has the Best Worship. The Lord's New Testament Church and Universal Spiritual Kingdom replaced the Old Testament physical National Theocracy of Israel. So we should expect Israel's physical and national religious places, structures, hierarchy, worship acts, sacrifices, holy days, etc., would also be replaced with spiritual and personal religious places, institutions, positions, days and acts of worship ... which are all **Better!**

For example, Israel had a physical temple; we have a spiritual temple: which is our bodies that are built into Christ's spiritual Temple. **That's better!** Israel had physical tablets of stone and portions of scripture written on posts and in containers on their arms; we have Christ's letters written on paper and in our hearts (Hebrews 8:10). **That's better!** They became Old Covenant Israelites when they were physically circumcised by men as babies, who had to be taught who Jehovah was. Christians become members of Christ's New Covenant Church when they are of sufficient age to know who Christ is, believe in Christ, repent of their sins, and then personally receive their spiritual circumcision by God in baptism (Ibid. 8:11; Colossians 2:11-12). **That's better!**

The entire nation of Israel had to be commanded to physically rest one day a week on the Sabbath day. Whereas every person in Christ's church wilfully and lovingly enjoys spiritually resting every second of every day in Christ's person (Matthew 11:29;

Hebrews 4:10). **That's better!** Israelites had to observe numerous holy days, including a national, annual, physical Passover by using the blood of physical lambs to recall their salvation from physical death from the Angel of Death. Whereas Christ's Church was given one weekly Lord's Supper that utilizes two common food items (unleavened bread and grape juice) to symbolize the body and blood of *"the lamb of God,"* who is their spiritual *"Passover"* that saved them forever from spiritual death (John 1:29; Acts 20:7; I Corinthians 5:7f; 10:16). **That's better!**

If you look up the word "Better" in your concordance, you will see that the writer of the Book of Hebrews (circa A.D. 68) used the word over and over to convince the Christian Jews that everything about Christ's New Testament Religion and Spiritual Kingdom, including its worship, was far ***BETTER*** than the Old Testament Religion and Physical Kingdom that was then being used to lure them away from Christianity. It is easy to understand why the Old Jewish Religion — with its ancient National history, voluminous Old Bible, elaborate physical Temple and Priesthood, and Holy City of Jerusalem — would appear to be a much more bona fide and attractive religion, especially to Jews, than the New Christian Religion: with its small collection of Apostolic letters, spiritual kingdom, temple, priesthood, simple worship and heavenly city. Jesus pointed out how this conversion to His spiritual kingdom would be difficult for traditionalist Jews when he said: *"And no man having drunk **old wine desireth new**; for he said, the **old is good/better**"* (Luke 5:39). But the problem these Jews weren't factoring into their temptation to return to Judaism was the rapidly *"approaching day"* of the destruction of the Jewish Religion, Temple and City in a few years (Hebrews 8:13; 10:25). Then they would see the prophecy of Haggai (2:6-9) come true when Israel's physical house was shaken away and the Lord's New Testament kingdom would be seen to be the kingdom that *"cannot be shaken"* (Hebrews 12:25-29; See my book on *The End of World...or AD70?*). Christ's spiritual church/kingdom, with all of its spiritual structures and worship, was **Better** in the beginning.

And it is still Better today, even though most so-called "Christian churches" — Protestant, Catholic, Cultic — still use the same Old Testament/Jewish-style physical buildings (Tabernacles, Temples, Elaborate/Crystal Cathedrals), dress, ceremonies, rituals, holy days, musical instruments, etc., to make their churches outwardly "<u>appear</u>" to be more religious and <u>bona fide</u> than simple Christian churches that do not. Inwardly, they are just *"<u>bone-filled</u>"* (Matthew 23:27f)! Personally, I'm not only content with what we see in the Lord's simple (yet profound) worship services, I have no desire to be bored to tears with endless arrays of human-contrived ceremonies, pomp and circumstance, which more belong in Caesars Court than Christ's Church. If the Lord's simple worship was good enough for Paul, it is good enough for all. Which brings me to the best reason to worship Christ's way.

All unauthorized worship acts are unscriptural. The Lord's true church is Christ's <u>New</u> Testament Universal Church, not a renovated <u>Old</u> Testament National Theocracy. Furthermore, Jesus said we *"**must** worship in spirit and **truth**,"* and not "you **may** worship in every way that makes you **feel** good" (John 4:24). When it comes to worship, *"it is better to obey* {God} *than to sacrifice"* just to please men or follow their traditions (I Samuel 15:22; Matthew 15:6-9). It is better to do it His Way than their way. And the Sovereign Son of God we worship made His Way of True Worship quite clear when He had it all written down for us! Let's see what kind of worship pleases Him (Hebrews 11:6).

When we look at what the Apostles instructed the Lord's church to do in worship, we find them being told to engage in the following practices.

(1) Singing praises to God. *"Through him let us offer up a **sacrifice of praise** to God continually, that is, the **fruit of the lips** which make confession to his name ... speaking one to another in psalms and hymns and spiritual songs, **singing** and making **melody with your heart*** {which literally means to "pluck the heart strings"} *to the Lord* (Hebrews 13:15; Ephesians 5:19).

You will not find one single New Testament reference to any church using, or being told to use, any of the musical instruments that had been authorized in Israel's worship to God. This personal worship is yet another example of how God changed worship from using external, physical music-makers in Israel to using our own voices and heart-strings to worship God. It would not have been difficult for Christ to tell his people to continue such acts of worship. But He didn't. Nor will I. Nor should all the churches that utilize every sort of musical instruments — towering organs, harps, tambourines, rock and roll bands and "cowbells" — to accompany their choirs in order to draw larger crowds to their religious operas, musical concerts and hootenannies!

The question that needs to be asked when this "instrumental issue" arises is not: "why don't New Testament Christians use them in their worship of God?" It should be: "where is Christ's New Testament authority for any church to use them?" If the use of them was to glorify or **please** God, God would have said so ... and we would all gladly include them in our "faithful" worship services (I Corinthians 10:31; Hebrews 11:6). But since God didn't tell us to do so, we must conclude that those who use them are more interested in pleasing themselves and others than they are in pleasing and glorifying God. If God said "sing," and man says "play," who are you obeying when you use them: God or man?

You could always make a *"joyful noise unto God"* by singing without instrumental accompaniment (Psalms 66:1-4). You could also do the same with instrumental music if God told you to do it (Psalms 81:1-3). But if He didn't, you're just making "noise!" Or, as those who opposed the late introduction of musical instruments into the church's acapella singing described it, "you're putting a cowbell in a symphony" (See my tract on Instrumental Music, *Three Strikes and You're Out*)! Singing is easier for individuals, cheaper for churches, more pleasing to God ... and **better**!

(2) Partaking of The Lord's Supper. Since we already discussed the time and elements of the Lord's Supper earlier — "unleavened bread" and "fruit of the vine" on the "first day of the week" (Acts 20:7) — the main thing I want to point out here is how superior the simplicity of The Lord's Supper of the New Testament is compared to what we often encounter in modern churches. The focus in Christ's church was/is not upon the living — those in charge of serving the elements, or those partaking — but upon Christ's death: his badly beaten, bruised and lacerated body and his freely flowing blood. Without Christ's blood-letting death, we would not have any hope in living or dying. None of this lends itself to any exaltation of any person on earth above another. As stated earlier, the ground is level at foot of the cross. And it is also level at the Lord's Communion Table: for even Judas was with the Lord at His Last Supper. This is **Better!**

(3) Praying. Jesus prayed often and taught his disciples to pray often, as well as how to pray. It was during his Sermon on the Mount that He delivered what is now called "The Lord's Prayer," the most repeated prayer of all time (Matthew 6:9-15).

Jesus' teachings on prayer in this text, and others, show how all disciples of Christ, regardless of their lowly status or isolated location, can go straight through Christ their Mediator to the Father in prayer and confess their sins, submit their petitions, and pray for whatever they desire according to God's will. They can ask other Christians to pray for and with them; but they don't have to ask any Christian to assist them in gaining access to God. That's something every sovereign Christian is able to do all by his lonesome.

This is all very liberating. We're all priests of God who, through our High Priest, Jesus Christ, can offer our bodies as a *"living sacrifice"* anywhere and anytime we desire (Romans 12:1). We can send, or blow as a kiss,* all of our spiritual sacrifices towards our Father in the Heavenly Holy of Holies by merely directing our thoughts, whispering our words, bending our knees, bowing our heads, singing our own hymns, or by winking and smiling at God whenever we choose to do so. (*The Greek word for "worship" is 'proskuneo' and means "to kiss towards God.") If need be, we can each partake of the Lord's Supper by ourselves on the "Lord's Day" by taking a piece of cracker and sip of grape juice. All of this religious freedom is **better** than being bound by walls, barred by closed doors or hindered by religious bureaucracy.

I'm sorry to have to say this, but much of this unrestricted prayer accessibility and freedom of worship is far better than what over a billion "Christians" all over the world enjoy. They have been told they need to go to "Mass," or make an appointment with the padre for a few minutes in the confessional booth down at St. Patrick's Cathedral at Fifth Ave and Elm Street in New York City, or wherever. Until their appointment arrives, they can count beads, "pray the Rosary," or relay their prayers through Mary or another superior saint, or first engage in a fast from food and booze, or pray they don't die before they make it to the confessional. This isn't Christian Sovereignty, this is Cultic Servitude! or Satanic Slavery!

Sadly, Satan can always find a way to turn something good, like prayer, into something bad, as we just pointed out. And, believe it or not, Satan actually found a way to keep people out of Christ's church/kingdom by misinterpretations of "The Lord's Prayer," itself. If you read that prayer, you'll read how Jesus told his disciples to ask the Father for: *"**Thy kingdom come**. **Thy will be done**, as in heaven, so on earth."* Of course, Jesus said this before his death, resurrection, ascension to his throne, building that prayed-for *"church **kingdom**"* and ratifying His, and his Father's, New Testament *"**will**."* Jesus promised to accomplish these epic achievements soon in Matthew 16:18f. So the prayer was answered forthwith! What a great example of answered prayer!

Well, not so fast. Here's what Satan's twisted logic has done to this simple prayer. His little helpers say: "Since Christians have been praying that same prayer from Jesus day till today, it shows that the Father's **kingdom** has not yet come and His **will** is still not being done on earth. So, consequently, **Christ is not ruling** in his kingdom on the earth, and Satan still rules the entire world (II Corinthians 4:4)!" All of this lying misinterpretation passes as "Gospel" today because so many people are willing to surrender their sovereignty, as well as the Lord's, to Satan and his little human servants: fast talking preachers and book sellers. For example, Hal Lindsey, in his 1970's book, *The Late Great Planet Earth,* predicted the end of our world would begin in 1988 with the Battle of Armageddon, then the Rapture, then Seven years of Tribulation, then Christ's rule in Jerusalem for a thousand years. The book sold tens of millions of copies, and it is still being revised and recycled in other titles. I suggest Mr. Lindsey entitle all of his books *Lindsey's Lies!* He certainly received his tortured Jewish/Christian nationalistic theories from the Father of Lies, Satan, and not our Lord of truth (John 8:44)!

So, now, about ninety percent of the so-called Christian world believes the "Lord's Prayer" Jesus told his disciples to pray wasn't fulfilled in their lifetimes, and still has not been fulfilled for almost two thousand years thereafter. What a lousy example of answered prayers! Wow! And now, twenty-six years since 1988 passed without incident, and Lindsey was once and for all proved to be a lying "prophet" (Deuteronomy 18:22), these same pulpiteers (or profiteers) are selling millions of their new books about the "soon-to-arrive" physical, visible, national kingdom of Christ!

Thank God we are water and blood-washed members of Christ's Best Church, Citizens in his Universal/Heavenly Kingdom, and Priests in His Best Temple: who can "pray without ceasing" or human interventions and interruptions, and enter into the very holy place of heaven from our closets (I Thessalonians 5:17; Hebrews 10:19-22). The only way it can get any better than this is for us to die and talk with Christ face to face in heaven (Philippians 1:23)!

(4) Preaching. It has been said that the most powerful position on earth is a pulpit preacher. It is a scriptural fact that preaching the true Gospel of Christ is the *"power of God unto salvation"* for the whole world (Romans 1:16; 10:17f). There's no other power on earth that can save souls. But may I expand the scope of this power beyond the pulpit to any Christian who shares the same Gospel that saved him/her — via simply talking about or sharing the word, or asking them to read one of your tracts or books — with anyone who will listen to you. Who knows whether you, like George Spurgin, will share that same powerful gospel with someone who will teach countless others also (II Timothy 2:2)?

But with that great power in our possession, we all have an equally great responsibility to preach the truth as Christ revealed it in his New Testament, and not the truth that's been revised and rewritten in denominational and cultic catechisms, creeds, manuals and perverted "versions" of the Bible. And here's an undeniable fact, dear reader, these ancient and modern "churches" that separate themselves apart and above others who claim to be "Christians" by calling themselves hyphenated-Christians — Catholic-Christians, Methodist-Christians, Baptist-Christians — would not exist if they weren't perpetuated by the dedication of their preachers, teachers and members to their peculiar, man-made, creeds and sects. This is indisputable. God did not author this confusion in his Word. Christ's prayer for unity amongst his people proves this sort of division causes disbelief in the world (John 17:20-21). Paul's condemnation of such *"divisions"* over personalities proves the entire "Denominational" process is sinful and unacceptable (I Corinthians 1:10-13).

And the fact that the Lord's true church is still present in the world today — right there in the pages of His New Testament, and still in every Church that proves all things by Christ's word (II Corinthians 13:5) — proves it doesn't have to be that way. But it is. For example, when a large denominational group calls itself "The Baptist Church," it not only calls the church something that it never was called in the New Testament ("John the Baptist's Church"), it also confuses people in the world as to who the true founder of the church was (not John the Baptist). Plus, even more confusing is the fact that those who call themselves "Baptists" don't teach or practice scriptural baptism. They say you're forgiven of your sins and saved before baptism. They say you can go to heaven without being baptized, but you can't be a member of the "Baptist Church" without baptism. Then they say it helps to be a "Baptist" to go to heaven. (So we must conclude it's harder to get into the Baptist Church than it is into heaven!) Sometimes this gets confusing to me! And it gets worse when you consider that the "churches of Christ" in the Bible believed and taught scriptural baptism, as they do to this day, yet never called/call themselves "Baptists" ... though the word surely applies to them more than it does to those who, ironically, call themselves such!

Baptists are falsely baptized, falsely baptize others, and are false "Baptists!" Sorry, I didn't write the baptism rules! Plus, Baptists won't debate the issue with those who challenge them on it. They bowed to men, not Christ. They obeyed men, not Christ. Christ wrote Acts 2:38 and 22:16, and He made it clear: *"be baptized for the forgiveness of sins,"* not "because your sins were forgiven." (*"For"* is "Eis" in Greek, which always takes the 'Accusative Case,' which demands "motion towards, into.") He said *"arise and be baptized and wash away thy sins,"* not "be baptized because your sins were already washed away" (See my Baptism book). A man wrote their teaching and founded their modern denomination. Scripture and history do not lie. They're not Sovereign Souls under Christ sole and absolute laws.

(5) Contribution. Christ's church has always needed money and/or necessities to support its leaders and its evangelistic and benevolent works (Acts 2:44f; 11:29f; I Corinthians 9:6-14; I Timothy 5:17f). Thus the Lord designated the collection of these contributions on the first day of the week when the Lord's people gather together to partake of the Lord's Supper and worship (I Corinthians 16:1-3).

The Lord, again, made this matter of spiritual service different from the Israel's Old Testament system of "Tithing," whereby the specific amounts of several different tithes to support the Levites (for priestly service), the theocracy and benevolence amounted to around twenty three percent (Leviticus 27:30-33; Numbers 18:21ff; Deuteronomy 14:22-29; 26:12). Instead of this national, controlled process of giving, the Lord made our giving of our means to support his church a more freewill, personal matter to be offered from our heart according to our purpose and ability (II Corinthians 8:11f). It is not an obligation to God, it is an offering for God's work. It is God's gift to help others and not a debt owed to a divine lender. We understand that all of our money, not a percentage of it, is "God's money." He gave us all of the physical blessings in life to earn every cent of it (Acts 17:25; James 1:17).

We also understand that God's material gifts to us are also for our own personal wellbeing and benefit and, consequently, we individual recipients have God-given personal property rights (Acts 5:4). All of "our" gifts and possessions were given to each one of us to use for our needs and to share with others as we cheerfully choose (II Corinthians 9:7f). This sovereign personal property right must be maintained if our charity is to be by choice and from the heart and not by legalistic levies, taxation and tithing. Remember the "widow's mites"... "All gave some, one gave all!"

Christ's Church is Best because it has the Best Unity. Jesus prayed for church unity, provided for church unity (via his Word) and prohibited church division (John 17:21-23; I Corinthians 1:10-13; Ephesians 4:1-5). But ... Jesus also said His Word would cause division between those in our families and churches who don't love Him and won't accept His Word (Matthew 10:34-37; I John 2:19). So how does this support the claim that His Church is the most unified church? Because Christ demands that all of His members love Him and "Agree to Agree" on everything He told them to do in his word. It is this love for Christ and his word that is the "Tie that Binds" them together. Any church member who decides to disobey Christ's Word will be sought, taught and/or marked as "divisive" and disciplined (Romans 16:17).

This is unlike denominational churches that don't accept Christ's Word as their final authority, and have thereby accepted doctrinal divisions and different churches. They are all held together by their "Agreement to Disagree" on anything and everything. Their Structural Unity is their Scriptural Disunity!

So the Best Church Unity is based upon our agreeing to agree on what each Bible verse says rather than upon what a hundred modern church manuals say. It is better to stand firm on one scriptural fact than on a hundred "theological opinions." We have a right to our own opinions; but not a right to our own scriptural facts (Daniel Patrick Moynihan). It is better to unite on one essential Bible Fact of Faith than upon a hundred extraneous fables and fictions of other faiths. It is better to be in fellowship with the faithful few sheep in Christ's Church than with the masses of sheeple in false manmade "churches."

Here's the FIRST ESSENTIAL KEY to Church Unity. The same Church *"KEYES"* that Peter used in Acts 2:38 — that first opened the door to get into Christ's One United Church — also kept all those who didn't accept his word locked out of it! Just as God locked the world out of the Ark when He locked Noah in it (Genesis 7:17; cf., Matthew 25:10)! Only those who *"received his word"* were added to Christ's True Church on Pentecost, A.D. 33. And only those who receive his word in Acts 2:38, today, will be in Christ's United Church. Acts 2:38 is also the text that will keep those who refuse to accept and obey it — whatever their church denomination — from being United in His Church or with His church. So it is better to be added by the Lord to His One True and United Church by doing what he clearly told us to do in Acts 2:38-47 than to join any of the Denominationally Divided churches who do not accept HIS KEY TEXT. Acts 2:38 divides them from Christ and Us, otherwise they would be *"of us and with us"* (I John 2:19)!

Christ's Church is Best Church because Christ's Church has Sovereign Souls. Though Christ's church members have different roles and responsibilities, they're all equal as joint heirs of life (I Peter 3:7). All Christians are naked in the eyes of God and are not supposed to seek to be above others because of their dress, office, demeanor or age (Hebrews 4:13). You never have to surrender your Bible beliefs on the basis of another's personal status or tenure in Christ's church. You never have to genuflect or bow to any person or kiss any rings. You remain sovereign in Christ's Church regardless of your race, gender or age. There's no pulling rank in Christ's Church. Christ is your Only Lord, and His

Word is the only Authority you need to support your beliefs.

Christ Church is Best because It is the Biggest Church. Christ's Church is the Biggest Church because it encompasses all of Heaven and Earth.

Christ's Church on Earth: Christ told his Apostles, and all of his disciples since, to spread His Church to every creature on earth. And His Church has been all over the world ever since. His Church contains all the true Christians throughout the entire world today. And the truth is we don't know how many members are in it. Only the Omniscient and Omnipresent God can know where and when every person truly believed, obeyed his Gospel, was added by Him to his universal church and was indwelled by His Holy Spirit to be another one of His individual holy temples (I Corinthians 6:19). No human being, or group of human beings, can know or do any of these divine deeds a single time for a single soul, much less for the entire world since the beginning of time. The true Church is too Big for Walls, and the Job of Universal Shepherd, Soul-Checker and Church-Caretaker is Too Big for a man or mankind!

As far as all of the manmade "churches," large or small, on the earth at any single time in history, including today, they are no more Christ's "Christian Churches" than were all those who called themselves "Israelites" true Israelites in Paul's day: *"For they are not all Israel, that are of Israel* (Romans 9:6). Manmade churches are not to be counted because they never counted themselves in. How Big they are is irrelevant. The Lord's Church of the Bible is not in competition with any or all of the manmade churches. First, because Christ did not authorize them to be in competition with unqualified participants. Second, because our job as Christians is to seek to save those in false churches, not beat them in some sort of "Mega-Church Contest."

Christ's Church in Heaven: The fact that it encompasses all of Heaven not only proves it is the Biggest Church, it is also another reason why Christ's Church is the **Best Church.** And the Best part about this is I'm amongst the *"ye"* in His divine description of it:

> *but ye* {and **"I"**} *are come unto* **Mount Zion**, *and unto the* **city of the living God**, *the* **heavenly Jerusalem**, *and to innumerable hosts of* **angels**, *to the general assembly and* **church of the first born** *who are enrolled in heaven, and to*

*God the Judge of all, and to the **spirits of just men** made perfect, and to **Jesus** the mediator of a new covenant, and to the blood of sprinkling that speaketh better than that of Abel* (Hebrews 12:22-24).

Notice that this text says the Lord's Heavenly Church is occupied by an *"innumerable host of **angels**."* We could point out all the millions of angels mentioned in Scriptures like Revelation 5:11, but this text says they are *"innumerable."* That means there were more angels involved in the Lord's ***heavenly*** church in the first century than there are people in all of the other churches put together today. And that means when we sing the hymn "Worthy Art Thou," the angels might be singing the "New Song" with us (Ibid. 5:9). That's why I believe this book will be reviewed by millions of joyful angelic reviewers when it is released (I Corinthians 4:9; Hebrews 1:14). This is one big reason why we preach and write books about Christ: to cause *"joy in heaven"* (Luke 15:7; See this personal claim on the back cover of my *The Supreme Scientist* book).

This text says the Lord's Church in Heaven contains all the souls of First Century Christians, who were the ***"firstborn"*** (baptized) ones to be *"enrolled in heaven."* That would include the Lord's Apostles, disciples, thousands of Jews and Gentiles mentioned in Acts and throughout the world (Luke 10:20). It also includes all the *"**spirits of just men made perfect,**"* meaning all the souls of all the true people of faith since Adam, including all of the faithful Jews under the Old Covenant, who were made perfect by Christ's atoning blood (Romans 3:25; Hebrews 9:15; 11:4-40). And it includes all the departed souls of Christians throughout the entire world since the First Century, as it will also contain all the souls of saved Christians until the resurrection at the end of time (I Thessalonians 4:13-17). We must also include all the souls of all the sinless (and spiritually "safe") children who died/will die from the beginning till the end of time. As Jesus promised, there's room for all of His "Sinless, Safe and Saved" Children in Our Father's Heaven (John 14:1-3). All of this repudiates the false teachings of churches that keep Christian souls in "Limbo, Purgatory" (RCC) or limit the number going to heaven to 144,000 selected, special or superior souls (JW's).

This text also says the Lord's True Church in Heaven and on the Earth brings us into the presence of **"_God_"** (the Father). Our God is Omnipresent and cannot be confined to this universe, much less to any earthly temples or church buildings (I Kings 8:27; Isaiah 66:1; Acts 17:24). Those who come into His Church by becoming His Sons when they were baptized call upon their "Heavenly Father" every time they call him *"Abba, Father"* (Galatians 3:26 thru 4:6). God the Father hears his Christian sons and daughters in their closets (Matthew 6:6); but He is far from those who choose to seek his ear in the world's largest "unwashed" churches and cathedrals (John 9:31; cf., Isaiah 59:1-2).

This text says being in Christ's Heavenly Church brings us unto **"_Jesus_"** — who gave us his New Testament and bloody sacrifice; who invited us to be his church-bride; who added us to his church; who sent the Holy Spirit to indwell us; who is also always with His *"Brethren"* on earth and, as our mediator and advocate: who is ever presenting our petitions, prayers and case to our Father in heaven (Matthew 18:20; 28:20; Ephesians 5:25-32; Hebrews 2:11f; II Timothy 4:17). Personally, I'd rather be attending or preaching in a small church where Christ is present, like the ancient church of Philadelphia, than in a mega-church where He isn't present, like the ancient Church of Laodicea (Revelation 3:7ff; 14ff).

This text says being in the Lord's Church brings the **"_Holy Spirit_"** into each one of us as His Spirit-indwelled Temple upon this Earth: which Spirit is also ever in Heaven interceding for us, explaining our prayers and problems; and who will raise our dead bodies at the end of time (Romans 8:11, 26). The Lord's Holy Spirit does not abide in false temples and churches (II Corinthians 6:16).

There's one prevailing truth and theme that jumps off the sacred pages in all of these teachings about the infinite room for innumerable spiritual beings and souls in Christ's Spiritual Kingdom and Church in Heaven: there's room for all who choose to go there in His Church ... but no room there (and no mention of such in a single text) for any sinner in any Church that isn't His Church Choice. So if you find yourself in any church that's not clearly approved in Christ's Holy Spirit inspired New Testament, *"Come ye out from among them"* (II Cor. 6:17) .... and then heed this Invitation from Jesus, His Spirit and Beloved Church-Bride:

*I **Jesus** have sent mine angel to **testify** unto you these things for the **churches**, I am the root and the offspring of David, the bright, the morning star. And the **Spirit** and the **bride** say, **Come**. And he that **heareth**, let him say, **Come**. And he that is **athirst, let him come: he that will, let him take of the water of life freely*** (Revelation 22:16-17). (I say, "Come, and Amen.")

Christ's Church is the Best Church because It is the Most Blessed Church. Though God showers his physical blessings — which include His air, water, food, life, written word upon the entire world (Acts 14:17; 17:28) — no one appreciates the Giver of them as much, and thus enjoys them as much, and uses them as well as those who're in His Church/Kingdom:

*But **seek ye first his kingdom**, and his righteousness; and **all these things shall** be added unto you* (Matthew 6:19-21, 33).

Plus, God's greatest spiritual blessings — forgiveness of sins, indwelling of His Spirit, adoption as sons and daughters, spiritual peace and rest in Christ, mediation by Christ, friendship and fellowship with Christ, talents and promotions (sainthood and priesthood), answered prayers, heavenly wisdom, angelic oversight and service, grace and mercy, on and on — are only bestowed upon those in Christ's church family, who are citizens in his universal kingdom.

*Blessed be the God and Father of our Lord Jesus Christ, who hath blessed us with **every spiritual blessing** in the **heavenly places in Christ*** (Ephesians 1:3; cf., vv. 4-14).

So whether we Christians live or die, every stage in our lives progressively proceeds from **"good, to better, to best."**

The first stage is good. This good stage is our physical life "in Christ." Paul said: *"For to me to live is Christ"* (Philippians 1:21). To live in Christ and in his church is to live the most enlightened, joyful, peaceful, content, confident, guilt-free, worry-free, purposeful, empowered, rich, freedom-filled and fulfilled ***"good life"*** (Philippians 4:4-7, 10-20; I Peter 3:10ff; John 8:31-36; 16:22-24).

All members of Christ's Church are free from being enslaved in and by all the BAD THINGS of life. They are free from being servants of sin and the wreck and ruin of unrestrained immorality. They are free from the lying superstitions and fearful false gods of paganism. They are free from all the legalistic spiritual shackles of Christless human religions, false churches and cults. They are free from the physical shackles of pseudo-scientific, earth-worshipping, body-centered atheistic and materialistic religions. If it's bad for Christians, they're free from it!

All members of Christ's church are free to enjoy all the GOOD THINGS of life. Unlike RCC priests, they are free to marry and have families. Unlike those of the Jewish faith, the Seventh Day Adventist church, and other Sabbatarians, they are free to eat all meats with their vegetables with thanksgiving towards God. They are also free to work seven days a week, especially on the Lord's day when they may travel near and far to worship, preach the word, and help the needy (I Timothy 4:1-4). Unlike many major cult members, they are free to read and study all the writings and books of cults, other religions and churches without fear of being chastised for doing so, or fear of being lured into the wrong church. Unlike other churches, they are free from bowing to other religious leaders. They are free from the fear of speaking openly about their biblical views. They are free from being accused of any sin that they cannot resolve by apologizing to the offended person, restoring what they can restore and repenting to their Lord.

The point is, to live outside of Christ is not a good way to live: whether that life is wasted in hopeless hedonism or vainly pursuing the false hope of pagan religions and pseudo churches (Gal. 4:8ff).

The second stage is **better** and occurs when we die and our spirits go to be with the Lord in Paradise/Heaven (Luke 23:43; II Corinthians 5:8f; Philippians 1:21-23; Hebrews 12:23; Revelation 6:9). See Psalms17:15; 139:8; Ecclesiastes 12:7 for O.T. texts on man's spirit.) Read these texts and rejoice in the Lord always.

Then the third stage is the **best** part of our existence and is realized when our dead bodies receive an immortal body like Jesus' at the resurrection (Romans 8:11; II Corinthians 5:1-7; I Thessalonians 4:13-18; I John 3:2). Rejoice in these texts now and live them later!

Considering all of this, why would any self-loving person trade any of these heavenly blessings for any of the materialistic scraps offered by any secular society or religious organization? Why would any Sovereign Soul allow his/her reception of these blessings to be doled out to him/her like some beggar in a Salvation Army soup line? or to be withheld altogether by any so-called higher religious benefactor? They're not their blessings to bestow, ration or withhold; they're Christ's! All the manmade churches put together didn't purchase any of them, nor could they ever afford to pay for a single one of these spiritual blessings. Forgiveness of one sin is above man's pay grade (Matthew 18:21-35)! Yet, "Jesus paid it all" up front at Calvary and freely gives every one of them to his brethren. It is Jesus, alone, who deserves to receive all the praise for every spiritual blessing we receive from him, especially our daily forgiveness of sin (I John 1:7ff).

Now unto him that is able to do exceedingly abundantly above all we ask or think, according to the power that worketh in us, **unto him be the glory in the church** *and in Christ Jesus unto* **all generations for ever and ever.** *Amen* (Ephesians 3:20f). Which brings us to our last point.

Christ's Church is the Best Church because It is the only Permanent Church. Jesus made it abundantly and prophetically clear, when he promised to build his church, that even his death would not prevail against his building of his church and eternal kingdom (Matthew 16:18f). The Hebrew writer made it clear to the Jewish members of Christ's church and kingdom, around A.D. 68, that — though the Jewish polity and religious kingdom would soon be destroyed in A.D. 70 — Christ's church/kingdom would never be removed, saying: *"Wherefore receiving a kingdom that cannot be shaken..."* (Hebrews 12:26-28). (They were receiving it, not waiting to receive it!) It would last until the end of the earth, and then be delivered up by God to heaven when all the dead are resurrected and the living saints are changed to immortality and taken to heaven. So we are Christ's Church-Bride in waiting until death do us all unite (I Corinthians 15:23-58; I Thessalonians 4:13-18)! Let's quote a few verses from these two major texts: to give comfort to those who're in Christ's church; and to give pause for concern to those who're in false churches which teach that Christ's kingdom has not come! Paul disagrees:

> *But now hath Christ been raised from the dead, the first fruits of them that are asleep* {dead}. *For since by man came death, by man came also the **resurrection of the dead**. For as in Adam all die, so also in Christ shall all be made alive. But each in his own order: Christ the firstfruits; then they that are **Christ's at his coming**. **Then cometh the end**, when he shall **deliver up the kingdom to God**, even the Father; when he shall have abolished all rule and all authority and power. For he must **reign** till he hath put all his enemies under his feet. The last enemy that shall be abolished is death.... Wherefore, my beloved brethren, be ye stedfast, unmovable, always abounding in the work of the Lord, forasmuch as **ye know that your labor is not vain in the Lord*** (I Cor. 15:20-26, 58).

> *For the **Lord himself shall descend** from heaven, with a shout, with the voice of the archangel, and with the trump of God: and the **dead in Christ shall rise first**; then we that are **alive**, that are left, shall together with them be caught up in the clouds, to **meet the Lord in the air**: and so shall we **ever be with the Lord. Wherefore comfort one another with these words*** (I Thess. 4:16-18)

Both of these texts support the Lord's church/kingdom being the one of prophecy and not a parenthetical afterthought. Both show the Lord coming to receive the immortal resurrected bodies of all saints of all time ... in the *"air"* and not on the earth. There's not a mention of Christ setting a foot on earth, much less establishing a physical, national (visible!) kingdom on earth for a thousand years. His present *"reign"* over all of his enemies will last until the *"end, when He will deliver up the kingdom* — {which universal Church-Kingdom has lasted for almost 2,000 years already} — *to God"* (and not deliver a smaller, earthly kingdom to mankind that will only last 1000 years... where Christ can't be a Royal King or High Priest!).

This all comforts true Christians in Christ's true church. They are already in a total "Win-Win" situation. As we discussed earlier, our lives already go from "Good to Better to Best" (Philippians

1:21-23). We already reign as Sovereign Souls and Soldiers of Christ above all earthly powers and authorities with our King of kings. We are already more than conquerors in Christ. We can't lose our royal life in His spiritual kingdom because it can't be destroyed or replaced by ANY type of kingdom, spiritual or physical. If they kill us, they bring about our ultimate victory and exodus to be with all our departed brethren and sisters of faith throughout eternity. You can't get any better than the "Eternal Life and Kingdom" we already know we're in via Christ's word:

> *These things have I **written** unto you, that ye may **know** that ye have eternal life, even unto you that believe on the name of the **Son of God*** (I John 5:13).

So millennialism is another sad demon-inspired doctrine that robs all those "Christians" who accept it of their ruling King and Kingdom now and of their Sovereignty in Christ by subjugating them to the ongoing rule of *"the god of this world"* (Satan). It also gives them no real connection to heaven or the powers and persons there. Christ's Church is by far and away THE BEST CHOICE in this life and in the life to come. If your Church is not His Church, your church is not the Best Church for you, your family & friends!

My Choice Confirmed

My choice of Christ's Religion and Church was a choice made of my own free will and without any outside human brainwashing, coercion or threats. I did not choose Christ's church because my best friends (George & Lucille) had chosen Christ's church, or because they convinced me to become a member of their church. Nor was my choice based upon my conducting a comparative survey of the many available churches where I lived, and then choosing the one that most agreed with my personal opinions, or tastes, or my parents' choice, or the one that offered me the most freedom to continue my sinful pursuits. I could have continued my old life as Jerry Neil Wright if I would have remained in my first church (my parents' church), or I could have chosen other churches that were equally "loose with the truth." But I didn't.

Instead, I chose the only church I read about in Christ's New Testament. Which was the church that scripturally stated that I had the "freedom" to make it my choice! <u>Which</u> was the church that also said there was not any other acceptable church to choose. <u>Which</u> was the church that would not make the choice for me! <u>Which</u> was the church that would not accept me if I refused to do, or change, some things in my life that I considered to be unnecessary to do and/or very difficult to change. <u>Which</u> was the church that told me I could not make this church choice for others, including my own children at birth or later.

So I exercised my freedom of religious choice and chose **Christ's Choice**: His One New Testament Church. His Whole Church built upon His Whole Truth. His church founded by Christ and no other. His church built by Christ and upon Christ and no other. His church headed by Christ and no other. His church that submits to Christ's authority and no other. His One Universal Church consisting of all of *"the churches of Christ"* (Romans 16:16). His church that doesn't have a single word from Christ that says any person has a right to expect Him to accept the "Church of My/Your/Their Choice" if it's not the "Church of His Choice!"

Now, having said that, Christ also gave all of us the freedom to reject Him and His Church in this life without immediately incurring his divine wrath and physical judgment (Hebrews 6:6). And I totally agree with Christ's offer of religious freedom without human coercion or divine retribution. And it is because of this Christian tenant that I do not believe in encroaching upon another person's sovereign right to choose their own religion and church, or their right to reject all religions and churches ... and even their right to challenge and criticize all religions and churches. Of course, this does not mean I accept their using their religious or anti-religious views and choices to infringe upon my sovereign right to practice and preach my religious faith and church as being Christ's Choice, and to also criticize all those who differ and challenge them to engage in orderly discussion and debate. This is what "Religious Freedom" is all about: "Freedom OF Religion" and "Freedom FROM Religion!"

But, again, I repeat that this freedom only pertains to our physical freedom to choose good or evil, right and wrong, the right church or the wrong church, and does not mean there are no consequences for making the **Wrong Choices**. A Wrong Church Choice can waste your precious time and life in a monastic, unmarried lifestyle, or engaging in nonproductive religious rituals and routines. A Wrong Church Choice can deprive you of many of God's physical blessings: like healthy food, meats, marriage. Wrong church choices subject people, including their children, to serious health risks: handling snakes, drinking poisons, using drugs, refusing medical care and blood transfusions. Wrong church choices sometimes lead to lawless behavior and even mass suicide (Jim Jones Church, David Koresh, etc.). Not to mention how all church choices which are not Christ's Choice have no scriptural objective hope of receiving any of His spiritual blessings on earth or in the hereafter. **No Choice** at all is often better than the Wrong Choice, because the wrong choice creates friendships, fellowships and even a family that they don't want to lose by changing churches. So why risk any of these physical and spiritual disasters when you still have the choice to choose "His Church Choice."

So when I, as a "Sovereign Christian Soul," say I respect every person's right to choose his/her own God, religion or church, that doesn't mean I believe one church is as good as another or that Christ will accept "your church choice" if it's not "His Church Choice." I don't speak for God or Christ! He has clearly told us that His Religion (Christianity) is the only accepted religion and way to heaven, and that His Church is the only church He adds saved people to and will save in the end. In light of today's era of Islamic Jihadism and other violent religious extremism, I must go further and say I don't remotely respect any religion's or church's right to sacrifice kids to their gods or persecute and kill those who won't praise their prophets or convert to their religion!

When I have the privilege to respond to those who don't/won't choose to accept the Christian faith or church, I tell them that I choose to uphold their right to choose which-ever God, religion or church they please. And sometimes, if they are receptive to having a religious conversation, I uphold my choice of Christ's Church by stating my own Sovereign Joshua & Jerry Principle:

> **Choose You** this day which Christ you shall serve and which Church you shall choose; but as for **me and my house**, we have individually chosen to serve Christ and to be in His Church ... *"The churches of Christ salute you"* (Joshua. 24:15; Romans 16:16).

CHAPTER FIVE
Sovereign Souls Choose Christ's Companionship

Whom you and I choose to be our friends and companions in life makes a difference.

*Be not deceived: **evil companionships** corrupt good morals* (I Corinthians 15:33).

*Walk with wise men, and thou shalt be wise; But the **companion of fools** shall smart {Heb. "be broken"} for it....*

*He that maketh **many friends** doeth it to his own destruction; But there is **a friend** that sticketh closer than a brother* (Proverbs 13:20; 18:24; see II Samuel 1:26 "David and Jonathan").

As I stated in the beginning of this book, I had more "friends" — or I should say "evil companions" — when I was a teenage rebel than good friends since I've been a Christian. And I can attest to the accuracy of the above passages of scripture as per evil companions corrupting good morals, for they corrupted mine!

As I also stated at the beginning of this book, I was a good little boy up until I was nine-ten years old. That's because in my childhood days (circa 1942-52), I was surrounded by good parents, relatives, siblings, cousins, school and Sunday school kids. Also, the radio and early TV programs weren't filled with bad people and evil influences, either. (Unlike today's media cesspools!) The good guys like Roy Rogers and The Lone Ranger always beat the bad guys. Evil wasn't promoted! Lawlessness wasn't encouraged. Sexual deviancies weren't displayed or exploited. The "Fifties" were the "Fabulous Fifties" compared to the "Sensuous Sixties & Seventies" and steady moral decline over the decades since.

As I look back on my childhood innocence today, I fully realize that it was my choice of evil companions and their domains of sinful activity that influenced and corrupted me into becoming a bad little teenager who ended up sowing way too many wild oats

... which no prayer for a crop failure his yet worked (Ecclesiastes 12:1f). And allow me to assure you that being forgiven of all of your past sins doesn't remove the scars from your body and soul: the bad physical and mental consequences, bad tendencies and temptations, bad memories and guilty feelings over those innocent young people that I, yes I, corrupted—who died for their sins and in their sins. The *"way of the transgressor is hard"* and often physically and spiritually fatal (Proverbs 13:15; Romans 6:23).

This is what makes me so sad when I visit suffering sinful souls in jails, prisons, hospitals and morgues who are paying/paid the ultimate price for their sins. I realize that they were all once good little boys like I once was. And I also realize that they were all introduced to the dark, seedy and sinful side of life by their so-called friends—their "evil companions." This is why I find myself saying: "There but for the grace of God go I" ... or "gone was I."

Oh well, since I can't change any of my bad past, let's flip this historical record over from the dark side of my life to the bright side of my life, and do what Solomon the Preacher did in his historical writings about life. After presenting all of the **"vanities"** he had pursued and experienced in his extravagant life *"under the sun"* (Ecclesiastes 1:2f), he concluded with a warning to young men about living an ungodly life (11:9-12:1) and encouraged them to live a God-fearing life instead (12:13f). And in our text above (Proverbs 18:24), after warning us about the ease we'll have in *"making many friends"* who are evil companions, Solomon said we can have *"a friend that sticketh closer than a brother."* And mark this well, you don't get many good friends like that, outside of your own loved ones, in your entire life. Like a *"good wife,"* they are precious and hard to find (Proverbs 18:22; 31:10-31). And they are almost impossible to find in brothels and bars!

And I thank God that I found a good wife (my best earthly friend) and a good friend, who also had a good wife, like George and Lucille Spurgin. They only came as a pair! They definitely stuck by my wife and me closer than a brother or sister. Of course, my mother and father, and daughters were, or are, my best friends!

Good friends can help you physically, mentally and spiritually in life. They can lift you up when you're down, feed you when you're hungry, house you when you're homeless, advise you when you're too emotional to make an objective decision, stand by you when others turn against you, praise you when others curse you, protect and defend you when you're attacked verbally or physically, on and on. And I've had such a great friend as that in George Spurgin, who did all that and more, including giving me and Brenda keys to his house to use when traveling, and even offering to sell his house to help us if need be. And I've had/have other good friends, like the Exums in foreign mission fields and in America, and Joe Buchanan in Hawaii, that blessed my life more than I can repay. For those friends, I'm extremely grateful to God.

BUT ... NONE of these earthly friends and companions, including the most beloved ones in my family, could/can save me from the inevitable problems of life and dying, salve my guilty conscience, or satisfy my yearning and hope for a more fulfilling and permanent existence than can be found on this terrestrial ball. By the time I reached eighteen years of age, I had either experienced most of life's typical physical pleasures or been around older folks who had experienced them fully; and, yet, they all still died (like Solomon). So I soon discovered that this worldly life was little more than "striving after wind" or chasing butterflies, and I was already asking myself: "Is this all there is to life?"

So I knew I needed something, or someone, in my life that I didn't have. But, for some reason, I wasn't able to see that that SOMEONE was the One whose name I had been taking in vain for years! And, honestly, I don't know if I found Him, or He found me. But I know God knows, and I now biblically know He had always known that one day HE would be my Best Companion, Counselor, Consolation, Comforter, Champion, Hero and Friend. For I — Jerry/Gerald Neil Wright — was:

CHRIST'S CHOICE

Here are Five Facts about Christ's Companionship that set Jesus' Friendship apart and above all others.

- *Christ's Friendship is First.*
- *Christ's Friendship is Foremost.*
- *Christ's Friendship is Failproof.*
- *Christ's Friendship is Fulltime.*
- *Christ's Friendship is Forever.*

Christ's Friendship is First

Jesus Christ's choice of Gerald "Jerry" Neil Wright as a friend was not like anyone else chose me to be his/her friend. He didn't choose me as a friend because He looked me over for a while, liked what he saw (especially my Harley!), and decided he wanted to pal around with me and "hang out" as friends. If truth be told, I had a few friends who only chose my company because they wanted me to haul them around on my Harley or to borrow (or bum) some of my caddy money! If Jesus had based his friendship upon anything my teenage friends based theirs upon, He wouldn't have given me the time of day, much less waste any of his time with me.

No, we need to examine Jesus' friendship with us through Jesus' own words in his Biblical Biography. Therein, we learn Jesus' friendship with us was based upon his eternal divine nature and not only upon his temporal human existence and experience amongst human beings. Which experience would have made most peace-loving people swear off being around human beings altogether! Right? Didn't Jesus' own race of religious leaders lie about him, mock him, abuse him, seek to kill him and turn him over to their worst enemies? Didn't one of his closest Disciples, Judas, betray him right during the Passover? Didn't one of his most loyal disciples, Peter, deny him three times when he needed him most? Didn't all of his Apostles leave him and flee when he was arrested (Matthew 26:56)? So Jesus' human experience with humanity was anything but "Jesus-friendly!" Didn't He know all of this before he became flesh? Yes, he did. Remember, He inspired Isaiah 53 and also knew He would be wounded by his friends (Zechariah 13:6)!

Which brings us to the Bible truth about Jesus' knowledge of each one of us individually — from our conception through our death, before the world was created — which must be considered when we examine his friendship with us (see Jeremiah 1:5). Just as He knew the name of Israel's King "Josiah" three hundred years before he was born, and the name of Persia's King "Cyrus" over a hundred years before he was born, so He knows our name, our entire life (good and bad), and whether we become his friend or not. And, now rejoice in this, He wrote each of his foreknown friends for life in his book of life before the foundation of the world (compare I Kings 13:2 with II Kings 22:1ff; Isaiah 44:28; 45:1-7 with Daniel 10:1ff).

*Blessed be the God and **Father** of our **Lord Jesus Christ**, who hath blessed us with every spiritual blessing in the heavenly places in Christ: even as he **chose us in him before the foundation of the world**, that we should be holy and without blemish before him in love: having **foreordained us** unto adoption as **sons** through **Jesus Christ** unto himself, according to the good pleasure of his will, to the praise of the glory of his grace, which he freely bestowed on us in the **Beloved*** (Ephesians 1:3-6).

*And all {not his friends} that dwell on the earth shall worship him {the dragon}, every one whose **name hath not been written** from the **foundation of the world in the book of life** of the Lamb that hath been slain* (Revelation 13:8; also 17:8).

So Christ, in his omniscient foreknowledge, first chose me to be his friend before time or I existed. Then Christ still chose me in real-life time — when I was running to and fro on this earth, sinning day and night before his face — to be his friend. Unbeknownst to me at that time, I was personally fulfilling a major Gospel Fact about the love of Jesus as per Romans 5:8!

Logically and emotionally speaking, if Christ still chose me to be his friend when I was so unfriendly towards him that I could have easily been called his "enemy," shouldn't I believe that he surely must now consider me to be one of his best friends when I tell everyone that I consider Him to be my best friend? I think so. And by saying this, I just fulfilled another scripture about the Best Friend of all of Christ's penitent sinful enemies:

*And you {brethren in Colossae...and Gerald}, being in **time past alienated** and **enemies** in your mind in your **evil works**, yet now hath he **reconciled** in the body of his flesh through death, to present you holy and without blemish and unreproveable before him* (Colossians 1:21f).

All this again reminds me of how our Bible is a love letter from God. I know I would have never known about our loving heavenly

Father and our loving divine-human friend without it. As Christ's incomparable majesty and glorious power is always on display in his miraculous work of physical Creation, so his incomparable love is always on display in his creation of His Loving History Book, the Bible (Psalms 19:1-4).

Christ's Friendship is Foremost

Christ not only talked a good talk about wanting this sinner to be his friend, he walked the walk. He proved it by walking to the gallows in my place. And as I said before, I believe it is quite clear in his Biblical Love Letter that he would have died in my place even if I were the only sinner in the world. *"Greater love hath no man than this, that a man lay down his life for his friends"* (John 15:13).

Other earthly friends can lay down their lives to protect my right to live in sinful tranquility (which is the case in any country), or die in sin with me, or die trying to save me from another person's sinful assault upon me ... but not one of them can die for my sins, purchase my forgiveness and suffer my punishment for my sins. When it comes to a soul-saving friend, Jesus on the Cross is lifted higher than all the friends the world has to offer. He is First and Foremost. He lifted and lifts me higher than any other friend, or all the friends I've ever had, ever could. As the song goes, *"There's not a friend like the lowly Jesus, no not one, no not one!"*

Christ's Friendship is Failproof

Christ is the only friend we can have who has the divine abilities to guarantee us that He will never fail us in our times of need and struggle:

> *Be ye free from the love of money; content with such things as ye have: for himself hath said,* ***I will in no wise fail thee****, neither will **I in any wise forsake thee**. So that with good courage we say, The Lord is my helper; I will not fear: What shall man do unto me* (Hebrews 13:5f)?

I know any person who has "friends in high places" has a major advantage over those who only have "friends in low places" (as per

Garth Brooks' claim about having friends in bars!). Well, every Christian has a Friend — or should I say "The Friend of All Friends?" — who occupies the highest position in the highest place in existence: Christ in Heaven. Who not only created everything and everyone, He and his Father and Spirit owns everything and everyone, in heaven and on the earth, controls everything and everyone, and thus can use them to assist us in overcoming all the obstacles we will ever face in this life. Listen to Jehovah/Jesus speak from on high:

> *For every beast of the forest is mine, and the cattle upon a **thousand** hills. I know all the birds of the mountains; and the wild beasts are mine. If I were hungry, I would not tell thee; for **the world is mine, and the fullness thereof*** (Psalms 50:10-12). (The word *thousand* is often symbolic of ultimate completeness, as it is in texts like II Pet. 3:8; Rev. 20:1-6.)

> ***Be not anxious for your life**, what ye shall eat, or what ye shall drink; nor yet for your body, what ye shall put on. Is not the life more than the food, and the body than the raiment. Behold the birds of the heaven, that they sow not, neither do they reap, nor gather into barns; and your heavenly **Father feedeth them. Are not ye of much more value than they*** (Matthew 6:25f)?

> *The God that made the world and all things therein, he being Lord of heaven and earth, dwelleth not in temples made with hands; neither is he served by men's hands, as though he needed anything, seeing **he himself giveth to all life, and breath and all things*** (Acts 17:24f; see Colossians 1:12-17).

> *What then shall we say to all these things? **If God is for us, who is against us?** He that spareth not his own Son, but delivered him up for us all, how shall he not also with him **freely give us all things*** (Romans 8:31f)?

And so we sing with joy and gladness in our hearts: "What a **friend we have in Jesus**, All our sins and griefs to bear ... Have we trials and temptations? Is there trouble anywhere?... Are we weak and heavy laden, Cumbered with a load of care! ... Can we find a friend so faithful, Who will all our sorrows share? ... Do thy

friends despise, forsake thee? Take it to the Lord in prayer" (excerpts from song, *What a Friend We Have in Jesus,* Joseph Scriven, Charles Converse).

Christianity is not a mournful religion, a chanting religion, a humming religion, a clapping religion, a dancing religion, a drug-taking religion, or a hating religion. It is a joyous, loving and, most of all, **singing religion**. It is a religion in which even a blind lady, Fanny J. Crosby, was motivated to compose in her mind and dictate the writing of over eight thousand of our best hymns and gospel songs. Christianity is such a religion of joy that even a man in prison would sing and say: *"Rejoice in the Lord always: again I will say, Rejoice"* (Acts 16:25; Philippians 1:14; 4:4)!

Christ's Friendship is Fulltime

Christ promised that He would be with us until the end of time (Matthew 28:20). Just as He was with Elijah when he thought he was all alone and running for his life from Jezebel (I Kings 19:2-4, 10). Or with King David <u>wherever he had ever been</u> ... or <u>whatever he was doing</u>: from his downsitting to his uprising, from his lying down to all of his ways, to all of his thoughts and words ... or <u>wherever he would go:</u> whether to heaven or down to Sheol, or to the uttermost parts of the sea ... *"even there thy hand lead me, And thy right hand find me"* (Psalms 139:1-12). He was with Shadrach, Meshach and Abednego in the fiery furnace and with Daniel in the lion's den and his every prayer (Daniel 3:25; 6:22; 10:12). He was with Jonah in the Sea and the belly of the Sea Monster (Jonah 1:11-17; 2:1ff). He was with the Apostles in jail (Acts 5:18f; 16:25f; II Timothy 4:17). He was always there.

Now that's a Friend that sticks closer than any brother ever could! That's a friend that no other friend can be because no mere human friend can be with every person, everywhere, all the time; yet our Omnipresent Lord can. And Is. And this is the Friend that all of those in Christ have and need. This is the friend I needed!

Christ Friendship is Forever

*Neither will I in any wise **forsake** thee*
(Hebrews 13:5)

I don't care how many good friends we have, nor how long we have had them as our friends, there's not a one of them that can help us as our friend after he/she dies. Oh yes, we can gain some comfort from our memories of our dearly departed friends, and even continue to be blessed by all their spiritual contributions to our own lives, but we can't communicate with them after they're dead. Regardless of what so-called psychics say about calling forth their ghosts or departed spirits, you can't really see or talk to dead people, as is found in Samuel's miraculous "disquieting" (I Samuel 28:7ff, see *Now That's A Miracle!* book.) Nor will any one of us be able to revisit any of those we leave behind after we die. So be good to your friends while they're with you and you're with them.

But, Gerald, won't we meet all of our Christian friends when we go to heaven? Well, that's something we can't say with absolute certainty until we die and meet them in heaven. Though we can hear people confess Christ, see them obey the Gospel, see whether or not they have physically repented of some of their sinful actions and if they faithfully attended church, etc., we still can't know what our omniscient judge, Jesus Christ, knows about the thoughts and intents of their hearts and whether their actions were sincere (Romans 2:15f; Hebrews 4:12). I can only know about my soul!

All of these spiritual uncertainties make up a good case for not making any public pronouncements about a departed person's final destiny. You can believe and assume a person went to heaven, but you can't know such. Actually, you can more know that a person is going to hell rather than heaven if you see him/her doing evil and never obeying Christ till the day he/she dies. (But you'd be wise not to say such about any person's loved one or friend at their funeral!) Tell me something, is saying a departed person has gone to hell anymore passing divine judgment than saying he has gone to heaven? It is not. Yet people still condemn people for saying a public sinner who died in sin went to hell ... but not for saying he went to heaven? Before talking more about going to heaven, let's talk some more about people going to **hell.**

(1) I know Jesus said a lot of people were going there (Matthew 7:13-23; 10:28). **(2) I know** that believing any person is going to hell is "heart-wrenching" for Christians who love all souls and want all to go to heaven. **(3) I know** many churches don't believe in hell (like JWs, SDAs). **(4) I know** many modern churches have watered hell down so much that it's a "cool place" to be. Which was well illustrated by my dearly beloved and departed teacher, Richard Rogers, who made up this quote about their preaching hell: *"Pardon me, if you please, but I'd like to suggest that, perhaps, unless you commence to begin to do a little bit better ... you might accidentally be lost for a short period of time in a cool hell, somewhere, maybe. In other words, unless you repent to a measure you will be lost to a degree!"* **(5) And I know** that many unbelievers have more faith that there is no unseen hell than they have about there being an unseen heaven. After all, I have observed that most newspaper obituaries covering even the most profligate person's demise ends with *"He/she is in a better place!"* How can they be sure of that?

The truth is that no person or preacher can say anything about any person that has any effect whatsoever on where a deceased person's soul has gone upon his/her demise. Every preacher on earth can say a benevolent and loving unbeliever must be in heaven, and it won't make it so or move God to transfer his/her soul from hell to heaven because of popular demand! Nor will it work the other way around and move God to transfer ole Gerald from heaven to hell because so many insist I am "Gerald Wrong" and keep telling me to "go to hell!" One thing is sure, I'll never get lost, because so many people are always telling me where to go!

Because of all this human speculation and emotionalism about the afterlife, including mine, I thank God that my Divine Friend Jesus, who is **"the same yesterday, today and forever,"** will be the only judge and person in charge of the transportation of my soul when I die (Hebrews 13:8)! And He has promised to be the Best Friend of all of his faithful brethren throughout their entire earthly existence, then through *"the valley of the shadow of death,"* then, finally, greet each one of them in heaven with open arms and praise, saying: *"Well done, good and faithful servant ... enter thou into the joy of thy Lord"* (Matthew 25:21). Though I don't pretend to preach any departed soul into heaven or hell when I preach funerals, I do tell the living that our faith has to be in Christ's word and perfect love for us, as he had for his best friend, Lazarus, and not in our perfect love for Him (John 11:3, 36).

To close this point, here are a few things I can know from Christ's Scriptures about my own future prospects of heaven. I know if I remain faithful to him till I die, He will remain faithful to his promise to usher me into heaven after I die (John 14:1ff; Philippians 1:21-23, Revelation 2:10). I know I can fall away from Christ, so I never take his grace for granted and use it as a license to sin (I Corinthians 9:27; 10:12). I know I don't want to go to hell. I also know I don't plan on leaving Christ for any other human being, pleasure or price. My soul is not for sale. I don't know what my future holds, but I know who holds the future. And I know that's not a worn-out cliché! I believe "If we live as though Christ never died, we will die as though he never lived." So I know whom I have believed and Why I Chose Him to be my BEST FRIEND in life and for life (II Timothy 1:12). That's why....

CHRIST'S CHOICE WAS MY CHOICE

Because I Chose to accept Christ's Choice. I chose Christ as my friend because, as we just discussed, He loved and chose me to be his friend first. Who can deny that Jesus Chose our friendship first? And that includes ME! Nor can anyone deny that Jesus wants us to choose Him to be our very best friend on earth. Who am I to reject the friendship of any _good_ person who says he/she likes/loves me and wants to be my friend, much less the greatest person who has ever lived on this earth? I mean, I have befriended people in this world who didn't really love me or desire my permanent and close friendship. And most of them haven't spoken to me in decades ... or are dead! (Several died young due to criminal circumstances!) Furthermore, I have to be honest and admit that I can't recall a single invitation from any rich or famous person ever asking me to be his/her friend, or offering himself to by my best friend. Though I went to see many Country and Rock & Roll Music Stars in my life, not a single one of them called me and asked me if I'd like to be his/her friend. Go figure?

Actually, a "Sovereign Soul" must not only make his/her own choice of Jesus Christ to be his constant Companion and Best Friend, he must also make his own wise choices of his earthly friends and not allow others to choose themselves and their friends to be his friends. He must decide whether or not he wants to risk being a close or constant friend with people who are of such poor moral character that they are always trying to tempt him to sin with them: to have just one little drink of champagne to celebrate their victory, promotion, anniversary or divorce; to listen to their dirty jokes or sexcapades; to seduce him to take a look at pictures of his nude Jezebels; to do anything that will compromise his faith. He must decide if he wants to constantly endure their insults of his Best Friend and Faith. Maybe I'm a little old fashioned here, but I don't long abide anyone talking trash (or "stink" as they say in Hawaii) about my mother, wife, daughters, grand/great-grand kids, and my Best Friend, Jesus. You can get by with badmouthing my looks and Southern-Hick dialect, but not without a serious rebuke if you put down my friends when they're not available to defend themselves. (Sometimes I tell those who ridicule my looks: "I may not have an attractive body, but I have a beautiful soul!")

So Sovereign Souls show their sovereignty by being in charge of their personal boundaries. Let me close this point with a little humorous personal anecdote that illustrates this last point. Again it has relevance to my young Harley days in the 1950's, when a popular Rock & Roll song was on top of the music charts: it was *"Blue Suede Shoes,"* written and recorded by Carl Perkins, and also recorded by Elvis Presley. The key lyric went like this:

> *You can knock me down, step in my face. Slander my name all over the place. Well, do anything that you want to do, But uh uh honey, lay off of my shoes ... Well you can do anything, But lay off of my blue suede shoes.*

Well, because of that song and my need for a new pair of shoes, my mother bought me a nice pair of real blue suede shoes. Unlike the shame I usually endured when I had to wear old shoes my dad brought home from the Veterans Hospital where he worked, I was proud as a peacock of those shoes. But you had to be careful not to get them wet or scuffed, or the suede would be ruined. Well, I was at the Monroe Junior High School gym a few weeks after I got the shoes, and my gym instructor came over to me and said, "nice shoes, Gerald." Then he put his foot on top of my right foot and twisted it around a few times and walked off. This stunt caused a slick spot right on top of my shoe that I couldn't sand or wire brush back into shape: the shoe looked like secondhand junk! I'm not going to tell you about the names I called him; but I can tell you I had my big school bully threaten him. (Again, I told you I was a little hoodlum!) Oh well, lay off badmouthing my loved ones and Best Friend ... and stepping on my "Blue Suede shoes"... or on my recently purchased Harley Boots. (Though I feel safe walking in Harley Boots, I no longer feel safe riding a Harley!)

I Chose Christ because He gave me that Choice. I chose Christ to be my number one companion and friend in life because He gave me the blessed privilege of personally making my own decision to accept his personal written (scriptural) invitation to be his friend. I'm very grateful that He treated me with respect as a responsible adult and sovereign soul and didn't make me jump through hoops or go through the proper political channels, priestly protocols or higher mediators to RSVP his most gracious invitation. Thank you, Jesus, for thinking of us little guys! Us nobodies! You're truly a "Man for all Seasons" and "God of all the People!" By the way, thank you again for your humble visit to this planet in human flesh. Sorry about all the indignities and cruelties you had to bear while here ... but it was what we needed to prove, once and for all, how loving our God and Savior really is! Our love, thanksgiving and awe to You, and our Father and Spirit!

I Chose, and still choose, Christ because no other person can make My Choice. I chose to be Christ's friend because that was a choice no other person could make for me. And that was a choice that I now know, as a longtime friend and Sovereign Soul, don't want anyone else making for me. As long as I'm on this side of the sod, I'll choose my own friends, thank you very much! Besides, as far as making an informed biblical choice of Christ as my blood-brother and friend, no other person could have been baptized for me while I was alive, much less after I'm dead.

Note: I Corinthians 15:29 — doesn't teach us to baptize people for dead people as some cults (like Mormons) teach. Paul was illustrating how those who were denying the physical resurrection were also repudiating the efficacy of their baptism. This was because their being buried with Christ into his death in baptism would be equivalent to being baptized for, or into, a dead person if He wasn't raised from the dead (see Romans 6:3-6). This false teaching is quite similar to the RCC teaching which has its members praying deceased people out of their mythical purgatory.

I Chose Christ because no other person can replace Me as Christ's friend. No other person, great or small, can replace me as Christ's friend. Though others may be better friends of Christ than I can be, none can be a friend exactly like me, or in my place. No person can love Jesus as I love him. Though all sinners are equally saved, all sinners are not equal in their other personal good or bad traits. Jesus recognized this when comparing the love of the Sinful Woman with the Self-righteous Pharisee. Here's what he said: *"Her sins, which are many, are forgiven; for she loved much: but to whom little is forgiven, the same loveth little"* (Luke 7:47) All saved sinners are equal as saints; but not all saints are the identical as sovereign souls. Each person is unique in Christ's eyes, and He will not accept substitutes for me as a friend. Nor will I accept any other person substituting for me as Christ's friend. Such is not what I chose. I chose to be Christ's personal spiritual friend, who has his own identity and name, so I can proudly and fondly boast to the world: "Jerry/Gerald is a friend of Jesus!" Nothing more, nothing less. So, obviously, I won't accept any vicarious friends of or for Jerry. In fact, I don't believe there can be a "Vicar of Gerald" any more than I believe there can be a "Vicar of Christ!"

I Chose Christ because no other person can replace Christ as my Best Friend. Just as I will not accept any other person taking my place as a vicarious friend for Christ, I will also not accept any other impersonal relationship with any self-appointed Ambassador, Substitute or "Vicar of Christ" as a replacement for Christ as my Friend. I chose Jesus Christ to be my friend; not Pope this, or Pastor that, or Reverend Nobody! I was promised, in writing by Christ, a personal relationship with the Omnipresent Christ as a Friend: who is always ready, willing and able be at my side, anywhere and anytime — whether I'm free or in jail, awake or asleep, 24/7, 365/6 days a year — to render immediate attention and aid to my personal spiritual needs and physical wants.

He's always fully informed about each one of his friends, including little ole me. He's always "on duty, on call," always available to hold my hand, along with the Father's (John 10:28-30). He's always engaged, always able to hear about my troubles and temptations, always able to answer my prayers and fulfill my petitions. (The knowledge that He always hears my prayers is a sufficient and powerful answer to me. Especially since no one else who can help me hears them at all!) He's always ready to comfort me, mend my broken heart or heal my sorrowful spirit. He's always ready to hear my case, forgive my sins and give me spiritual peace and rest. So Jesus will always be my First, Foremost, Fulltime and Failproof Friend. The Choice of 'Gerald's Best Friend' has already been made. The Position is filled. Jesus is My Friend. My Companion. My Champion. My Hero. "Hey, Pilate, 'Behold My Man Upstairs'" (John 19:5; Revelation 12:5)!

So, obviously, I'm not open to accepting any Feeble Friars, Magnanimous Mahatma's, Popular Pulpiteers, Pseudo Pontiffs or Venerable Vicars, who are unable to be anything like the Friend I already have in Jesus. For they are incapable of doing anything like my Friend Jesus did or can do. In fact, they can't do anything for anybody that you or I can't do! I can get in touch with the Almighty God by simply calling upon Jesus (in thought or vocally), the ONLY Mediator between all men and God, in a heartbeat ... or when it's skipping beats (I Timothy 2:5)! I can pray for myself, you or anyone else I chance to meet, all by my lonesome. I can teach anyone how to be saved, worship and be a Christian all from my own copy of Christ's Unabridged Bible Handbook, or even from my memorization of its very memorable passages. I could've called 911 when I was having a heart attack (as we'll discuss soon). But since I didn't have my phone handy, I'm glad my golfing friends did it for me without going through any of the "priests" here or at the Vatican who don't know me.

Please understand my purpose in saying all these harsh words. For I'm not saying them just to **put "powerful people" down**. I'm trying to say **I'm not willing to put myself down** (or the 99% of the world's 'Peons' like me), or make myself dependent upon anyone when it comes to looking out for my best spiritual interests. When it comes to knowing and helping little old me, all of the world's famous and "great" religious icons and leaders are, by comparison with Jesus, out-of-touch, out-of-reach, long-distance strangers who don't anything about me or my problems.

Of course, I'm sure these leaders would say they would've helped me if they had known me and about my problems; but that's really their problem, now isn't it? They shouldn't set know themselves up as the greatest religious "Friends of the World" and some sort of "Divine Mediator" between all people and God if they don't have the ability or desire to be either. It's not my fault that I can't get in touch with Arch Bishop "So and So" or Pope "What's His Name?" The truth is I couldn't get in touch with any of these so-called great religious leaders if I wanted to: "No not one!" They wouldn't accept my phone calls if I hacked into their big switchboards. They'd say: "Gerald who?" My verifiable truth is, I was at the Vatican in 1967, and the Pope didn't even know I was there! (Though I did get to come face to face with a few dead popes "under glass" while there! See them on UTube if you dare!)

So here's the end of the matter with me: if any highfalutin, religious world leader didn't die for my sins, can't walk on water, can't be my constant friend and companion just like Jesus — who can't hear my loudest cries (Jesus can hear my whimpers and whispers), and can't be my light in my darkest hours or at the end of my tunnel — he can forget about it. I'm sick of these "Jesus Wannabes" telling me I need to go through them or utilize their religious relics — crucifixes, statutes, pictures of Christ, Saints, or even "Mother Mary" — to access ALL of the spiritual blessings of God (Ephesians 1:3). I don't, and won't, accept "symbolism over substance." I don't/won't accept substitutes or 'standins' for Jesus Christ. HE is my real personal, Divine-Human Friend, Mediator, High Priest, Lord and Savior. Ah...what a friend I have in Jesus! *"There's not a friend like the lowly Jesus, No not one, No not one!"* (In case you haven't noticed, this is very personal with me, as it should be with all "Sovereign Souls of Our Savior!")

I have Chosen to keep Christ as My Best Friend because He has always proved He's My Best Friend. Jesus has been my Best Friend for 52 years. I have no doubts that I made the right choice when I made Jesus the Number One Friend in my life. I fully believe I wouldn't even be alive today if I hadn't chosen to follow His Word and walk in his steps. I can't even imagine what my life would be without Him. There's no other friend on earth that can compare or compete with all the blessings of having Him as my friend. I've never done anything physically or spiritually harmful to myself or others by following His word or walking in his righteous paths (John 15:14). I doubt I'd be married or have great children (Stephanie and Melissa). I know I wouldn't be an evangelist and author of a dozen books proclaiming and defending his Gospel. Preaching His Gospel is the Greatest Career on earth (see next Chapter)! No one is more surprised at what I've accomplished than am I. Truly, I'm not what I should be or want to be, but I am not what I once was. I'm not a Punk Criminal. And though John Butterfield — the Daytona motorcycle racer and owner of Butterfield's Harley Davidson Store in Roanoke, who sold me my Elvis Harley — said he thought of me every time he heard an ambulance siren, I'm not dead ... yet!

And I have never had to fear being without my Best Friend (Jesus) standing at my side because He was too far away to help me or had died. My "Nest Friend," my wife, is with me most of the time now, but not all the time. My best earthly friend, George Spurgin, died! Popes die, too, and stay dead. (As I said, I saw some long-time dead popes in the Vatican!) Jesus has never failed or forsaken me. He has been with me in twelve countries, through good times and bad times, through temptations and triumphs, sins and sermons, here, there and everywhere. He's been my Constant Friend. He is my Life (Colossians 3:4).

When I was arrested for his sake, He was there. When I've been lonely or worried, He was there (Philippians 4:5f). When others forsook me, He was there (II Timothy 4:16f). When I needed rest from my burdens, He was there to take a load off of me and give me rest ... as He promised (Matthew 11:28). When I came near the valley of shadow of death, He was there (Psalms 23:4). Speaking of which, I now would like to share with you:

"My Near-Death Experience"

I, as many others, have had the providential privilege of surviving what some call "a near-death experience." You might be asking what this has to do with Jesus being my friend as a "Sovereign Soul." Well, **first** of all, being at death's door is an experience that you usually don't live to tell about. Usually the event kills you. **Second,** such rare experiences often reveal something to you that you will never otherwise learn. It did to me. **Third,** you learn that though your friends can try to save you physically, you know they can't actually stop you from dying. **Fourth,** I would never have written this book if I hadn't gone through that experience. Most of my books were generated by my experiences in life and out of religious drama, debates and demands. This book was to a large degree generated out of my "near death experience" and the life changes it brought about. Historically speaking, I began preaching the major points in this book a few months after I arrived home from the hospital.

Before going into the details, first allow me to clarify what I'm talking about here. I'm not talking about **"near death events"** wherein you come close to getting killed while engaging in risky occupations or activities: like military combat, fire-fighting, mountain-climbing, surfing or riding motorcycles. You know, those "close-calls" you live to tell about and glibly say: *"Close only counts in horseshoes and hand grenades!"* For life is fraught with "accidents-waiting-to-happen" in the lives of those who live dangerously or go where eagles dare. When David was fleeing from the wrath of King Saul, he said *"there is but **a step** between me and death"* (I Samuel 20:3). Of those kinds of experiences, I have had many. The three most memorable "Close Calls" occurred when I was a young teenager in a hurry to get to work (caddy) or play. The first two occurred before I got my first motorcycle and had to walk or hitchhike to work or wherever I was going.

My First Close Call: My first brush with death occurred when I was almost run over by a train. I was around thirteen years old and in a hurry to get to the golf course to caddy (about five miles from my house). When I heard the whistle of the long coal train coming, I knew it would delay me for 15 minutes or more. So I decided to see if I could beat it. I ran for about a quarter of a mile up the street, across the fields and down the steep embankment to the two sets of railroad tracks. Upon arrival I saw the train was only a few yards away on the first set of tracks and, without even slowing down to consider the risk, I dove across the tracks in front of the train. Though I sustained some scrapes and bruises due to the "belly-landing" on the gravel between the two sets of tracks, I made it. Barely! What a little "Daredevil" I was! I still ponder at how "lucky" I was to escape getting run over by that train that was going faster than I thought. Whew, Close Call! Indeed, there was "only a step between me and death" on that day!

My Second Close Call: The second time a similar near-death occurred was when I was almost run over by a bus when I was in a hurry to get to the highway down from my Junior High School so I could hitchhike to the golf course. I don't remember even seeing the bus approaching. But just as I stepped off the curb, the wind of the passing bus blew me back upon the sidewalk! (I only weighed 118 pounds!) Another close call! "Only a step from death!"

My Third Close Call: Though there were many other "near-suicidal" experiences during my teen years — almost falling off cliffs, almost drowning swimming in flood-swollen rivers, being in a head-on car crash in a car I had hitchhiked from the golf course, almost hitting a tractor trailer truck at Hilltop Restaurant on my Harley, being chased by the police at 100 mph in the dark on my Harley, shot at by irate neighbors who hated my Harley, etc. — I suppose the closest, witnessed "brush with death" came when I launched ole "Houndog" across a four-lane intersection in Salem, Virginia. The instant the stop light turned green, and without looking both ways, I went full throttle across two lanes of traffic and crashed into a car on the other side of the median that ran the red light. The driver was the Mayor of another city. I struck his car in the rear wheel well. My Harley stuck in the wheel well, and I was propelled upwards and over the car, two lanes of traffic and about eighty feet (total) into a service station. Unbeknownst to me, there was a police officer on the opposite side of the highway who witnessed the entire accident. He said: "though you were turning the Harley on, the Mayor did run the red light and caused the accident." He also told me I was doing summersaults through the air over the car, two lanes of traffic, and all the way until I landed on my butt near the entrance of the service station's grease rack.

Though we didn't wear helmets and protective leather gear back in the 'Fifties,' I didn't get a scratch! (Though I don't remember doing the summersaults through the air, I thank God I didn't land on my head!) The Mayor gave me a hundred dollars to replace my front fender and bent forks (still rideable), and I continued on my way to Brenda's house for our date. Another "Close Call!" But when you're young and stupid, it would take more than a **"near-fatal"** crash to stop me from riding Houndog! (Unbeknownst to me, my right leg was numb because I had compressed a disc in my lower spine, which has served as a painful and debilitating reminder, or "thorn in the flesh," for me for the last 56 years!) Now back to my definition of a "Near Death Experience."

What I mean by a *"Near Death Experience"* is your suffering what could be a mortal wound or serious organ failure in your body. One in which your "golden hour" is fast ticking away, and your life's breath is fading away. One in which you'll likely die. And one wherein some say they actually died, saw a "bright light," floated on a cloud into heaven and saw Christ. Then they came back to life and returned to earth to tell us what heaven is like and sell millions of books! (II Corinthians 12:1-4 says such heavenly experiences and revelations are not naturally possible or lawful.)

My "near death experience" was one wherein I never went unconscious, never saw any lights, never went to heaven—though I thought I was near my departure; but one which could have been as deadly as if that bus, train and car ran over me back when I was a teenager. My near-death experience was a massive heart attack in which my left anterior descending artery — the so-called "Widow Maker" — suddenly became one hundred percent blocked. Why did this happen?

Well, though my dad died of a heart attack at the age of fifty eight, he was a heavy smoker, and I was not. My health was pretty good for a seventy-one year old man. Of course, I can thank Jesus for that. Because of my Christian beliefs, I hadn't had a drop of booze or a cigarette for over fifty years. And I had also worked out with weights for fifty years to keep my bodily temple in good shape. That helped. My cholesterol was low (126) and my blood pressure was normal. Besides, I had a treadmill test and echocardiogram on my heart done a few years earlier that was so good the cardiologist said I'd never have a heart attack. (He was obviously not omniscient like my Lord!) My only worrisome health problem was my platelet count was low due to recently diagnosed thrombocytopenia, which made me tire easily and caused me to stop using baby aspirin. (Which guards against heart attacks!) In spite of this unnoticeable problem, I thought all bodily systems allowed me to go ahead "full throttle" in my life: running two secular businesses, doing construction, preaching and writing.

I did most of my writing of new books and revising my older books from 11:00 P.M. to 3-4:00 AM every night. I was literally burning the candle at both ends. I spent much of 2011 and 2012 writing *The Supreme Scientist*. Then in the Spring of 2013, I decided to write yet another book. As usual, unfolding religious circumstances precipitated that decision. For when I saw Bill O'Reilly on his TV Show, The O'Reilly Factor, touting his upcoming book, *Killing Jesus - A History,* as going to be the most historically accurate story about Jesus ever written because its content would come from secular history books and not "inaccurate, contradicting and allegorical religious books like the Gospels," I felt that "fire burning in my bones" and could not let his outrageous claim go unchallenged. So I decided to write a book entitled, *Killing Jesus - The History,* which would simply present the facts as written in the Gospels and related scriptures. I spent the next eight months writing the book, as well as collecting all of O'Reilly's quotes and reading his book when it was released in September. I then included a refutation of all of his erroneous verbal quotes and unhistorical, contradictory written statements in my book. I finished my book a few weeks before I had the heart attack. (The stress of writing the book may have caused the heart attack. If so, it was worth it!) The day before the heart attack, which was a Sunday, I preached that morning and spent another typical late night session revising one of my other books for reprint. All is well ... tomorrow's my day of Golf ... before lighting up the midnight candle again! Or so I thought.

The Place of "my near death experience" was "The Muni Golf Course" in Hilo, Hawaii, which is about 21 miles from my home in Pahoa, Hawaii. I was playing in our normal foursome: Myself, Jerry Bragdon, Mike Leverette and Arthur Freschette (who didn't show up that day). My wife used to play with us every Monday as well, but she had been sidelined from playing golf for a few years because of intractable vertigo and Meniere's Disease. I was not feeling "up to par" from the start, but had walked fourteen holes (3 miles) playing hard and walking up and down hills in the hot sun.

Suddenly, on the fifteenth tee, I felt clammy and couldn't seem to get my breath. I sat down on the bench, then asked Mike, who was riding in a motorized cart, to take me to the clubhouse. I got in the cart, and then fell out on the ground, gasping for air. Mike called the clubhouse and asked them to call 911 and get an ambulance to the fifteenth tee. He also called my wife and told her to call me on my cell phone. For some reason, the person in the clubhouse thought Mike had already called 911 and didn't make the call. So for about twenty minutes I was laying on the ground gasping for air, telling my wife on my cell phone that I was having a heart attack ... and talking to my Friend Jesus!

What was I talking to Jesus about? What were my emotional feelings? Well, at that moment, and afterwards, I was asking Jesus: *"If this is it, would you please take me home to be with you? Please be with my wife and family."* Though I already intellectually knew, from Psalms 23:4, that the only person who would be able to go with me through *"the valley of the shadow of death"* would be my Shepherd and Savior, I didn't know from any previous experiences how I would feel when I got to the edge of that valley! Like most people of age, I had wondered how my faith would hold up if I was conscious when my final moments of life arrived, or at least what I thought were my final moments. Well, I'm glad I was wide-awake and fully cognizant to experience these memorable moments for over five hours from ground zero to the operating room at Queens Hospital. I wasn't fearful and didn't feel all alone like some "Solitary Soul" or stranded pilgrim on this spinning coffin we call earth. Quite the contrary, I felt like one of our "Savior's Sons." This reaction sort of surprised me, as I "thought" I'd be more fearful if anything like this ever happened to me. But the opposite was true: I felt more hopeful!

This experience of actually calling upon Jesus as my lifelong friend in what I thought were my final prayers was a unique blessing I had never experienced in my entire life, and it actually calmed me and likely aided my survival. In my heart of hearts, I believed and felt more like "there was but a step between me and God" rather than just "a step between me and <u>death</u>" as per that previous quote by David. It was more like David's comforting words in Psalms 17:15, wherein he said: *"As for me, I shall behold thy face in righteousness; I shall be satisfied, when I awake, with beholding thy form."* Well, since I was still awake, I will continue with a few more details about my confrontation with the "Grim Reaper" on my way to the operating table. (Which is where many surgical patients see the bright white light and white-robed images hovering over them: which makes them think they are in heaven!)

Mike called the clubhouse again and asked them where the ambulance was. They said they thought he had called 911. He said, *"Gerald's lying here on the ground dying! So call 911!"* I was listening to him screaming at them, and my wife screaming on the phone,*"Call 911!"*. Again, I thank God I never lost consciousness during the entire ordeal so I could/can recall all the conversations they were having ... and I was having with my wife and Friend! As an aside: I am also grateful that I wasn't grasping for a Saint Christopher Pendant, or calling for any priest to rush to my side in case I needed to be given my "last rites." As a priest, I was doing my own!

The ambulance couldn't find a way to get out on the golf course. So they went to the clubhouse, took a golf cart and traveled about a mile to where I was lying on the ground. To make a long story a little shorter, they picked me up, put me in the cart, gave me aspirins (!) to chew and squirted nitro into my mouth. When we arrived at the ambulance in the parking lot, the emergency medics increased their treatment measures, more nitro and clot-buster drugs, which cause me to vomit and think, again, "this is it!" They then raced me to the Hilo Hospital. My daughter, Stephanie, had arrived there from her nursing job at the Gastro-Center in town.

While in the Hospital Emergency Room, I over-heard them say I had suffered a massive heart attack (STEMI) and would have to be medivaced to the Island of Oahu (several hundred miles away) to undergo surgery. When I heard them say that, and knowing it would take hours, I told my daughter: *"I'm not going to make it. But that's Ok ... I want to go home and be with Jesus. I'm ready to go."* This upset her greatly, but it came straight from my heart and head. Now, though I'm sure my biblical brain full of texts like Philippians 1:21-23 had something to do with the words that were coming out of my mouth, I was also sure at that time that the words were based upon the historical truth and influence of Jesus Christ's life upon my life and ongoing death throes.

Time seemed to stand still between my arrival at the Hilo Hospital and my arrival at the operating room at Queens Hospital in Honolulu. I thought the total time was around an hour. But the entire trip from the arrival of the plane from Honolulu, to my transport on a stretcher in an ambulance to the Hilo airport, through my being loaded into the slender tube-like plane — which had no seats, which meant my daughter had to be tucked in the tail of the plane — through the bumpy flight, transfer to another ambulance, long trip through heavy Honolulu traffic to Queens actually took five hours. My "Golden Hour" was rather long ...

which would have been too long to have survived from the get-go if I would have been at my home twenty-five miles away from the Hilo Hospital instead of a few miles at the Golf Course! But I survived because I was golfing at The Muni. Maybe that's why I still feel safer when I'm there on Monday's Golf Day!

If the attack had never occurred, plus all the complications since, I would not have been forced to close down my two secular businesses which required so much of my time, which also kept me away from my wife more than I desired, and I would not have as much time to focus on my preaching and publication efforts as I do now. (Sometime you just have to be stopped from chasing too many butterflies!) And I know I would've never written this book, **"The Sovereign Soul,"** if I had not had the heart attack and been forced to realize that, in the final analysis, life is all about you and your sovereign spiritual relationship with your **Sovereign Lord,** and not about trying to please all the world's many material, or better yet, "immaterial," masters. And with that thought, let's look at some of the Ways we can Declare to the World that Christ's Companionship/Friendship is First in our personal, everyday lives, and not just for an hour or so on Sunday.

"Declarations of Friendship."

We Declare Christ's Friendship when we gladly Keep his Commandments. Jesus said: *"Ye are **my friends**, if you do the things I **command** you"* (John 15:14). It is interesting to note that Jesus earlier said *"If ye love me, ye will keep my commandments"* (Ibid. 14:15). The best way we can be Jesus' Best Friend, and thereby say He is our Best Friend, is to love him. And one of the best ways to show that friendship is to listen to Him and obey Him. And the Only Way we can do that today is to read his New Testament. If we choose not to obey him, we show we do not love him enough to be his friends, and we become his enemies (Colossians 1:21). We're either for Christ or against him (Matthew 12:30).

There are no fair-weather, fence-riding, two-souled, two-master, double-minded Friends of Jesus Christ (James 1:8; 4:7). Sovereign Souls owe their existence as such to Him. And without Him and His Words, our saying we are "Sovereign Souls" would just be another egocentric vanity of life. He is the Vine, we are his branches. He is the Fountain, we are the springs flowing from Him. Apart from Him we can do nothing, be nothing and are nothing (John 15:5). His infallible and immutable word is the *"anchor"* of our souls, and without Him and his divine directions we would be adrift at sea, *"tossed to and fro and carried about with every wind of doctrine, by the sleight of men, in craftiness, after the wiles of error"* (Hebrews 6:18f; Ephesians 4:14).

We Declare Christ's Friendship when we put His Fellowship First. Putting His fellowship first includes putting fellowship with His friends (fellow Christians) — like in communion, worship and social fellowship — above the offers and requests of fellowship from all of our non-Christian friends (Galatians 6:10). The Hebrew writer exhorted and admonished Jewish Christians in the First Century to seek out fellowship with their brethren.

> ... *and let us* **consider one another** *to provoke unto love and good works;* **not forsaking our own assembling** *together, as the custom of some is, but exhorting one another; and so much the more, as ye see the day drawing nigh* (Hebrews 10:24f).

Though the historical context (Circa, A.D. 68) of this passage is referring to how some Jewish Christians in Jerusalem were *"forsaking"* Christianity altogether and returning to all the external trappings of the Jewish religion and temple in Jerusalem — which city and temple were fast approaching *"the day"* of destruction in A.D. 70 — it is applicable to how most Christians who fall away from the faith begin by failing to assemble with the saints on the Lord's Day or other scheduled assemblies throughout the week (see Hebrews 10:25 discussed in *The End of the World,* pp. 54ff).

With whom we spend our time speaks volumes about Who our friends are, and especially about whether Jesus is really our Best Friend or not. There is a saying that is sad but true: "If some professing Christians were put on trial for being a Christian, there wouldn't be enough evidence to convict them!" God forbid!

We Declare Christ's Friendship when we Talk about Him at every opportunity, personally or publically. It is great to see people "walking the walk," even if they are unable to talk at all. It is also great to see and hear people who are "Walking the Walk" also "Talking the Talk!" In fact, Talking the Talk is part of Walking the Walk. Jesus told us to go ***"preach"*** the Gospel to the world, not just practice our faith in the world. He told us to go ***"convict"*** the world's sinners of sin, not just convince them of Christ's love for sinners. (The word "Love" is not in the Lord's history book of world evangelism, The Book of Acts!)

It's amazing how so many people of faith — who say they're not good at quoting scriptures and discussing or "arguing religion" with other individuals — can be found jabbering incessantly and passionately about who's the best politician, professional golfer, baseball or football player, music and TV star, etc., and spitting out statistics like a professional auctioneer. The Lord wants us to "shout his name from the rooftops" if we can shout at all. He wants us to make a "joyful noise" if we can. He wants us to Talk the Talk and "Declare His name" in the midst of all of our friends, just as He declares God's name in the midst of those he calls his *"brethren"* (Hebrews 2:11f).

I hate to admit it, but the blame for many of the moral and doctrinal problems that plague the "Christian Religion" and so-called "Christian Nations" must be laid at the feet of the all too "Silent Majority." Sometimes "Silence is Golden," but sometimes it's just yellow, especially when it doesn't warn others of impending disaster and doom because we're safe and sound, or we fear getting involved in other people's problems (Obadiah 10-11). My Sunset teacher of the Book of Obadiah, Richard Rogers, called this sin of neutrality, "The Violence of Silence!" And this sad reality reminds me of the famous poem by Martin Niemoller, that's displayed in the US Holocaust Memorial Museum:

> *First they {the Nazi's} came for the Socialists, and I did not speak out—Because I was not a Socialist. Then they came for the Unionists, and I did not speak out—Because I was not a Unionist. Then they came for the Jews, and I did not speak out—Because I was not a Jew. Then they came for me— and there was no one left to speak for me.*

I'm grateful to God that my friend George spoke out to me! And because of him I can now speak out for Jesus, my Best Friend in the world ... A Jew! Who's Apostles were Jews. Who's first church was made up of Jews. Who is still the Messiah and only hope of the Jews and all the races in this world. Who wants us to Go into all the world and Preach his Gospel to every lost soul. Preach On!

We Declare His Friendship when we Follow Him wherever He goes. Throughout the Gospels we find Jesus going to the synagogue every Sabbath. We may not see Him, but we can still find him in places of Bible study and worship today. We can be sure that, since Jesus only walked in righteous "straight and narrow pathways," we could follow him anywhere he went without fear of ending up on streets of sin or in dens of sin. As the hymn says: "Anywhere with Jesus I can safely go." By following Jesus we will always lead our friends down "The Way" as we've been charged: *"make **straight paths** for your feet, that that which is lame be not **turned out of the way**, but rather be healed"* (Hebrews 12:13).

We Declare His Friendship when He can Follow Us wherever we go. When we "Christians" go anywhere, we not only physically take the name of Jesus Christ with us, we are also spiritually taking Him via His indwelling Spirit with us. If Christ's Spirit-indwelled Christians don't want to take Jesus to idols' temples, bars or bad movies, don't go there and grieve His Holy Spirit, thereby (Ephesians 4:30). As Paul said:

> ***Be not unequally yoked with unbelievers****: for what fellowship have righteousness with iniquity? or what communion hath light with darkness? And what concord hath Christ with Belial? or what portion hath a believer with an unbeliever? And what agreement hath a temple of God with idols? for we are a temple of the living God; even as God said, **I will dwell in them**, **and walk in them**; and I will be their God, and they shall be my people. Wherefore **Come ye out from among them, and be ye separate**, saith the Lord, And touch no unclean thing; And I will receive you, And I will be to you a Father, And ye shall be to me sons and daughters, saith the Lord Almighty* (II Corinthians 6:14-18).

Our feet are not to be swift to run to mischief, or to make any provisions for the flesh (Proverbs 6:18; Romans 13:14). Our footsteps need to be beside the footsteps of Christ so others will also be following Him when they follow us (Hebrews 12:13).

We Declare His Friendship when we Talk as He Talked. We do this when we use His logic and words to teach others His truths or to repudiate the doctrinal errors of those led astray by false teachers and teachings. If our words are exactly His Words, they are as authoritative as His! His words in John 1:1-3 and 8:58 will stand forever against all human attempts to strip Christ of His Deity and Universal Friendship. So quote them, then quote them in Greek if possible, and repeat them line upon line, phrase upon phrase, precept upon precept and word by word. It will educate you and those to whom you speak. Preach His word!

We Declare His Friendship when we Imitate Him. Paul said we should imitate him as he imitated Christ (I Corinthians 11:1). They say imitation is the sincerest form of flattery. In Christ's case it is the sincerest form of Friendship. I make no apologies for liking Elvis Presley (as you've probably noticed by now). I went to see him in a concert in Lubbock, Texas shortly before he died. My mother loved Elvis and our house was an Elvis Museum! She had tickets to his last scheduled concert in Roanoke, Virginia ... which he couldn't keep because of his unscheduled death! My mother kept the unused two tickets and gave me one (See in Research Sources). And I still listen to his music and watch his videos. Sales of his recordings are still at record highs, and now total over a billion!

But ... Elvis never knew me and was not my friend. And though I know of no person who has been more imitated after his death than Elvis Presley, I know his imitators don't compare in love, sincerity, numbers or in any other way to those who imitate Jesus. The difference is that Elvis is being imitated by people singing the songs he sang when he was alive almost forty years ago; Jesus is being imitated by people who are singing songs **about** Him because He lived, died and was resurrected for our benefit almost two thousand years ago. (You know you are great when people sing songs <u>about</u> you!) That's why many of our songs about Jesus joyously proclaim: *He Lives! He Lives!* In fact, Elvis loved to sing songs about Jesus! (As did his mother, who was a member of the Lord's church.) And Jesus' songs and books are still Number

One worldwide. His Friends and Fans on earth and in heaven are countless!

As far as addressing all the ways we can imitate Jesus in our lives, everything I'm writing about in this book is about ways to imitate Christ. So to sum this point up simply, I'm going to give you my own revised version (WDJD - "What Did Jesus Do?") of the once popular acronym (WWJD - "What Would Jesus Do?") to help you know you're correctly imitating Christ. I believe this approach is better because it objectively compares our words and deeds with the historical words and deeds of Christ on specific issues rather than subjectively pulling Him into our general situations. My revised way asks us to walk in His historical shoes rather than seeking to get him to walk in our hypothetical shoes.

For example, if you have the opportunity to help a person in a specific physical or spiritual problem, ask yourself WDJD ("What Did Jesus Do?") in that specific problem? Then look it up in the Gospels and do likewise. If you have an opportunity to teach a person on any biblical subject, ask yourself WDJT ("What Did Jesus Teach?") on that specific subject, look up the subject in the Gospels and teach the same. Or ask yourself WDJS ("What Did Jesus Say?"), and quote his exact words to the person. If you're facing a temptation to go into a specific sinful place, ask yourself WDJG ("Where Did Jesus Go?"), and look into the Gospels and see if He ever went there. Though some "well-meaning" preachers go into bars and houses of prostitution to teach people actively involved in sinning, you won't find Jesus doing either or telling you to do so. Imitate Him ... not them! Do it His Way.

We Declare His Friendship when we Introduce Him as our Friend to our friends and associates. There are all sorts of ways we can introduce Christ as our best friend and insert Him into our conversations. We can so in both positive and negative situations.

<u>Positive Situations</u>: If you are talking with others about having or making good friends, tell them your best friend is Jesus Christ Tell people all the things you like about Him. Tell them why and how He's always proved He was your best friend. Tell them you read His Books, tell him all your plans, tell him you love him, trust him and follow him. Tell others Jesus loves them and wants to be their best friend. Then lovingly share Christ's helpful advice about

any of their physical or spiritual needs. Introduce Jesus whenever you find yourself in any "friend-to-friend" or friendly situation.

<u>Negative Situations</u>: If someone asks you why you won't go to certain questionable establishments (like bars), tell them your friend, Jesus, wouldn't approve and won't go with you. If you encounter anger over your refusal to endorse certain questionable religious/political beliefs and practices — abortion, "born Gay," polygamy, drug use — be sure to introduce them to Christ as a friend of all little children, regardless of the sinfulness of their parents or if they were "wanted" (Matthew 18:2-6). Aren't you glad Mary didn't believe she should abort Jesus because he wasn't planned by either parent (See my *A Mother's Son*)? Tell any person, who believes he/she was born "gay," that your friend is the Creator who made their bodies either male or female, created their spirit, and loves them and wants to be their friend regardless of what they believe. Or tell them Jesus is a friend of all sinners: who wants to save all sinners from sin (not in sin) and wants to make each sinner His friend—if he/she will accept His friendship by accepting and keeping his word (John 14:15; 15:14). The best way to introduce Jesus to your friends and associates is to tell them to befriend Him. (The modern "Facebook" phenomenon might be applied!)

We Declare His Friendship when we seek his Consolation. That's what friends are for. Especially One who can stick closer than any human friend or brother because He is our Human-Divine Friend and Brother (I Timothy 2:5; Hebrews 2:11f)! There's no one who can mend a broken heart better than Jesus Christ who, while enduring a massive "broken heart attack" when he was being crucified by his own people, said: *"Father, forgive them, for they know not what they do."* And there's no friend who loves you, his Christian brother or sister, more than Jesus—not even you yourself. For he will forgive you even when your heart condemns you and you can't bring yourself to forgive yourself (I John 3:20f).

We Declare His Friendship when we put Following Him First above our worldly Pursuits and Possessions. We may not have great possessions to offer in our service to Him, as did the Rich man (Matthew 19:21f), but we have some things which are just as precious and priceless: our time, our mouths, our hands, our hearts, our help! How can we say "Christ is our life" and His Church is our First Choice if we always have some excuse for not seeking fellowship with Him, His Church and His Causes, saying:

> *I have bought a **field**, and I must needs go out and see it; I pray thee have **me excused**. And another said, I have bought **five yoke of oxen**, and I go to prove them; I pray thee have **me excused**. And another said, I have **married a wife**, and therefore **I cannot come*** (Luke 14:18-20).

It is obvious that all the special "Invited Ones" in this text above had an *"me-myself-and I first"* problem—which was the real reason, not an excuse, they could not come.

Our Lord deserves better than our spare time, our seconds, our leftovers, our hand-me-downs, our used and worn out items like many send to "Goodwill." He deserves the best we have to offer in everything we have been so blessed by him to possess. He, himself, said this to his chosen Jewish people: *"**Is it time for you yourselves** to dwell in **your ceiled houses**, while **this house lieth waste?**"* (Haggai 1:4).

Though we Christians don't have to spend all of our treasures to build a costly and elaborate temple as did the Jews, we do have a universal spiritual kingdom/church and Great Commission to support. Those people in the world, who don't have our king and friend to honor and support, may have an excuse; but we do not. For if we, his most precious people and friends, won't do his work where we are and when we have the opportunity, he will find others in the church to do it ... but it might cost us dearly. For if we squander his blessings in physical pursuits, He might just remove them and give them to someone else (Esther 4:14; Matthew 25:24-30). Again, let's continue with Christ's words on both sides of this issue, beginning where we left off in Haggai 1:4-6.

> *Now therefore thus saith Jehovah of hosts* {the Pre-Incarnate Christ}: *Consider your ways. Ye have **sown much**, **and bring in little**; ye eat, but ye have not enough; ye drink, but ye are not filled with drink; ye clothe you, but there is none warm; and he that **earneth wages** to put it into a **bag of holes**.*
>
> *Be not therefore anxious, saying, What shall we eat? or*

What shall we drink? or, Wherewithal shall we be clothed? For after all these things do the Gentiles seek; for your heavenly Father knoweth that ye have need of all these things. ***But seek ye first the kingdom****, and his righteousness; and all these things shall be added to you* (Matt. 6:31-33). Thank you, my Friend, for my blessings and this privilege.

We Declare His Friendship when we always have Him in our Hearts and Minds. That means Jesus' life and teachings occupy a large portion of our thoughts, souls, songs, plans, thanksgivings and prayers. Christ expects us to thank him for our blessings and healings (Luke 17:17f; I Timothy 4:4). Though others cannot read our minds and will not see most of these declarations, we know they're there, the Holy Spirit who searches our hearts knows, Christ knows, and even the angels know some of our prayer requests and holy actions (Luke 15:7; Romans 8:27; I Corinthians 4:9; 11:10; Hebrews 1:14). For it is out of our hearts that all the other issues of life — good and bad things, small and great plans — spring forth (Proverbs 4:23; look up all the "heart" passages in Proverbs; Matthew 15:18f).

In order to think about Christ and like Christ, we will have to be reading about Christ and what he said and did. And when we spend our time reading and thinking about Christ, we'll be thinking "larger than life" and "out of this world" thinking. For He knew and revealed things, far and future, we could never know, and He can do things we cannot possibly do. That's why I sometimes ask the Lord to send Gabriel to help me in my struggles to serve Him and His People (Daniel 9:17-23). Who else can I call upon in the middle of the night? I can't get in touch with my Congressman, the President or the Pope ... who actually aren't able to help me with the staggering, mind-blowing requests I often make. Think Jesus! Think Big (Ephesians 3:20)! Pray often! Otherwise, you might *"have not because ye ask not"* (James 4:2-3; also 1:5-8).

I know the Lord knows our thoughts and knows what we want to do. And that's all well and good. But He still wants us to talk to Him about it and ask for providential help concerning our well-thought out plans. The very fact that He always hears us is an answer in and of itself. Of course, if we have studied prayer, we know we sometimes don't know what to ask or ask amiss. We also will learn that the Lord often gives us something different or better in his answer. For example, I had received offers of preaching jobs in Perth, Australia and Durban, South Africa when I was nearing graduation from preaching school. And I was seriously thinking about going to one of the two. Then a friend invited me to check out two preacher jobs in Hawaii: one in Kailua, Oahu and another in Hilo, Hawaii (Big Island). A brother in Texas offered to pay my airfare to go to Hawaii and investigate the jobs. So I went to Hawaii in 1971, checked out both, and finally decided to take the Hilo job because the church there was smaller and seemed to be more in need of a fulltime evangelist.

So what's that got to do with wanting to preach in Australia or Africa? Well, since my work in Hilo was less demanding than in the larger congregations, I decided to write tracts and books. I once preached for three years in a larger church in Florida, and didn't have the time to write anything due to the many "pastoral" demands. I haven't written any books anywhere but in Hawaii. This book I'm writing will be my twelfth published book. The other books have been selling for up to forty years and are around the world. One church sent a thousand copies of my Sabbatarian book to Africa. Hundreds, or maybe thousands, of my books were sent to the number one missionary in Africa, George Funk and his "Gospel Chariots." And I not only know (from the internet) that my books are in Australia, I recently sent six of my JW Books to a Roman Catholic person there. So, in the Lord's own way, I am working in both countries, Africa and Australia, spreading the Gospel and related truths to the glory of our Lord and Savior.

We Declare His Friendship when we're willing to Risk our Lives for Him. Jesus' dying for us proved his friendship with us was based upon his personal love for us, and not only upon a divine plan or duty (John 15:13). In like manner, our willingness to risk our lives for Him shows our friendship with him is based upon our personal love for him, and not just out of religious duty or following our religious friends. David and Jonathan, two of Israel's greatest warriors and best friends, had this life-risking love for each other (II Samuel 1:25-26).

Though Christ is talking about the highest form of spiritual love (Greek "agape") for all human beings in John 15:13, He, being a normal human being, also displayed the affectionate love (Greek "phileo") of physical friendship towards his earthly friends. **Lazarus** and his family were his closest familial friends (John 11:3,11,36). **The Apostle John** was obviously Jesus' most beloved friend in every way (Ibid. 21:20). **The Apostle Judas**, whom Jesus knew was a thief and betrayer from the beginning, was Jesus' worst "friend." And, after Judas betrayed him with much kissing and calling him "Rabbi," Jesus said unto him, *"**Friend**, do that for which thou art come"* (Matthew 26:49f). It is most revealing that Jesus didn't use the affectionate word ("phileo") for "friend" there, but rather the word "hetairo," which means "comrade" and conveys Jesus' disappointment over Judas' betrayal (see pp. 176f in my *Killing Jesus* book).

Of course, the **Apostle Peter** was the most outspoken person amongst the Apostles, who said that if all the other Apostles forsook him at the night of his arrest, he wouldn't (Matthew 26:31-33). And even after Jesus told him he would deny him three times that night, he said he'd rather die with Jesus than deny him (Ibid. 26:34-35). (To be fair, the other Apostles repeated Peter's brave claim, verse 35.) Yet we know Peter not only forsook him as did the others, he also denied him three times (Ibid. 26:56; Luke 22:54-62). Then after the resurrection, Jesus afforded Peter with the opportunity to repent of his three denials by asking him if he loved him three times (John 21:15-23). Let's look more closely into this classic scriptural "Tough Love Story" about the friendship of Jesus and Peter. Please turn to **John 21:15ff** and read it all.

Verse 15 — Christ's First Question: *"Simon ... lovest thou me more than these?"* First, Jesus used the highest word for love, agape. Second, He used it comparatively to point out how Peter's denials proved he didn't love Jesus more than his life, much less more than the other Apostles loved him. Though the other disciples were offended and fled for their lives (Matthew 26:56), Peter followed Jesus and his captors from afar, but did not step forward to defend Jesus against the false charges and abuse and, instead, denied he even knew Christ and cursed and swore about it (Ibid. 57-75). So Jesus' prophetic statement was right ... Strike One!

Peter's First Answer: *"Yea, Lord; thou knowest that I love thee."* First, Peter lowered Jesus' highest word for love, "agape," to the lower physical word of friendly affection, "phileo," because he knew his abandonment and denial proved his love for Jesus was not that which put his own life on the line for Jesus. Second, Peter's omission of his previous elevation of his love above the other disciples is tacit admission that he knew that had been painfully disproven as well.

Jesus' Response: Jesus told him to *"Feed my lambs."* Jesus switched to a positive response by telling Peter to feed his lambs (new disciples) rather than putting them down. Jesus used similar responses to all three of Peter's answers. This context of Peter's rebuke, repentance and being humbled not to elevate himself above the other Apostles, can NOT be twisted into being a promotion of Peter as the "Chief Shepherd" and Apostle above and over all the other Apostles—as is asserted by the Roman Catholic Church. It is exactly the opposite of that: Peter's personal elevation above the other Apostles was the very problem that caused all of these mea culpas on his part to be necessary.

Verse 16 — Jesus' Second Question: *"Lovest thou me."* First, Jesus repeated the question, using the same highest word for love, "Agape," because Peter had not really answered that question at all. Second, the fact that Jesus dropped the comparative part of the question, *"more than these,"* implies that Jesus accepted Peter's obvious failure to answer the charge as his admission, or confession, that he was wrong to make such unproven, untried, and condescending statements.

Peter was not a *"swift to hear, slow to speak"* kind of guy (James 1:19). And this was not the first time Peter had quickly fired from the hip (spoken from the lip) without thinking. And it got him into trouble every time. **Matthew 16:15-23** is a classic example: **V.18** — Peter made the greatest confession of his life about Jesus being the Christ and Son of God. **V.19** — Then Jesus told Peter that He would give him the keys to the kingdom. A good assignment. **V.21** — Then Jesus told Peter that He had to die before any of these things could come to pass. **V.22** — Peter then rebuked Jesus and told him that wasn't going to happen. Whoops, his outspokenness just overruled his knowledge. **V.23** — Then Jesus told Peter: *"Get thee behind me, Satan: thou art a stumblingblock unto me: for thou mindest not the things of God,* *but the things of men."* My beloved Bible teacher, Edward Wharton, used to ask us: "Why did Jesus say that to Peter?" Then after we went into our varied explanations, he would say: "Because Peter was minding the things of men and not God!" In other words, Peter was speaking from his human-emotional heart and not his divinely-directed-objective head. Peter was promoting Peter and Satan, not Christ or us! Thank God that Peter was allowed time to repent and grow in Christ's grace. He was not an infallible human being. Thank God Peter was wrong!

Peter's Second Answer: *"Yea, Lord: thou knowest that I love thee."* Again, Peter didn't really answer the Lord's question because he used the word "phileo" and not "agape," which has him actually saying "I like you" and not "I love you." But he was right when he said *"thou knowest"* because: Jesus knew that wasn't what he asked; and Jesus knew that Peter needed to be asked the same question again, yet, this time, using the same word for love Peter continued to use. (Next)

Verse 17 — Jesus' Third Question: *"lovest thou me?"* This time Jesus did not use the high word for love, "agape," that he used in His first two questions. This time he used the same word Peter was using for love in his answers, *"phileo,"* and is equivalent to saying: *"Do you even have true affection for me?"* This was brutal! This was tough love! This was true. For true friends do not do what Peter did, now do they? This is why John showed us how heart-rending this third question was to Peter by adding: *"Peter was grieved"* over Jesus' third question because He asked him *"hast thou phileo for me?"* And Peter's third answer reveals how Peter had finally gotten Jesus' point! (Next)

Peter's Third Answer: *"Lord, thou knowest all things, thou knowest that I love thee."* This time Peter simply confirmed that he, at least, had friendly affection ("phileo") for Jesus. Again, Peter was right, Jesus knew that. And we also know, as we'll see from Jesus' response to this entire episode in Verses 18-23, that Jesus knew *"all things"*—including how Peter was growing in love as they spoke and would, in fact, become a full-fledged, agape-loving friend who would lay down his life for Jesus. (Next)

Verses 18-23 — Jesus' Response: Jesus, via his divine foreknowledge, told Peter that when he would become old he would die for Him via what most interpret as being crucifixion (read Verses 18-19). Early writers say he was crucified about 33 years later, during Nero's reign, and requested he be crucified upside down because he was not worthy to be crucified as his Lord. This is not surprising since Jesus had proved that he knew Peter's entire future when he had earlier (in **Luke 22:31-34)** told him: **(1)** That Satan was going to *"sift him as wheat"* to see if he could shake his faith. (As He tried to do with Job.) **(2)** That his faith would falter (which would be his three denials). **(3)** That his faith would not *"fail"* because Jesus had prayed for him. **(4)** That his denials would occur between the crowing of two cocks: the first at the late evening hours, and the second at the early morning hours around dawn (Mark 14:30). **(5)** That Peter would *"return to his faith,"* or "repent." Peter's godly sorrow and tearful repentance was facilitated by his remembering Jesus' prediction about the cock crowing when Jesus' turned around and looked upon him just as he denied him the third time and the cock crowed (Luke 22:60-62). **(6)** That he would afterwards firm up the faith of his brethren, who also, in like manner, had been weakened in their faith by Satan's attack. **(7)** And that after his death Peter would sit on one of the twelve thrones (with the other Apostles) judging the Twelve Tribes of Israel (Luke 22:29-32). This they do through their word (I Corinthians 5:3).

After Jesus' Response, Peter then displayed that he still wasn't where he needed to be in the growth of his faith when he questioned the final fate of John. Jesus basically told him to leave John's fate to him, mind his own business and follow Him (John 21:20-23). (Peter's full spiritual understanding came in Acts 10.)

We Declare His Friendship when we read His books. Jesus is the best-selling author and publisher of all time. He has sixty-six of the best-selling books of all time, neatly packaged in his Bible. It covers all the burning issues of all time. We'll never be able to know how great our Divine Friend is without reading his biography: which historically begins with us in Genesis One, gets more personal in Matthew One, and will get even better when He comes to receive his faithful friends — living and dead — to be with him in heaven forever (I Thessalonians 4:13-18).

Again, it is amazing how we can find people reading an endless assortment of "People" type magazines in every store and office, and yet not one Bible about the greatest person who has ever lived, and still lives in Spirit and in us on this planet. Read the only Book that will never be out of date. Read the only book which will always be about you if you are His Friend. This is why we write books that include voluminous quotes, stories and facts from His books in our books: it makes our books more timeless.

We Declare His Friendship when we Talk to Him. Of course, this includes talking to him in private prayer; but it also includes talking to him when we walk around during our busy day as if He were at our side (He is!). It includes having a heart to heart, raw (I didn't say "raunchy!"), candid conversation with him as if we're talking to our best earthly friend. It could include giving Him a "thumbs up," or "Shakha Sign" (Hawaiian style), when you want to quickly convey your friendly appreciation for something good that just happened to you: like eating one of His tasty foods. It could also include singing a song to Him. I suggest singing one of my favorite friendship songs, *My God and I.* What a lovely God-Friendly song this is. Sing Verses One and Three with me now:

***My God and I** go in the fields together, We walk and talk as **good friends** should and do. We clasp our hands, our voices ring with laughter—My God and I walk through the meadows hue. We clasp our hands, our voices ring with laughter—My God and I walk through the meadows hue.*

***My God and I** will go for aye together. We'll walk and talk and jest as **good friends** do. This earth will pass, and with it common trifles—But God and I will go unendingly; This earth will pass, and with it common trifles—But God and I will go unendingly* (I B Sergei, Austris A Whitol).

We Declare His Friendship when we attend the Church of His Choice. Since we've already discussed this at length in Chapter Four, a few friendly reminders will do. Since our Friend, Jesus, made it clear that His Church — which HE promised, founded, built (keeps building), patterned, purchased, wedded, named, populates, protects, attends, loves, cherishes, and will save — is His Choice, I personally think it would be a good idea to attend and give our utmost attention to it. Especially since all "church choices" outside of His Church, are not <u>His</u> Choice, but <u>their</u> choice. If you go to their choice, you might be with some of your friends, but are you going to be with Him, who should be your Best Friend, and with His spiritual brothers, sisters and Best Friends? As long as MY Best Friend is there, I plan on being there!

Also, it does not matter if His Local Congregation is small or large. Remember, if Jesus is there, it doesn't matter where "there" is. Also, it doesn't matter how many dignitaries and popular friends of the world are at any of the other churches if Jesus isn't there. Don't get me wrong, large churches are great, and in the past I regularly attended a wonderful large church for years; but small churches — even "house churches" — are still His church, and He is always present at each one of them (Acts 20:20; Romans 16:5) Remember a true small church like Philadelphia is better than a mega-flawed or false church like Laodicea (Revelation 2-3).

We Declare His Friendship when we Love Lost Souls as much as He Does. Jesus loved and loves every person who's ever been conceived on this earth. That's right, I said "conceived," and not just those born on the earth (Jeremiah 1:5). But speaking of adult "lost souls," God's biblical love letters tell us that God/Christ/Holy Spirit "loves" every sinner equally and wants them to be forgiven and saved eternally (John 3:16; Romans 5:5-8; I Timothy 2:4). Christ died and proved he wants every person to become his saved brother, sister and **friend** for all time and eternity. So if we hate what he hates (sin), we must love what he loves (Sinners). If that's his heart's desire, it must be our heart's desire. If that's His Commission for us to accomplish on this earth, that must be our Mission on earth. And that, my friend, brings us to our Next Chapter.

CHAPTER SIX
Sovereign Souls Choose Christ's Commission

CHRIST'S CHOICE

18 *And **Jesus** came to them and **spake unto them**, saying, **All authority** hath been **given unto me** in **heaven and on earth**, **19 Go ye therefore**, and **make disciples** of **all the nations**, **baptizing** them into the name of the Father and of the Son and of the Holy Spirit:* **20 *teaching** them to **observe all things** whatsoever I commanded you: and lo, **I am with you always**, even unto the **end of the world*** (Matthew 28:18-20).

NOTICE that Christ spake unto *"them,"* to the Eleven Apostles (Ibid. v. 16). This took place after his resurrection and after they had finished worshipping him as God (v.17; see also Mark 16:14-20; Luke 24:36-52). Thus this is God speaking (Hebrews 1:1-2)! This Great Commission wasn't of this world, nor was it given to this world to fulfill. It was, as we will see, a Divine Directive from heaven: which was delivered to Christ's Holy Spirit-Inspired and Empowered Apostles to fulfill by preaching, miraculously confirming and infallibly recording Christ's word. He did all of this so Christians down through the ages could continue to preach the same soul-saving truths of Christ to the world (see v. 20). Christ chose to do this for us because He loves us so!

NOTICE that Christ claimed to have *"all authority."* That means Christ had one hundred percent of the authority in and over his church and its mission, which does not leave any command authority being left for others to seek, claim, contemplate or argue about. Christ said He was The Supreme & Sovereign Power in his church-kingdom, period. Therefore, He did not delegate any of this authority to another Apostle. Rather, He inspired all the Apostles to know, write and teach His authoritative words, not their words!

NOTICE Christ said this absolute authority *"hath been given unto me."* Here He is referring to his new role as the God-man, since he already had that authority in the Godhead prior to his Incarnation (Matthew 11:27; John 17:21-23; Philippians 2:5ff). He is also revealing the involvement of the Godhead — Father, Son and Holy Spirit — in this universal and heavenly work of redemption, as he states later in verse nineteen. It was not *"given"* to Jesus as a gift. Jesus had kept the will of the Father perfectly, suffered and sacrificed his physical life to bring about our salvation and ratify his New Covenant, and proved his deity thereby in order to receive His New Kingdom and Authority. The truth is that all kingdoms, nations and leaders on earth are under God's authority (Romans 13:1ff). Thus we find that when **Pilate** told Jesus *"I have power/authority to release thee, and power to crucify thee,"* **Jesus** replied, *"Thou wouldest have* **no power/authority** *against me, except it were given thee from above..."* (John 19:10f). God rules over all kings and rulers on His earth, not men.

Now if Christ deemed it necessary to reveal God's delegation of divine authority to rulers in physical kingdoms, then surely He would have clearly pointed out any delegation of divine authority to any human ruler over His Spiritual Kingdom, Elect Nation, and Church. Yet, he did not. And Matthew 16:19 does not remotely teach such (See Supplemental Studies). Christ has ALL Authority.

NOTICE that Christ said the scope of His authority and jurisdiction was/is *"in heaven and on earth."* So Christ retained "all" of his authority on earth after he went to heaven, and will keep it unto the end of the world (v. 20). He did not need to delegate any of his absolute authority to any human "Vicar" or "El-Papa" (pope), for He was/is able to be with us in His Omnipresent Spirit and in us via the Holy Spirit (Romans 8:11; Galatians 3:27-4:6). And Christ returned to His authoritative throne in heaven when he ascended to heaven (Acts 2:34-36). This comprehensive authority and universal and heavenly rule of Christ again shows that only the Eternal, Omnipresent, Omnipotent and Omniscient Christ can be understood to be the "Head" and "Commander-In-Chief" of His Christian Church and Calvary.

For only this Divinely Endowed Christ knows each one of us by name, knows all about our personal needs and struggles, and can be with each and every one of us at the same time: to hear our prayers, answer our calls for help, heal our broken hearts, forgive our sins, provide ways of escape from temptations, supply our needs, strengthen and stand with us. No mere man — and I don't care who he is, thinks he is, or pretends to be (king, high priest, pope) — can know all of us, much less be with each one of us. I can assure you that I couldn't get in touch with the Pope if I wanted to, even in this day of electronic communication, and I can assure you He doesn't know me from Adam! Nor could he help me if my life was depended upon it, or upon him!

Furthermore, only Christ, the Supreme Being, had the superior person and power to command heaven's angels to support us (Hebrews 1:14). Only Christ could send the Holy Spirit to supply the Apostles' need for divine inspiration of their words, miraculous powers to confirm their authority, and even spare their lives until Christ's New Testament was completed and his church was actively involved in world evangelism (Romans 10:17-18). There is no power — good or bad, Satan or demons, seen or unseen, known or unknown — that can separate us from Jesus Christ our Lord and Conqueror (Ibid. 8:37-39)! Indeed, Jesus is the Jehovah-Nissi of the Old Testament, which means "Jehovah my Banner," in this world conquest for Christ (Exodus 17:15; See "Jesus is Jehovah" in Supplemental Studies).

Now though some may think Christ has an "authority problem" on earth today, he really doesn't. I know it might look like man is in control of Christ's church all around this earth: with so many so-called "Christian churches" having human founders, heads and doctrines that have enslaved people to parrot their falsehoods rather than freeing them to seek and speak Christ's truths. But they are counterfeit churches, regardless of the age/date of their founding, size of their buildings or membership rosters. But that's not new, and they are no more Christ's true Church now than were the false heretical churches during John's lifetime:

> **They went out from us**, *but they were **not of us**; for if they had been of us, they would have **continued with us**: but they went out, that they might be **manifest that they all are not of us*** (I John 2:19).

This text tells us that the very fact that they/we can use Christ's scriptures to show how some individuals/churches/congregations (then and now) have gone so astray from Christ's teachings that they manifestly are not Christ's church proves that there was/is an identifiable Original Church and Church Pattern to do such. False churches don't disprove Christ's true Church. Just as false Christ's (or Vicars of Christ) don't disprove the true Christ. Just as churches that deny Christ's Deity do not disprove Christ's Deity. John called this teaching and its teachers ***"antichrists"*** (I John 2:18; 4:1-3). So what shall we call so-called "Churches of Christ" ("Iglesia Ni Cristo") and cults that deny Jesus Christ was God Incarnate: "Anti-Christs?" Certainly not "Pro-Christs!"

The truth is still the truth. Christ's church was the first church. And it will be the last church! And the fact that Christ's New Testament is still with us, and his first Church can still be duplicated by its pattern, shows Christ is still in charge! I know this: He is still the Only Authority in all matters of religion and life with me and my house (as we'll see at "My Choice.") So Christ fully provided the necessary "Presence of Divine Power" that must continually reside and rule on earth if we expect any such worldwide crusade for Christ to endure unto the end of the world.

NOTICE that Christ told them to *"Go ye therefore, and make disciples of all the nations."* Herein, God's chosen people up until that time, the Jews, had just been told they had a New Leader (Jesus and not Moses), a New Covenant and a New Commission to fulfill on the earth. As the Theocratic Nation of Israel, the Jews were to remain pure by staying separate from all the foreign nations of the earth, only welcoming into their Theocracy those who would become Jewish proselytes. Yet now these same Jews were told to go into all the world and make converts of all the nations, which is from the Greek "Ta Ethne," meaning to "every ethnic group." Mark uses the Greek word "Ktisis" to stress the whole creation, or every human creature in the world (Mark 16:15). They would be going to the nations to invite them to become disciples in Christ's Universal Church right where they were living and not sending out Church invitations to come to some Big Jewish Temple in Jerusalem or Catholic Cathedral in Rome!

It is interesting to note that the words *"Go ye"* are not in the imperative mood as a command, but a participle ("as you are going"), which assumes they would want to tell everyone in the world about the Good News of Christ. Much like the Samaritan woman at the well quickly went out and told others (John 4:28f). Then those Samaritans who heard her went out to see Jesus and became believers, who would also tell others (Ibid. vv. 39-41). Also, the Jews, who saw the resurrection of Lazarus, went out and quickly, without any command from Christ, told others about it (John 11:45; 12:9-11). In like manner Jesus' Apostles, who had seen Christ perform more miracles than any other group of people on earth, as well as the resurrected Christ, would naturally be so on fire for Christ that they would be "chomping at the bit" to race off in all directions preaching the Greatest Good News of all History: "He arose, He arose, Hallelujah, Christ arose!" It was so great that at first they thought it was too good to be true (Luke 24:41). But that evidence, plus Christ's ascension before their very eyes, couldn't be denied by anyone, friend or foe (Acts 1:9; 2:22). So they began their mission to turn the world upside down, beginning in Jerusalem. The calendar would be changed; it was the dawning of a new age—The Christian Age!

So thousands of the millions of Jews who had come to the City of Jerusalem from all over that part of the world to celebrate the Jewish Day of Pentecost, heard Peter's First Gospel Sermon, became Christians and members of the first church of Christ, and went throughout Jerusalem, then to Judaea, Samaria and unto the uttermost parts of the world to invite thousands upon thousands of Jews, and eventually those who were *"afar off"* (Gentiles!), to become a part of the heavenly city of Jerusalem in the Messianic Kingdom of God (Galatians 4:24-27; Hebrews 12:22). Follow their phenomenal success in Acts 1:8; 2:1,5,37-47; 4:4; 5:14; 6:7; 8:4-8; 9:15-19, 28f, 41f; 10:44-48; 11:19-26; 12:24; 13:12, 43f; 14:1; 15:30; 16:32-34; 17:4) ... until it was said of Paul and Silas in Thessalonica: *"These that have **turned the world upside** down are come hither also"* (17:6). And this they continued to do the next day when they came to Beroea (17:10-12). And this they surely did every day until Paul would say: *"So belief comes by hearing, and hearing by the word of Christ. But I say, Did they not hear? Yea, verily, **Their sound went out into all the earth**, And their **words*** *unto the ends of the world"* (Romans 10:17f). All of this is just as Jesus had promised before he Ascended to his throne (Acts 1:8). And because of them, we are in His Church today!

NOTICE that Christ told them to *"make disciples...baptizing them..."* Mark's Gospel has Jesus saying this: *"He that **believeth** and is **baptized** shall be saved; but he that **disbelieveth** shall be **condemned**"* (Mark 16:16). Though I don't know how Christ could have made the necessity of baptism any clearer than He did in these two simple verses, to millions of Christian "believers" these verses are very controversial and not clear enough to prevent hundreds of false churches from teaching that the act of baptism is a meritorious work that cannot precede being saved by *"faith"* alone (Romans 10:17). They often point out that Jesus did not say *"he that disbelieveth* and is not baptized *shall be condemned."* A brief analysis of the texts and their arguments will show the only problems are in their additions and subtractions to/from the texts.

First, everyone who reads Matthew 28:19 and Mark 16:16 will have to agree that both put baptism before discipleship and salvation, not after. (As does every baptism verse in the New Testament). Mark's spiritual equation is as clear as One plus One equals Two: One Mental Act (*"he that believeth"*) plus (*"and"*) One Physical Act (*is baptized*) equals (*"shall be"*) Two (*"saved"*). So when you have an opportunity to talk to members of any church that denies baptism precedes salvation, have no fear of bringing up this text and guaranteeing them that they and you will agree on what it has to say about baptism. For God did not author confusion.

Here's how to proceed. First, read the verse from your Bible (a standard text like KJV or ASV is best). Then ask them to tell you what the verse says. If they begin telling you what they think it means, or what their church thinks it means, politely tell them you didn't ask them what the text means. You just want to know what it says. If they go off into whether its talking about water or Holy Spirit baptism, again tell them you just want to know what it says ... and it doesn't mention or deal with what kind of baptism it is in that verse. (Nor does it deal with repentance.) There are other verses that deal with that. One verse and issue at a time.

Now it may take some time, but eventually you might have to tell them what the verse says by simply reading it out loud, word for word, and then reply: "That's what it says, right? It says what it says and means what it says. And regardless of which baptism it is, a baptism is necessary in order to be saved, right?" Then you might go to Ephesians 4:5 and read how there is only *"one baptism"* that we must teach and obey. Then you might point out that Holy Spirit baptism is not what we must do, but what God did, and eliminate all baptisms but water baptism. Then go to the water baptism and salvation passages — like Acts 2:38; 8:37f; 9:18; 10:48; 16:33; 22:16 — to reinforce the point. They must agree with what Mark 16:16 says, or reject the text altogether. Which, believe it or not, they often do by saying some ancient manuscripts don't have Mark 16:9-20. Then go to other texts and show how the texts all agree and cannot be misconstrued if allowed to speak for themselves. Now let's address other ways to deal with the false teachings they use to "muddy the waters" on water baptism.

Second, if Jesus had added the words "and is not baptized" after the word "disbelieveth," he might have prevented some confusion amongst Bible novices; but he would have been adding redundant and ridiculous words since no one would get baptized for any reason if he "disbelieved" in Christ and his word!

Third, the absence of their additional words ("is not baptized") in Mark is not the only cause of their confusion in this simple text. There are three contributing problems: **(a)** Their adding the word *"alone"* after the word *"faith"* in Romans 10:17. It isn't in the text. **(b)** Their narrow definition of faith as mere "mental assent." Bible "faith" is a package word that covers everything we believe and do to be saved and stay saved: from believing - to confessing - to repenting - to being baptized - to walking in the light (compare John 3:16 with 3:36; Romans 1:5 *"obedience of faith;"* I John 1:5-10). **(c)** Their using scriptures that don't even mention the word "baptism" to teach anything at all about any kind of baptism!

Fourth, there is no meritorious or laborious "work" in getting yourself baptized. The ones commanded to do all the physical work in Matthew's account were to be the Apostles doing the baptizing and not the recipients. Baptizing the three thousand on the Day of Pentecost was a lot of work for the Apostles and others that assisted in that monumental task (Acts 2:41). As far as the work of the baptismal recipient, it is entirely a work of ***"faith in the working of God"*** and not in one's self (Colossians 2:12).

Obviously, baptism was a whole lot easier than becoming an Israelite or proselyte to Judaism by being circumcised! And there is no question that the act of baptism is much less of a physical effort and work on our part than "repenting of our sins" (stopping all kinds of sins, working off unpaid debts, etc.), which also precedes being saved in Acts 2:38.

The truth is this entire discussion about working for forgiveness is shamefully insulting to Jesus. If Jesus our loving Lord had commanded us all to travel to Israel and dunk ourselves three times in Lake Galilee to receive his blood-bought forgiveness, he had the authority to do so, and we should thank him every day of our lives for giving us the blessed opportunity and privilege to have done it to show our faith in and love for HIM!

Fifth, you would no more be able to be baptized as a "meritorious work/act" after your initial forgiveness from your past sins than before. For all of our obedience of our Lord's commands — from our first belief to our last breath — are *"obedience of faith ... from faith unto faith"* and not legalistic works that merit the forgiveness of one of our sins, before or after we are initially saved (John 6:29; Roman 1:5, 17; Ephesians 2:8). Water baptism is always referred to as an act of faith, and not a meritorious "work" (See "Faith contains Obedience Passages" in my *There Has Always Been One Baptism* book, pp. 149-152*).*

Sixth, this sort of scriptural wrangling over a simple one-time act of obedience that we have to submit to in order to be saved, really misses the main point of the entire text: which is Christ's divine authority to tell his Apostles and us to go into all the world and make disciples of people by preaching, baptizing and teaching them to observe all of Christ's commands and words. NOW THAT'S A WORK! But we do that evangelistic work because we're saved by grace through faith and not because we're working to merit anything by doing it.

Seventh, not a single sinner will be ***"condemned"*** because he/she did not "Hear" about Christ, "Believe" in Christ, "Confess" Christ, "Repent of his sins," be "Baptized for his sins" or be added to "Christ's Church." Each sinner is already condemned because he/she is a sinner (John 3:18; Romans 3:9-20). Belief in Christ and being baptized is His Salvation Solution for all sinners. Thus condemning Christ's Salvation Solution is a Great Sin!

NOTICE that Christ told them to be involved in ***"teaching them to observe all things I have commanded you."*** We must connect this Apostolic charge to teach everything Christ commanded them with Christ's earlier promise to send the Holy Spirit to inspire and teach them *"all things,"* to bring to their remembrance *"all that I said unto you,"* and guide them into *"all truth,"* so they might infallibly record all of Christ's truth for us in His New Testament (John 14:26; 16:13; also see Galatians 1:11-17 for Paul's direct inspiration and revelation from Christ).

Christ's comprehensive charge as per their teaching ***"all things"*** also means he didn't leave the door open for any later self-proclaimed apostles or prophets to teach us any new things that His Twelve Apostles (and Paul) didn't reveal and record in His New Testament. And, again, that precludes any later changes or new revelations from any later prophets, popes or preachers (See Galatians 1:6-9). If we are to be Christ's Sovereign Souls, we cannot possibly serve two Masters, Kings, Church Heads or Testaments. As for me, if I am faced with choosing Christ and His New Testament versus Moses and the Old Testament, the Pope and his Papal Decrees; Joseph Smith and his Book of Mormon & Doctrines and Covenants, Ellen G. White and her false prophecies and teachings, or any other imposter that comes along in our turbulent times, it's a no brainer: no way, no how, not now, not ever! Or to put it in my Southern Lingo: "It ain't happening!"

The Entire Christian Faith was *"once for all"* time and people delivered to the saints in the first century (Jude 3). And this means we can know of a certainty that we have obeyed the truth and can preach and teach it to others without fear of bringing spiritual harm to them or ourselves (Luke 1:4). And if they are faithful, they will do likewise (II Timothy 2:2). This circle cannot not be broken!

Paul even told us HOW we can use God's authoritative and inspired word to fully accomplish Christ's Commission to teach His Whole Truth to the Whole World:

*But abide thou in the things which thou hast learned and hast been assured of, knowing of whom thou hast learned them; and that **from a babe** thou hast known the **sacred writings** which are able to make thee wise unto salvation through **faith in Jesus Christ**. **Every scripture inspired of***

God {mgn.,*"is inspired of God"*} *is also **profitable for teaching**, for **reproof**, for **correction**, for **instruction** which is in righteousness: that the **man of God may be complete, furnished completely** unto **every good work*** (2 Tm. 3:14-17).

First Paul tells us about the importance of Timothy's Bible heritage and training. Since Timothy was a *"babe"* he had been taught the *"sacred writings"* by his Christian mother, Eunice, and his grandmother, Lois (II Timothy 1:5). According to Luke's history in Acts 16:1, Timothy was a young Christian Paul had possibly converted earlier in Lystra, whose mother was a Jewish Christian and his father a Greek unbeliever (see I Corinthians 4:17). He became one of Paul's closest companions throughout his missionary travels unto the end of his life (II Timothy 4:11).

One thing that will help us fulfill the Great Commission is to teach our own children the Scriptures, so they will know the truth, become Christians and add to our efforts to evangelize the world (Ephesians 6:4). Another reason to teach your children while they're young and innocent is to give them their most important education before they go to the world's schools, where they will be told not to read or believe anything in the Bible. (Seriously!)

That the *"sacred writings"* {letters} largely included the New Testament Gospels and Epistles is evident by the fact that Paul said they were able to make Timothy *"wise unto salvation through faith in Jesus Christ"* and into a complete *"man of God"* and preacher of *"the word"* of Christ. Though we can learn many things about God, Creation, law, and the coming Messiah from the Old Testament (Romans 15:4); we can only fully learn about that Messiah — his name and title (Jesus Christ), his sacrifice, his absolute authority, his plan of salvation, church, teachings, etc. — from his New Testament.

Notice that Timothy's obedient faith in Christ was not grounded in his mother's or grandmother's words, but in the same inspired and authoritative scriptures that created faith in them and him. Our faith in Christ is grounded upon our objective knowledge and trust in God's inspired word and not upon our subjective feelings about the religious beliefs of our families, preachers or churches.

"Every scripture inspired of God is profitable" means just what it says: It is profitable for God and us. God's word is living and

active (Hebrews 4:12), and it will be profitable to God as far as accomplishing His purposes. God, via Isaiah (55:11), said so:

*So shall **my word** be that goeth out of my mouth: it shall not return unto me void, but **it shall accomplish that which I please**, and **it shall prosper** in the thing whereunto I sent it.*

And God's Word will profit us. God didn't give us his word just to give us a good book to read. He gave it to us to profit our lives and the lives of the whole world. He gave it to further reveal His person and all of His plans for mankind, and to fulfill all of man's physical and spiritual needs. He gave the Old Testament to His Theocratic Nation of Israel in order to showcase the true Creator-God's Creation, Commands and Promises of the coming Messiah to save fallen mankind through that Nation (Romans 3:19). He spoke to us in Person through His Son in His New Testament, and therein revealed all the truth that we'll ever need to know about the Messiah who came, about how to be saved, how to remain saved and save others through his word (Hebrews 1:2). Paul then proceeds with the specific ways we can profitably use God's word to fulfill Christ's Great Commission. Here they are:

Every scripture is profitable for teaching. Just as Timothy and his mother and grandmother had been taught about Christ's plan of salvation and all of his teachings, so we also can teach others. The New Testament Scriptures do not teach that anyone learns anything about Christ's life, divinity, plan of salvation and teachings by direct revelation from God, or visions, or a subjective experience with Christ in the middle of the night. If God had wanted to save people by such individual divine visitations and experiences, He could have. And if He had done so, He would have told us about such in writing, as well as how we could prove the validity of the visitation. But He didn't do any of this. So this sort of personal proof of salvation is, on its face, without any scriptural authority or support. It is yet another cause of confusion based upon the endless changing personal testimonies of fallible, fantasizing and often fraudulent men and women.

I bring this up because I have faced it many times in doing door-to-door personal evangelism. One in particular was with my next door neighbor in Lubbock, Texas. He admitted he couldn't deny the clarity of the plain teaching of Christ in Mark 16:16 and Acts 2:38; but said he just couldn't accept the fact that his late night encounter with Christ on a Navy ship at sea, and his immediate salvation by accepting Christ, could be a figment of his imagination and insufficient to save him from his sins without any further obedient acts: like repentance or baptism. Also, I had a woman reject the truth of the Gospel because of her personal "Holy Ghost" experience, wherein God immediately healed her toothache! I lie not, you can't make this stuff up!

Every scripture is profitable for reproof/refutation. Christ didn't just provide us with scriptures to teach ignorant and indifferent sinners how to be saved; He also provided us with scriptures and scriptural arguments — used by Himself and his Apostles — to reason against, dispute and refute false religions, teachings and teachers (Acts 6:9; 9:29; 15:7; 17:17; 19:8-9). When you see large cults and denominations, it is not because God authored this division and confusion in his word. It is because ignorant and often "charismatic" men and women twist the texts to teach what they want them to teach in order to entice and seduce unstedfast souls into their evil designs and/or doctrines (I Corinthians 14:33; II Peter 2:14-19; 3:15f). Only God's complete and unadulterated truth can set any sinner free (John 8:32f; 17:17). I've written most of my books refuting cultic founders, churches, "bibles," translations and false teachings (See in Research Sources). There are new "Christian Cults" coming out every year!

Every scripture is profitable for correction. The scriptures give us inspired truths that will correct, or restore, the world's fallen sinners and straying saints to their correct upright position more quickly and permanently than anything the world's greatest physicians and psychiatrists have to offer. The winsome healing and restorative powers of the Great Physician's love, rest and forgiveness corrected me! There's no profligate sinner that Christ can't raise up to walk a new life via being buried with him in baptism (Romans 6:3-6). And there's no prodigal son that the Father won't restore to his old place in God's family via returning to his church family, repenting and confessing his sins (Matthew 18:15-17; II Corinthians 2:6-11). <u>Note</u>: This forgiveness and restoration by Christ and the members of his church does not mean that a leader in the church, like an elder or evangelist, has to be immediately restored to his previous position of trust in the church.

Every scripture is profitable for instruction in righteousness. The Bible profitably educates every person who chooses to learn and live by its laws and principles of what is right and wrong, good and evil, faithful and faithless, godly and ungodly, charitable and selfish, wise and foolish, purposeful and vain, expedient and excessive, helpful and hurtful, healthy and unhealthy, honorable and dishonorable, redeeming and ruinous, living and dying. A Bible education creates a Spirit-controlled life of self-discipline and control over our tongues, tempers and temptations (Romans 1:16-32; 6:12-14; 8:12-14; James 1:5-27). It creates Christian Character, Integrity and Fortitude. Without a Bible education, no person is fully educated, and no other education is nearly as profitable. (It continually educates me!)

Every scripture makes the man of God complete, furnished completely unto every good work. Consider this: Christ's holy scriptures made every lost sinner a saved sinner, every child of the devil a child of God, and every child of God a Christian, Saint and Priest. No other power, philosophy or person on earth could have done that. So now we learn that Christ's New Testament scriptures can make any Christian who chooses to diligently study them, and have his spiritual temple *"furnished completely"* thereby, into a **"complete man of God."** This is not a title or rank by which an elite "clergy" might seek to elevate themselves even further. Rather, it is what every Christian actually is in potential and can realize in practice as a spiritual being and servant of God.

As we must keep Christ in focus and His future promises ever before us while running the Christian race until we finish the course, we must keep Christ's past history and precious payments to provide us with such scriptural and spiritual blessings in our minds until we die. As we each seek to add all these Christian virtues and victories, we must never forget the cleansing of our old sins and the price He paid to provide for it (II Peter 1:9-11). We can only be complete men/women of God because Christ completed His Salvation Mission and Saving Message as the Son and Messenger of God by shedding his blood (Hebrews 9:15-22). We can only be the "profitable" servants Christ deserves, and the

Father expects in return for His investment in us, because of what God did for us and gave to us in Christ and His New Testament (John 3:16; Matthew 25:27).

And this is not the end of the human sacrifices that were required to give us our New Testament. Paul fought the good fight and offered his life as a sacrifice upon this scriptural altar by giving his physical life to fulfill his ministry, preach Christ's message and write 13-14 books of Christ's New Testament. Can you imagine Paul saying *"the free gift of God is eternal life,"* and then giving the rest of his entire life to get it? And as we already presented, this human sacrifice holds true for all the Apostles who preached and delivered Christ's word. We have been <u>bought</u> by Christ's blood, and <u>built</u> upon the Apostles' blood. And, because of all of these divine blessings and divine-human sacrifices, I must preach more about our debt of gratitude to our Lord and Savior and His Apostles for giving us His New Testament "Words of Life" ... which saved us and completely enables us to be ready, willing and able to do *"every good work"* (Titus 3:1).

Read it and weep. As we become complete men of God by reading Christ's New Testament history of His life, let us take it to heart that the Son of God spent thirty-three years living and sacrificing his life for us sinners/enemies to give us that history (Romans 5:7-10; Colossians 1:21). If He was willing to do all this to give us His New Testament to read, is it asking too much that we, his friends, take or make the time in our busy lives to read His Book? A few lyrics from two old hymns will answer this for us: *"I gave, I gave My life for thee, What hast thou giv'n for Me?... Jesus Paid it all, All to Him I owe"* (from "I Gave My Life for Thee," Havergal & Bliss; "Jesus Paid It All," Hall & Grape).

In like manner, if Christ's Apostles gave their lives to give us their history and Christ's history, is it asking too much for us to set aside the time to read their letters? Is it asking too much of us to turn their dead letters into living voices so others might hear and read them? One way God's Word is living and active is through us when we become walking and talking Bibles (Hebrews 4:12)! And the only way you and I can become a "Living Bible" and be a completely prepared and approved ***"man of God"*** and ***"workman that needeth not be ashamed"*** is to *"**study** to show ourselves approved unto God"* (II Timothy 2:15, KJV).

We don't need to seek a greater goal in life, or a higher office or title in the church, or better education credentials, or for more authority to speak for God, or for more divine help in world evangelism ... because God has *"furnished completely"* his church members with all the godly goals, Positively Heavenly Degrees (PHDs) in scriptural education, and Christ's universal/heavenly authority and assistance to get the job done. We Christians have the rank, right and might to do the job. We can do all these things through Christ who strengthens us because God has blessed us with every spiritual blessing in the heavenly places in Christ (Philippians 4:13; Ephesians 1:3).

Sing and rejoice. When we sing *"Break Thou the Bread of Life, Dear Lord, to me,"* we need to rejoice over how it is through consuming Christ's *"words of eternal life,"* the manna and "meat" of our lives, that Christ's words actually become a part of our minds and beings and we become like Christ (John 6:52-68; Heb. 5:14, KJV). The more we consume a daily diet of Christ words, the more we will begin to think like Christ, reason like Christ, argue like Christ, talk like Christ, walk like Christ, talk about Christ, pray like Christ, love like Christ and preach like Christ, as did Paul and Timothy. Then we can Stand up and Sing <u>for</u> Jesus.

Arise and work. We will become productive "men of God" when we rise up from studying the Scriptures and do the *"good works"* God's Words can accomplish in and through us. We can Stand <u>with</u> Jesus (Ephesians 6:13f)! We will be able to do what Paul said Timothy would be able to do with the Scriptures. We will be able to take our New Testaments in our hands and go about *"teaching"* the world how to be saved. And we can teach them such because we were taught such to be saved and have studied every scripture on the matter since being saved. We will have divine answers to all their important questions about God, Creation, life, sin, salvation, the church and heaven. We will be able to offer them complete divine solutions to all of their spiritual or physical problems. It is not that we claim to have the answers to everything; we claim to know where the answers to everything is (in the Bible); and we know where to find them in His Scriptures.

We will be able to take our New Testaments and *"reprove and correct"* false teachers and teachings, and make Methodists, like I was, into New Testament Christians. We can reprove and correct with the same scriptural words that reproved and corrected us. We can even learn from those whom we correct: not only about their false teachings, but also about how clever the ones who led them to believe their lies were at twisting and tweaking the truth (I Timothy 4:1-2).

For example, I'm amazed at how many false teachers actually quote Satan's words to Jesus during His Temptation — wherein Satan offered to give Jesus *"all the kingdoms of the world"* if Jesus would worship him — to prove God did not rule the worldly kingdoms then or now (Matthew 4:8-9). This not only contradicts all the scriptures that say God has always ruled over the world's kingdoms, good or bad, it also ignores the fact that Satan always lies: just as he did when he told Jesus the kingdoms of the world were his to give (John 8:44)! We learn about Satan's clever devices, like about "lust & pride," when we confront them face to face (II Corinthians 2:11; I John 2:16). President James Garfield said: *"A brave man is a man who looks the devil in the face and tells him he is the devil."* You don't do that by quoting Satan like he is the God of the physical world rather than just the demi "god" of the wicked spiritual world (II Cor. 4:3-4).

On the more positive side, we will be able to take our New Testaments and offer complete ***"instruction"*** to the young and mature, weak and strong, tired and energetic members of Christ's church. We can increase their knowledge and encourage them to be the best personal soul-winners, teachers, preachers, elders, priests, saints and Christians that they, for Christ's sake, can be. Teaching other people is a joint effort. We never get too old or smart to grow in the grace and knowledge of our Lord. It takes all kinds of people with all kinds of talents to make Christ's true Church function like the dynamic Living Body of Christ it was created to be (I Corinthians 12:12-31; Ephesians 4:9-31). All of God's children can become better "men of God" and better Sovereign Servants as we help each other to be better Christians in every way.

Finally, God's word makes us ready to do ***"every good work."***
* Becoming a ***"man of God"*** is in and of itself full of Good Works. Being proficient with Christ's Scriptures and thereby becoming able to teach, reprove, correct and educate searching souls and saints are all good works.

* Everything Christians do in the name of Christ, unto God's glory, that saves a single sinner and edifies His saints is a good work (Romans 14:19; I Corinthians 10:31; Colossians 3:17).
* All the good changes within a Christian's life constitute a good work. We're all to be "works in progress" (Philippians 3:12-14).
* Being evangelists, elders, deacons, teachers, song leaders and church building janitors are all good works.
* Being a good Christian mother, father, son or daughter is a good work.
* Writing biblical books is a good work. All the well-written secular history, science, medical and non-Christian religious books in all the libraries in the world can't make a single person *"wise unto salvation;"* but one book that repeats and reaffirms the Bible can make millions of people wise unto salvation. (I hope this book helps you grow in the Lord! Writing it has helped me. Writing books is my "Soul Food" and "Food for other Souls!")
* Doing voluntary *"almsdeeds"* (acts of mercy) at every opportunity, like the widow Dorcas did, is so dear unto our God who is full of mercy. Luke said she was *"**full of good works** and almsdeeds"* (Acts 9:36). Her Christian cup of love, compassion, sympathy, empathy and helpfulness was always full and running over to help others. Even so we should always be so full of good works, physical and spiritual, that we are always apt and able to *"be ready unto every good work"* (Titus 3:1-5). Always ready to give a thirsty soul a cup of water, offer a shoulder for a sad soul to cry upon, a loving hand to hold in times of sorrow, a caring voice of spiritual hope and freedom to those in prison, Christ's spiritual rest to the lost and weary, something to eat when they are hungry and the free gospel of Christ when they are lost (James 2:14-26).
* Seeking to fulfill the Great Commission is a Great Work! We'll look at ways to fulfill the Great Commission later in this chapter.
* Progressively living for/like Jesus, and pressing towards the goal of His perfection and prize of life is the greatest work of all:

*Not that I have already obtained, or am already made **perfect**: but **I press on**, if so be that I may lay hold on that for which I was laid hold on by Christ Jesus. Brethren, I count not myself yet to have laid hold: but **one thing I do**, **forgetting** the things which are **behind**, and **stretching***

forward** to the things which are before, **I press on toward the goal unto the prize of the high calling of God in Christ Jesus (Philippians 3:12-15; Matthew 5:48).

It is indeed a pity that so many successful and sinful unbelievers, who give their lives in pursuit of vanity and sinful pleasures, will have to be judged by God for all their past sins in the future. Thank God the Christian life is not so. The Christian's life is not to be lived in the **past** by dwelling on our past failures and sins or resting upon our past successes and laurels. And thank Jesus that we Christians who seek to walk in the light don't have to be judged in the future by God for any of our past sins (I John 1:7-10).

That being said, though we Christians are not to dwell on our past failures; we are to learn from them, lest we repeat them! And though we can't rest upon our past successes or achievements, we can build upon them today so tomorrow (the future) we'll be able to use the past day's progress to build upon today. As the saying goes: "Today is the tomorrow you worried about yesterday." We don't live in the past, but we're almost certain to relive it! And if we waste today, we may repeat it tomorrow. If we use it to glorify God and grow in his grace and knowledge, it's called one more day's progress towards our higher calling. And with that goal before us, we now progress to the last words, and perhaps the best, words, of our Lord's Great Commission.

NOTICE that Christ promised to be with them *"unto the end of the world."* Since the Apostles' written Words are Jesus' Inspired Words, and since their words are still on the earth in our New Testaments, and since they will reign with Christ in heaven till the end of time, this promise is true in every way (Matthew 19:28). Again, this proves no mortal man, who is here today and gone tomorrow, could have been our religious leader and Christian Commander In Chief for almost two thousand years, already. Even Methuselah couldn't have passed muster for that position! Only the God-man, Emmanuel, could be with the Apostles then and with us now ... and until the end of the world.

This again reassures us that we are involved in the Greatest Work and Career on earth: a work wherein we work for God and with God in order to bring others into this Divine Partnership. And since it is a Divine Work, it is a work that will never be overthrown by any person or power (Acts 5:39). And since this Loving God and Gospel of Christ is the only GOOD NEWS for all the inhabitants of this BAD NEWS World — full of fearful-false gods, prophets of doom, religious jihadists, baby-killing doctors, truth-hating atheists, pseudo-science professors and hoards of *C.A.D. Teachers from the Planet of the Apes — we should all thank God daily for all the Faithful Souls who brought it down to us some two thousand years later. (*Confessed Ape Descendants!)

Now, we must not shrink back from fulfilling Christ's Great Commission just because there are many adversaries and the armies allied against us are also formidable, or because the times are dangerous and difficult. Nor should we pray for the "End of the World" to come quickly, as so many are wont to do during such tumultuous times, and even write best-selling books to promote. **First**, because there have always been such trying times, trials and tribulations facing Christians who marched for the Master. None really worse than in the First Century. The world didn't end then, yet some were predicting and preparing for it then (including giving up working) just as now, often misinterpreting the same prophesies of Christ (in Matthew 24) that predicted the destruction of Jerusalem in A.D. 70 and not the "Second Coming" at the end of time (II Thessalonians 2:1-11; 3:10; see my *The End of the World: Jewish Calamity or Universal Climax?*). **Second,** because we don't want the world to end just to spare our physical lives at the expense of the loss of billions of spiritual souls who have not heard the truth. **Third,** when Jesus comes at the end of time, all those who ever lived — dead or alive, good and bad, saved or lost — will confess that *"Jesus Christ is Lord to the glory of the Father"*... and then receive their just judgment and eternal recompense or reward (Philippians 2:11). Then will Christ's Great Commission be fully and finally completed.

Until then, Christ's Church of Sovereign Souls must press on with fulfilling the Great Commission, and pray for more time to preach to the lost, so all others may at least have the chance to hear the Gospel once before we hear it hundreds of times in our church services. If the Lord's primary purpose for Christians and his Church on earth had been to be a worshipping society that glorifies his name, rather than getting others to become Christians who will glorify his name now and forever, it would be better if we all died upon conversion so we could worship much more intimately with Him in heaven. This is what the Apostle Paul was referring to in Philippians 1:21-25.

> *For to me to **live is Christ**, and to die is gain. But if to **live in the flesh** {on earth},—if this shall bring **fruit** from my work, then what I shall choose I know not. But I am in a **strait betwixt the two**, having the desire to depart and be with Christ; for it is very far better: yet to abide in the **flesh is more needful for your sake**. And having this confidence, I know that I shall abide, yea, and abide with you all, **for your progress and joy in the faith*** (See also Acts 20:24; 21:13).

So our Sovereign Lord and Commander In Chief has already made the <u>major career choice</u> in life for all of his Sovereign Souls: **"Choose My Commission!"** It is also one of our wisest choices: *"He that winneth souls is wise"* (Proverbs 11:30). And He has a place, purpose and position for each one of us in his kingdom. He has a job that fits the talents of each one of us (Ephesians 4:11-13; Matthew 25:14-30; I Corinthians 12:4-11). There are no Zero Talented persons mentioned in Matthew 25:15. Remember the value of the "Widow's Mite." Or the success of the simple words — *"He told me all things that I ever did"* — of the Samaritan lady at the well (John 4:39-42).

Remember that only you, as His Sovereign Soul, can do your job for yourself. No one can take your place, bear your personal responsibility or receive your blessing in doing it for the Lord you love (Galatians 6:4-5). There are teaching opportunities wherein you might be the very person the Lord has providentially placed at the right place at the right time in another person's life to reach him, teach him, and do the Lord's bidding. Remember these words of Mordecai to Esther: *"Who knoweth whether thou art not come to the kingdom for such a time as this"* (Esther 4:14)? (I'm glad I was "lucky" enough to bump into George and Lucille in Bermuda in 1963!)

Here are some of the positions Christ has qualified us to fill, and tasks He has provided us with all we need to accomplish, as his fully Commissioned Church members, Covenant-Keepers, Cross-Bearers and Gospel Preachers.

(1) He enrolled us as *"Fellow Citizens"* in His Kingdom so we might seek his kingdom first and spread it all over the world (Ephesians 2:19; Matthew 6:33). He wants his kingdom to be first in the whole world. Do we? Is this our mission or omission?

(2) He, as our Commander In Chief, commissioned us as soldiers in his Army. He gave us the offensive weapons (*"loins girded with truth, feet shod with the gospel, sword/word of the Spirit"*) and defensive armor (*"breastplate of righteousness, "shield of faith, helmet of salvation"*) to defend the Faith, defeat Satan, capture souls and win the war of all wars (Ephesians 6:10-18; II Corinthians 10:3-5; Jude 3).

(3) He charged and challenged us to be His preachers and teachers of His Gospel Principles and Promises, who are ever ready, willing and able to give answers for all of our beliefs and hopes (I Peter 3:15). He's provided us with the most effective life-changing Word in existence. If Saul — the *"Pharisee of Pharisee, Chief Sinner,"* Chief Christian Persecutor and Murderer — could be changed to Paul the Chief Christian Evangelist, Persecuted One and New Testament Author, anyone can be saved and at least learn and share his many letters (Acts 7:58; 8:1-3; 9:1-30; II Corinthians 11:16-33). We, like Paul, don't depend on how "able" we are without Christ; we depend on how much Christ and his Word has *"enabled"* us to serve him successfully; and we trust and thank him daily for that blessing and ability (II Cor.12:9; I Timothy 1:12-17).

(4) He told us to be His Seed Sowers and not personal Soil Inspectors, who try to prejudge who the "good prospects" and likely conversions are (Matthew 13:18-23). Leave that to God, for He's the one who gives *"the increase"* (I Corinthians 3:6). Saul was not a "good prospect." Nor was the thief on the cross. But God's Word is powerful and can save and change the worst sinner. If we get confessing, penitent believers to the water, He will take care of supplying them with his forgiving blood.

But, having said that, we also need to know that God has not promised that every person we share his word with will be converted or stay faithful. If you will read the Parable of the Sower, you will see that most of the seed we sow will not bring forth lasting fruit. But, in spite of that, it will still accomplish His purposes (Isaiah 55:11). Sometimes, unfortunately, our preaching only ends up warning and indicting people so God can tell them at judgment that He tried to save them (Ezekiel 2:4-7; 33:7-9).

(5) He's told us we are *"the light of the world"* and are to be the highest and brightest bulbs wherever we might find ourselves, even if we are (or "you are") the only light in the entire city on a hill (Matthew 5:14-16; II Corinthians 4:3-6). Better to light one candle than to curse the darkness. But, caution, if you shine your light on Christ and all of his moral goodness in a place of evil and darkness, there will be those who hate you for it ... but some will be saved. Remember they killed Peter and Paul; but millions saw their light and have been saved by their words, like me and, hopefully, you (John 3:19-21; 15:20).

My Choice

As I chose to heed Uncle Sam's call to enlist in America's military service in January of 1962, and chose to be a member of the Lord's Church in October of 1963, I chose to heed the Lord's fulltime "Great Commission" Call in 1970. Though I had been successful in my eight plus years of fulltime active duty in the Air Force — had good pay, good promotions, good security, great assignments (Bermuda, Germany and three States), and a promised retirement pension in less than twelve years (by age of forty) — I chose to leave the Air Force to accept the opportunity to pursue the Greatest Career Choice on earth: being a fulltime, often unpaid, self-supporting, struggling missionary! All the later money-making "side jobs" that I have been forced to do since becoming "Self-Employed," or "Christ's Employee," were for the purpose of promoting world evangelism and pursuing the Greatest Career Change and Choice I could have ever made in my life! The day I made that choice I received an immediate promotion from a worldly Staff Sergeant to an Officer and Gentleman in the Lord's Army!

This again reminds me of America's twentieth president, James A. Garfield — March 4, 1881 to September 19, 1881 — who had been a Brigadier General in the Union Army and traveling preacher for the Christian Church before getting into politics. He has been quoted as saying he was actually stepping down from the highest position of Preaching to become President. After being elected, he was assassinated within his first year! Personally, I'm also glad I stepped up to the highest position in life, a preacher, but it might not be the safest position I could have chosen!

Since being fulltime missionaries, pulpit preachers or Bible school teachers aren't the only ways one can be involved in the Great Commission of World Evangelism, let's discuss a number of ways everyone can always be involved in spreading the gospel throughout this world. Before discussing them, there are some tried and true formulas that we might keep in our minds as we present each method.

First, remember that people are usually converted one at a time. So start by seeking one person you know who might listen to you.

Second, remember that your goal is to have the person you teach become a teacher of another person he/she knows (II Timothy 2:2). Do the math. If you and every person you teach teaches one other person every year, and each taught-person does likewise, by the end of thirty years over ten million people will have been taught the Gospel of Christ because of what you started and do!

Third, seize every opportunity every day, no matter how insignificant it seems to be, to share the Gospel or any Bible truth. For great projects are often best tackled in small increments. Otherwise, we will likely become overwhelmed at the enormity of the task. Even the Great Pyramids of Egypt were built one huge stone at a time. As the Lord taught, live life one day at a time (Matthew 6:34). Another is, *"redeeming the time,"* or "buying up the opportunity" (Ephesians 5:16, also margin, ASV). Or as they said at my old alma mater, the Sunset School of Preaching, "Inch by inch it's a cinch; yard by yard it's too hard."

Fourth, realize that you are not alone in this labor of love. The Lord is always with us (Matthew 28:20). Remember that He who knows where the fish in the sea are also knows where souls seeking salvation are (Matthew 7:7f; 17:27; Luke 5:4ff). He also knows he has many soul-seekers helping us, about whom we know nothing (I Kings 19:10-18; John 10:14-16). Plus, don't forget his angels are also involved behind the scenes (Hebrews 1:14).

Fifth, remember that you will get better at whatever you're doing with practice. You'll have to crawl before you walk. Then you will have to take baby steps and grow in the grace and knowledge of the Lord before you run (II Peter 3:18). Then after running with the Lord for a while, you'll know you're a solid Bible student ... and err long you will think you can fly with the eagles: *"but **they that wait for Jehovah** shall renew their strength; they shall **mount up with wings as eagles**; they shall run, and not be weary; they shall walk and not faint"* (Isaiah 40:31).

Sixth, then know that none of your works, or even your great plans and intentions for the Lord, go unnoticed or unrewarded, whether they materialize or not, and whether the ones you lead to Christ remain faithful or not (I Kings 8:18; I Corinthians 3:15; Hebrews 6:10). We get "E for Effort" with our Lord. Remember you might be the one who caused the conversion of a great gospel preacher. Though everything in life is vanity without the Lord, no work or effort in the Lord is vain for those who keep on keeping on until death (I Corinthians 15:58).

Seventh, know that those whom you lead to the Lord will, possibly, be with you in heaven. That will be the Reunion of all Reunions. There's a Great Day Coming for all the Participants and Recipients of Christ's Great Commission! Until then, let's look at some of the ways we can be more involved in our Greatest Career every day of our lives.

Be Prayerful

Begin and end every day talking to your Lord, best Friend and Commander in Chief, Jesus Christ. (Remember all those ways we just discussed about declaring our friendship with Christ.) **Pray** for Christ to lead you to the sinners seeking salvation, or them to you, that He knows are within your reach each day. **Pray** for lost souls and soul-seekers you know by name. **Pray** for open doors and opportunities to teach someone every day (Acts 14:27; I Corinthians 16:7-9). **Pray** for peaceful political situations that will allow you to preach in politically unstable places (I Timothy 2:1-4). **Pray** for missionaries to be safe and successful (Ephesians 6:18f; II Thessalonians 3:1-3). **Pray** for every specific evangelistic work you know about. **Pray** for financial blessings to support your efforts. **Pray** for the wisdom to do all of these things scripturally and expeditiously (James 1:5).

This last prayer for ***wisdom*** sums up the attitude we need to possess when it comes to all of our prayers in such great endeavors as World Evangelism. We each must remember that God knows more about what's best for you, as well as which one of your choices are best for Him, you and others. Sometimes our best intentions and choices to do this or that for the Lord, or go here or there for the Lord, aren't the best for us or the Lord's work. Sometimes the "best answer" to our prayers is "No!" As Garth Brooks' song, 'Unanswered Prayers,' says: *"Some of God's greatest gifts are unanswered prayers ... Sometimes I thank God for unanswered prayers."* I know that's been true with some of my prayers. Here's a classic case where I thank God my prayer to do something to spread his Creation Story worldwide was not answered.

"My Challenger Moment"

This moment occurred in 1985 when I was preaching in Hawaii. Since Hawaii is the most remote place on earth as far as its distance from any other continent, some get what we call "Rock Fever" and want to get off the rock every now and then, or reach out beyond the scope of their mission field. This was my desire and prayer.

So, being a Christian preacher and missionary, as well as an avid Creationist, I came up with the "crazy idea" that I should apply to fill the spot that was open for a teacher on the Challenger Shuttle. After all, one of the Astronauts, Ellison Onizuka, was from Hawaii. So I sent a letter to Washington, DC, and to get an Astronaut Application Form. You may read the letter I sent on October 30, 1985, as well as the reply from NASA in the Research Sources section.

I received my reply from NASA sometime in early December, which was a month or so before the launch. There I learned that they had already chosen a history teacher, Sharon Christa McAuliffe. So my brooding about this rejection began and continued all the way up until launch day on January 28, 1986. And to make my disappointment worse, my mother called me and told me she was going to take a vacation to Florida (from Virginia) so she could see the launch.

So when this Challenger launch was counting down I was not only watching it to see what I had missed, I was looking to see if I could find my mom amidst the crowds of spectators. I actually was picturing myself on the Challenger when it blasted off and soared upward. I was telling my wife how I could have been on that space ship IF they would have chosen me instead of her. IF the Lord would have answered my prayers to go and spread His Creation story as the other astronauts — William Anders, Jim Lovell and Frank Borman — had done on the Apollo 8 Mission when they were in Lunar Orbit. But they didn't choose me ... "Why not me?"

Then, as I intently watched the flawless launch up to around 10-12 miles above the earth, I heard those now famous words from Mission Control: "Go with throttle up"... and then Challenger Commander Dick Scobee say, "Roger, go at throttle up!" So I thought to myself, "they're committed and on their way to where I wanted to go, to where I could view the entire earth from space."

Then, before I even got those thoughts out of my mind, I saw the catastrophic explosion and destruction of the rocket booster and shuttle ... which led to the death of all seven of the "lucky" occupants of the Challenger. Which could have been my "Challenger Moment." First I was shocked and saddened. Then I said "thank you Lord for not answering my prayers!" And so, once again, I learned "Father Knows Best," and being a Sovereign Soul means you need to entrust your life to God — His Will, Word and Plans — and not other humans, including yourself!

But, though all of this seemed to be bad for America, the words of its President, Ronald Reagan, at the Commemoration of this sad event, lifted us above it. Take a look and see what you think:

> *Sometimes, when we reach for the stars, we fall short. But we must pick ourselves up again and press on despite the pain.... The crew of the space shuttle Challenger honored us by the manner in which they lived their lives. We will never forget them, nor the last time we saw them, this morning, as they prepared for the journey and waved goodbye and* **'slipped the surly bonds of earth' to 'touch the face of God'** (emp. mine).

On and On we can go with the need for prayer in every part of our life's work for the Lord ... which is why we've been told to *"pray without ceasing"* ... which means without long intermissions I Thessalonians 5:17). Having done that, we prayerfully go to the next point.

Be Prepared

(1) Pray (see above). Since Prayer should always be an integral part in all of our preparations, plans and actions for the Lord, always pray before, during and after you act in His behalf. And this is especially true when it comes to seeking and saving lost souls.

(2) Read God's Word. Take the time, make the time, prioritize your time, schedule the time, and even redeem the time (borrow or buy some time from other time-consuming activities by utilizing the lag times, travel times, lunch breaks, bedtimes, etc.), and be sure to highlight study of God's word on your daily list of pressing things to do. King David said: *"Mine eyes anticipated the night-watches, That I might meditate upon thy word"* (Psalms 119:148).

I don't say this so you might satisfy some self-imposed, time-management schedule or legalistic requirement; but to learn how to become a more faithful Christian and better Bible teacher every day. Remember, *"faith comes from hearing* {or reading} *the word of Christ"* (Romans 10:17). If you want to *hear* the word when you read it, read it out loud! It will help you remember it. You can never replace the objective faith of knowing the truth with the subjective faith of feelings. You must download Christ's word into your brain if you expect it to flow freely from your mouth. Especially if you come face to face with a cultic or atheistic enemy of Christ's truth. Trusting in an empty gun is not wise! As Sir Oliver Cromwell charged his troops: *"Trust in God and keep the powder dry!"* Therefore, our objective faith in Christ — from our initial faith through all of our spiritual growth thereafter until we die — must spring from our growth in *"in the grace and* **knowledge** *of our Lord and Savior"* (II Peter 3:18).

So the more you learn how to use your Bible, as well as all of the good Bible research tools we have at our disposal today (like Strong's Exhaustive Concordance, Bible Dictionaries, Lexicons), the more you will be able to be your own student, the more you'll always be ready, willing and able give an answer for your faith (I Peter 3:15), and the more you will become a faithful and fact-based Bible teacher of any person you meet in the public and private places of life (Luke 14:23; Hebrews 5:12).

(3) Study other religious beliefs and church doctrines. Right up front, let me assure you of one positive thing you will almost immediately realize when you engage in any serious study of denominational and cultic churches: that the New Testament truths of Christ on every issue are much easier to understand, accept and teach than their false teachings. Quite frankly, reading the Book of Mormon is much like reading redundant and sophomoric gibberish. You will run into so many repetitions of the phrase *"And it came to pass"* that you will lose all sense of where you are and what is being discussed! The only time the Book of Mormon comes near the linguistic, logical and historical content of the Bible is when it actually quotes the King James Version of the Bible verbatim, as it does of Isaiah 53. (Which is a dead giveaway of its fraudulent claim of being directly transcribed from "Reformed Egyptian Hieroglyphics" thousands of years ago!)

A word of caution is in order here. Though it is good to be well-versed in the false teachings of major religions and churches where ever you find yourself, it is usually not possible to know as much about their teachings as the devout members in those religions, churches and cults, especially those who are leaders, preachers and missionaries. So the best preparation we can all do is become so well-versed in the truths and teachings in Christ's New Testament that we can immediately detect their false teachings and use them to segue into the truth on the matter. Then you can remain on offense and in the Affirmative in your presentation of the clear scriptures on essential subjects, rather than spending all your time on defense and in the Negative repudiating their endless false doctrinal, worship and organizational teachings.

This is how those who study how to identify counterfeit bills operate. They learn all the details about the true bills, and then simply compare any of the other possible counterfeit bills with them, and then they identify any bill that is in any way different from the true bill as being counterfeit. This approach works every time. It is also best to focus on the first essentials in the Plan of Salvation — belief in the deity of Christ, repentance and baptism — than to engage them in every difference on other subjects (like worship acts, elder qualifications, etc.), which are best studied after they realize they need to leave their false religion or church and become true New Testament Christians.

Be A People Person

What I mean by this might not be what you think. I am not

talking about becoming the "center of attention" and "life of the party" here. Nor am I talking about every Christian becoming a handshaking, crowd-comfortable, public-speaking person or preacher. For not all people are so inclined, or even able to do such in many situations, like people with physical communication disabilities. God can use people who are not eloquent to do his leading and bidding, as He did with Moses, by appointing his brother, Aaron, to be his mouthpiece (Exodus 4:10-17). He can also use deaf, dumb and blind people to do amazing things: e.g., the blind man in John 9:13-38; or Helen Keller. So it is obvious that God is able to use those who are timid, or not that outspoken in public, in many more private and personal capacities that most do have to offer in fulfilling Christ's Great Commission.

And I, again, personally thank God for that fact. For the man that led me and my wife to Christ, George Spurgin, was not a person who would do any public speaking in or out of the church assembly. When I first became a Christian in Bermuda, George explained to me why he didn't feel comfortable doing any public speaking, leading prayers or serving at the Lord's Supper during the worship services. His embarrassing public incident occurred in a church in the United States during his early years in the USAF. He worked at the AF Base gymnasium in athletics just as he did in Bermuda when I met him. He had advised the leaders in the church where he attended that he didn't do public speaking in the assemblies and requested that he not be called upon during the services. Well, during one Sunday morning service, someone who didn't know about George's reticence about public speaking, spontaneously called upon George to lead the closing prayer. Everyone immediately bowed their heads. George was embarrassed, yet unable to courteously decline. So he bowed his head and somehow his familiar vocation words just came out: *"Athletics Department, Sergeant Spurgin speaking!"* Haha (This is painfully hilarious!) That was it. And, THAT WAS IT for good!

BUT, though public speaking was not George's "strong suit," he was very powerful and articulate, in his own Texas style, when it came to persuading a person to be his own Bible student and check out the scriptures on all the essential issues. He was the exact kind of "preacher" I needed to run up against: a straight-talking, tough-loving, rough person versus a smooth-talking, mild-mannered and soft-handed preacher like Reverend Star! And because of George's unique talent and effectiveness, George's wisdom and verbal contributions in fulfilling Christ's Commission are being spread through a person (named "Gerald") who isn't that restricted when it comes to such public presentations. I do it for Christ and George!

Before leaving this sidebar and expanding our 'Be A People Person' point, I'd like to put myself in George's shoes: because I once was much like George when it comes to being in the public spotlight. It might not seem to be so now, but it is true. It is true that I've always been a very talkative person, even from a baby. For my mother had to take me back to the hospital shortly after I was born because I wouldn't stop screaming...wouldn't shut up! And seldom did I ever get a report card in elementary school that didn't have a note to my mother written on it saying, "talks too much." However, though I've always been a very talkative person, I've also always been a very private person. I'm not a person who likes to be in the middle of crowded situations and events, or the center of attention. I'm not a "Facebook" kind of guy. (Which is why my picture on the back of all my books is thirty years old, and counting!) But, for Christ's sake, I'm willing to put myself in those kinds of public situations and even be a speaker in public events. Because of my desire and burning fire within (Jeremiah 20:9), I must speak up, speak out, and speak for Christ at every opportunity, private or public. Because of that personal trait, I have been a preacher, publisher, and even a politician (ran for political office twice), who has had the opportunity to speak to small and large audiences. I'm willing to be a "fool for Christ's sake" ... or make a fool of myself for Christ's sake! So much so, that now "talking" is what I do for a living: I talk, talk, talk!

This reminds me of what Lee Trevino, a notorious incessant talker on the PGA Tour, said to one of the big-name professionals who didn't talk much when playing golf, and had told Lee he was annoyed by his constant banter. Lee (paraphrased) said: "That's ok, you just listen and I'll talk enough for the both of us!" Point: if you're a natural talker, use it to talk about and for the Lord.

But if you're not all that talkative, remember being a "People Person" also means you have to be a good listener as well. As James said: *"But let every man be swift to hear, slow to speak, slow to wrath..."* (James 1:19). So you might be just the person who can listen to talkative people, and then talk to him/her in private or convey his/her views and questions to someone you know who will be more capable of dealing with his/her many ideas. Though I do talk a lot, I also listen well to what others are saying. I do this because being a Bible student and teacher means we must listen to what a person says, how he says it, and why he says it in order to know how close to the truth he is. If I find some point of Scriptural agreement, I usually begin the discussion with that first and build upon it. If all a person says is unscriptural, then I respond to the most essential issue he brings up. So listening well is half the battle of being a good People Person.

Having said all of this, what I really want to get across in this 'People Person Point' is how we Christians simply need to be going to places where people, besides members of the church, gather together for lawful, healthy and morally upright activities. A few examples of this would be going to shopping centers, sporting events (my golfing at the "Muni" or surfing at "Kaimu"), parks, neighborhood social events, etc., where you might meet and greet your neighborhood friends, or lonely/needy people, or people seeking the truth: *"he that seeketh findeth"* (Matthew 7:8). Or just go to Oahu, Hawaii which means "The Gathering Place," and give me a call: We'll talk story in person. (Lord willing!)

Be Peaceful

We're always supposed to be loving and kind towards our neighbors and fellow human beings. We've been charged to speak the *"truth in love"* towards the persons we're trying to teach and correct, and not just express our hatred of false religions and ideologies (Ephesians 4:15; Psalms 119:128). Christians are never encouraged to be hateful, hostile or combative against people over religious differences. We've not been told to go and punish the world for being sinful and wrong. We've been told to go preach to the world and save sinners by telling them what's right. We're not supposed to brow-beat people into scriptural submission. As the saying goes: "He who is convinced against his will is of the same opinion still" (Borrowed). But we should seek to powerfully persuade them to consider becoming a Christian, as did Paul (Acts 26:28-29). God's world will become more peaceful because of it.

In this regard, notice I said "more peaceful" and not a "peaceful world." For we world evangelists must come to the biblical realization that true "World Peace" will never become a reality: not so long as there's sin and hatred — towards God and man — in this world. Not as long as there's larceny in the heart, or ignorance in the mind, of one of our fellow human beings. Not as long as religious strife and wars are as much a part of the problem as secular strife and wars. And praying for world peace, or singing songs wishing for world peace (like "Imagine"), will never create any true peace all by itself. We must work with God and pursue His plan for making peace: which means we must preach the Gospel of Peace and Divine-Human Reconciliation via the *"**Christ** of reconciliation, the **ministry** of reconciliation, and the **words** of reconciliation"* (II Corinthians 5:18f). More Christ = More Peace!

This is not just religious "pie in the sky" stuff here. It is proven by history. The spread of True Christianity promotes individual, national and worldwide peace. Christ's New Testament and Great Commission can't be misunderstood. His command is universal Gospel "Good News" communication, not the "bad news" of universal religious conquest. Christianity IS a religion of Peace headed by the **"Prince of Peace."** And Christ's Church offers sweet and loving invitations of "Come to Jesus" to *"whoever will ... come and take the water of life freely,"* without force or charge (paraphrasing Revelation 22:17). It is not like "Islam," which means "submit" (or possibly be killed), which was founded by a warrior and physical conqueror, named Muhammad: who said he had been made *"victorious by terror."* And which, to this day, has as its core teaching: convert or die, "kill infidels" (Quran) ... and is still most busy with doing just that! We need to convert them so they won't continue killing us by bombing church buildings, butchering Christians and flying planes into our towers. (See Supplemental Studies on false charges against Christianity by President Barack Obama.)

Be Pragmatic

"Be ready unto every good work" (Titus 3:1). Whatever works, that's good and practical in today's modern world, do it. I saved this one for last because all the talk about scriptural inspiration and mission techniques will not replace the work and perspiration that's required to get the job done. Becoming proficient in

evangelism is like any other profession: OJT — "On the Job Training" — is essential to getting the job done. Evangelism requires work and not just talk. Unfortunately, all too often, "when all is said and done, there's more said than done." So we need *"a mind to work"* to motivate us to use our methods of work (Nehemiah 4:6). And I can think of no greater thing to make us set our minds to do Christ's work than the love Christ had for us, which we have already experienced, and which love *"constraineth us"* — holds us together in this mission, and compels/propels us ever onward, forward, outward — to share His loving Gospel with the world that He so loves (II Corinthians 5:14; John 3:16).

I am only going to list twelve ways that I have been involved in, or have seen to be effective, because I don't believe in telling other people to do what I won't do, or haven't done. I'm sure you can expand upon the number or applications of these suggestions as you consider your abilities and situations in your local area and life.

1. Volunteer to help out in any way you can in local Gospel Meetings and Campaigns for Christ. Knock doors and hand out personal invitations in the neighborhoods near the church that's sponsoring the event. Though knocking doors is not the easiest thing for me to do, I have knocked doors in many cities and some countries, and can tell you it is as effective as any other method of advertising. One time in Hawaii, when times were hard, I even knocked doors for a few weeks to sell Kirby Vacuum cleaners ... until I remembered my long-standing personal caveat: "I will only knock doors for Christ!" (So I quit Kirby that day!) The reason most Cults, especially the JW's and Mormons, have grown so much around the world is their daily door-knocking regimens. Another way to advertise Gospel meetings is to put up signs and posters, or even putting bumper stickers on your cars. A good example of the effectiveness of this was the phenomenal success realized by the "I Found It" bumper stickers utilized by the Campus Crusades for Christ back in the 1970's.

Since I'm writing this book during a Presidential Election in my *"Country Tis of Thee"* America — which nation was built upon Christian Principles, which has "In God We Trust" on its coins and "One nation under God" in its Pledge of Allegiance — I would like to make a bumper sticker that says: "Could Jesus Get Elected in this Country?" I could even ask: "Could Christ be hired as the Preacher in your Denominational or Catholic Church?" Or "Could Christ host your big TV or Talk-Radio Show?" I doubt it! (I called Sean Hannity's Radio Show right after I wrote this part of this book — on December 22, 2015 — and asked if I could discuss this very subject ... I was not allowed on the show!) Let's close this point by hailing Christ as our "banner" going before us in all of our endeavors in his Church, wherever it is.

2. Keep Christian tracts available on your person, at home, at your job, office, in your car, and give them to anyone who will take them upon your request. Or leave them anywhere you can lawfully do so. I was told (but never checked it out) that a great preacher in Spain, Juan Monroy, found his way to the truth via a tract! Or, write your own tract and do the same thing. You might be surprised where it might end up ... but you won't if you don't give it a try. Or, if you have the option, you can direct a person to your personal or church website to get tracts or answers to Bible questions. You and your friends and contacts are herein invited to go to my website — www.Biblical-Books.com — and read my two tracts, and then tell others to read them free of charge. (They're not for sale. But I will allow you to reproduce them upon request.)

3. Make your own Christian business cards to hand out. I have cards for my website and books which I hand out to every person I meet and have a chance to strike up a religious conversation with. Sometimes I offer a free book of choice to any person who goes to my website and asks for one. Soul-winning costs money ... but each soul led to Christ is priceless.

4. Write in your local Newspapers. Most local papers include an 'Opinion Page,' wherein you can submit your opinions on many social and even religious issues. You can receive an amazing amount of free newspaper print by doing this. I have used this approach for over forty years throughout the State of Hawaii. I still try to get my letters published, but they are now few and far between because I have been banned by some papers who have become anti-Christian over the years. The previous Editor of our largest newspaper here used to print about anything I submitted, up to half a newspaper page in length. If free Op Ed letters aren't your choice or available, you can usually get special church events or new books published as "news" for free. Or you can purchase advertising space in the newspapers. I have done this on a limited scale, but my beloved Publisher, Alvin Jennings, has done such on a large scale for eight years in Fort Worth, Texas, with his "Paper Pulpit." You may access this on line and even buy his book on it.

5. Use local radio and TV religious broadcasts and ads. Run a low-priced, one-minute Bible "sermonette," or an advertisement for any true Christian radio broadcasts: like "Herald of Truth, World Radio, World Christian Broadcasting" and such.

6. Call local and national Radio Talk Shows: like Rush Limbaugh, Mark Levin, Sean Hannity, Michael Savage. Again, this is yet another way to receive amazing amounts of free exposure of your conservative Christian religious and social views. I've been on several national and state talk shows over the last few years, and I am seeking to get on others. Why not seize upon every opportunity to talk to millions of listeners all over the world (because of computer podcasts). I can assure you that getting on such shows will inspire a personal reality check within you as to your participation in "going into all the world" for Christ! (I'm not saying any of these Radio Talk Show Hosts are conservative Christians, or that they will let you "preach" the Lord's New Testament church or push your books on their shows. But they will usually allow you to get your name on their shows and push for conservative Christian principles in America, or for the need to return to our Christian and Biblical Roots. If you ever get one of them to advertise your book, it will sell thousands immediately!

7. Financially support Christian schools, colleges, and mission programs. Of course I, being a *Sunset School of Preaching graduate, support their many missionary efforts around the world when I can, including giving them permission to print and sell some of my books and keep the profits. (*Sunset was renamed, "Sunset International Bible Institute," years after I graduated.) Sunset came up with a novel idea of sending Solar Powered Players that play Gospel teachings to parts of Africa that don't have electrical power. There are many great local churches of Christ that support missionaries all over the world. So to participate with them in any small or large way is to seek the kingdom first and pursue the greatest Career one can pursue until the day he/she dies. Actually, many churches accept contributions from personal estates after you die. And I pray I'll be able to set my physical house in order in such a way that I'll be able to do likewise. (You need to put such in your "will" to do so.)

If you have the desire, ability and aptitude to teach, preach or be more prepared in these great mission works of the Lord, you might consider attending one of these Christian education institutions to get the training in how to use the tools of the trade: meaning the Bible, original languages, lexicons, etc. Some of the Schools of Preaching charge no tuition to attend. You must either have the funds to support yourself or seek other like-minded brethren to support you. I attended the Sunset School of Preaching via the GI Bill and raising church and individual support. Though my beloved friends, George and Lucille Spurgin, supported me and my family at Sunset and throughout the rest of their lives on earth, I still had to travel near and far seeking support from other churches for additional support to continue there and also for later mission works.

Travelling to raise financial support proved to be a challenging and sometimes lonely and inspiring experience in and of itself. One road trip to Oklahoma, away from my wife and kids in Lubbock, Texas, stands out. On the second night I began to write a little song that reflected my emotional struggle with loneliness at that time. I'll now share that unpublished song with you. (Well, I guess after I have this book published, it will be published!)

Another Lonely Night

Well it's another lonely night ... Past a day that wasn't right ... Seems like I've been gone, a long long time. Well, I know here in my heart, It's not good when we're apart ... Tell me Dear, do you miss me when I'm gone?

Now the daylight I can see ... Just spent eight hours of misery ... Seems like I've been gone, a long and lonesome time. Well, one thing I know sweetheart, I'm no good when we're apart ... Tell me dear, do you miss me when I'm gone?

Well there goes the sun it's setting fast ... I sure hope this one's the last ... Seems like I've been gone, forever in my mind. Well, I know here in my heart, I really miss you when we're apart ... So I'll tell you dear, I miss you when I'm gone ... Yes, I tell you dear I miss you ... I really miss you .... and I'm coming home.

I so much wanted to find another way to raise support for my ministry besides travelling all by my lonesome that I decided I would try to get this song published. So I had one of my Sunset teachers, Jim McGuiggan, who sounded like Paul Williams, to record it on a little cassette tape. Then I took my wife and kids and drove about a thousand miles from Lubbock, Texas to Nashville, Tennessee in order to submit it to one of the largest recording companies in the country: Tree International Publishing Company.

When I arrived in Nashville, I immediately went to Tree International and took my little tape to the front desk. I was told that they only accepted reel type tapes and not cassette tapes. I told them about my long trip, and they agreed to have their A&R man listen to it on my little recorder. (I later learned A&R means "Artist and Repertoire!") While waiting on him on their nice leather couch, and looking at all the gold records hanging on their walls (like Roger Miller's "King of the Road" at that time), Chet Atkins walked in, looked over at me, and I felt like slithering under the couch! I think I also began to question my sanity!

Well, the A&R man listened to the tape, said it was a good song, but didn't have a "bridge." I asked him what that was, and then felt worse! (It still doesn't have a bridge!) He then laid these record selling facts on me: Tree International receives hundreds of songs a month to review for recording. Of that large number, only one gets contracted. Of the large number of those contracted, only one gets recorded. And of that large number of recorded songs, only one makes any money! Then he closed off the conversation with this kicker: "If Loretta Lynn had brought this song in, Tree would probably record it." Hey, anyone seen Loretta around here?

Believe it or not, Loretta did have a home on the Big Island back in those days, but I never had the chance to meet her. But I did meet Country Music Star, Don Williams (a member of the church), a few times when I was preaching in Kailua Kona on the Big Island, but never had a chance to bring this song up ... but I'm not dead yet! Sovereign Soul Winners never quit! Quitters never win!

8. Visit prisons, assisted care homes, widows and orphans. Besides such being the pure religious and loving thing to do (James 1:27), these places are often times the best place, and even the final place, on earth to reach desperate and dying people. (As I mentioned, I have had the painful privilege of watching a number of poor sinners die in their sins in the hospital!) To say we have a "captive" audience might sound calloused, but it is true.

One of my first "converts" in Hawaii, was a young prisoner, George Manos, at the Kulani Correctional Facility about thirty miles from Hilo. He had been studying with Jehovah's Witnesses for weeks when I arrived there. He was to join their church the next week. I asked him to put it off till I could return the next week. He did so. I returned with nothing but my Bible and the JW's New World Translation. To my surprise, four JW's with a load of books were with George when I arrived. Right away I asked them to explain the Watchtower's addition of four words — (*"other"*) — in the NWT of Colossians 1:16-17, which changed Jesus from being the Creator of *"all things"* to being a Created Being who created "all "other" things." They couldn't answer and left without further ado. George became a Christian soon afterwards, and I wrote another book, entitled: *The Perversions and Prejudices of the New World Translation.* See their perversions of Colossians 1:16-17 on pages 41-45 of that book. Just another day in the Career of Christians who're always on Call!

9. Rent a space, booth or stall in the Market Place: like at the County/State Fairs, outdoor 'Farmer's Markets,' and other social events, like Hilo's block-festival, Ho'olaule'a. I once had a very successful booth in Hilo's County Fair a year after I came to Hawaii, in 1973. I built a large wooden "Computer" (enclosure), put Christmas lights on the front, and a sign telling people to put their religious questions on the old computer cards I provided and insert them into the small slot. I was hidden inside and looking up the answers in my Bible. It attracted so much attention I had to get my Christian brother, Joe Buchanan, to help me. It was a "good biblical work"... and a good mental workout!

10. Utilize conservative Christian books. Though E-Books are becoming more and more popular, real paper books are still best in this area. First of all, because Bible students like to highlight and add notes and other scriptures in these books. Secondly, you can loan your books to others (tell them there's no charge for your notes!), give them away and even leave them in some public places for another person to read. (I know, it also means another person will throw it in the trash!) You might want to check the pulse of the city or neighborhood where you live and leave books that deal with the dominant religious group there. I would not recommend writing your home address or even your home phone number on any book you leave in any public place. It would be better to include a P.O. Box number, your website or even the address of your local congregation.

I would also recommend writing your own book/s. I believe every Christian who has the time, talent and desire to write a book that will steer people to the Scriptures for all their answers in life is a "good work." Plus there are other advantages in writing your own books for the Lord. **First,** your book will be unique and, believe it or not, might work wonders with someone who has an affinity for people from his/her home town, background, culture, age, and suchlike. Just as I liked Wayne Newton because, during his early recording years, he lived and sang in my hometown of Roanoke, Virginia. **Second,** you will become a better Bible student and teacher. Doing the required research to write a book will increase your knowledge and confidence on your chosen subject. And you will become humbled as you see how the Lord's inspired words prove that uninspired human beings could not have written His Bible. **Third,** it will keep you busy, often day and night, in your greatest career challenge: fulfilling the Great Commission. Since "idleness is the Devil's workshop," thinking about holy and heavenly things when you are writing a biblical book will become what you want to do in most of your spare time (Philippians 4:8f). It may start out like a part-time or spare-time hobby, but, believe me, writing and finishing a book can easily become one of the most difficult things you can do in your life, and even a taskmaster (Ecclesiastes 12:12). Winston Churchill had this to say about writing books:

> *To begin with, it is a joy and an amusement. Then it becomes a mistress. Then it becomes a master. Then it becomes a tyrant. And the last phase is that just as you are about to be reconciled to your servitude, you kill the monster and fling him out to the public!*

Of course, when you are writing a book about Jesus, for Jesus, and from His Book, the joy will not only remain as you progress, but when you finish it and watch it go where you cannot go, you will rejoice and begin planning on writing your next book! Being a shining light, or star, for Christ is not like being a Hollywood Movie Star, Music Star, or Secular Author — whose fame often doesn't last past their last hit movie, song or book/novel — because if your book accurately presents the scriptures in a personal, passionate and powerful way, it will be around for ages to come. (Some of the books that I consult in my research have been selling for centuries. Some of mine for over forty years.)

11. Teach your children to be Christians and train them to be soul-winners for Christ (Ephesians 6:4). Solomon said: *"Train up a child in the way he should go, And even when he is old he will not depart from it"* (Proverbs 22:6). There's a lot of truth to this ... but maybe not all the truth that's in this English quote. For the Hebrew for the words *"in the way he should go,"* as is found in most Bibles, is actually *"according to his way"* (see margin note in ASV). That also is true. For if you allow your child to choose his own stubborn way in life, he might just remain that way until he dies. So, contrary to what some of our "progressive parents" (pathetic parents) teach about allowing your children to grow up to adulthood, then choose whether they want to learn about religion or just be free happy hippies hooked on life and love, it is our parental responsibility to teach our children the truth from a baby and train them to live for Christ (II Timothy 1:5; 3:14f).

12. Run for political office. I placed this option last because it is the most limited position you can seek to serve the Lord. It is not the most limited as far as your influence can be if you run or get elected; it is the most limited because of election cycles, qualifications for office, etc. I know that though most people don't feel qualified for higher political offices, most people are "armchair quarterbacks" and believe that can do a better job than the person who was elected to the office! I also know there are as many people who insist we should not mix politics with religion as there are people who say we should not argue politics or religion!

But I, being a "Sovereign Soul" under the "King of all Kings" and Universal "Commander-In-Chief," as well as an old student of "Divine Politics," know full well that not only can God's religion be mentioned in politics, our God and Lord is the One who rules in all of the political affairs of men upon this earth. And I know He wants us to do whatever He allows to keep governments in harmony with his People, Church and Divine Mission (Daniel

4:25-37; Romans 13:1-7; I Timothy 2:1-4; see *God Among the Nations,* in Research Sources). If we Christians have been told by our God to pay taxes to all governments and pray for our rulers, then, "By God," we can have a political say and position in all governments. Thus all the screaming about "Separation of Church and State" and "keeping God out of politics" is just another way of saying "keep only secularism and atheism in politics."

Though America's Constitutional First Amendment prohibits the State from meddling in God's affairs and religion, it does not prohibit God and his Religion from being involved in the State's Affairs. In fact, that very Constitution was drafted by professing Christians who confessed Christ as Lord at the end of it, saying: *"In the year of Our Lord, 1787."* One of the largest churches in America was in the Halls of Congress. America's Coins say "In God we Trust" upon them! It's National Anthem and Pledge of Allegiance have the God of the Bible in them. Many of our Founding Fathers and Courts said it was a "Christian Nation." Does that sound like "Separation of Church and State" to you?

So my personal view is, "why would anyone bother to be involved in politics if it weren't for religious reasons?" Yes, including religious moral reasons! Again the old bromide that "you can't legislate morality" is a Devil's lie. The famous Judge Robert Bork said this to those who say you cannot legislate morality: "You can't legislate morality?; we legislate little else" (See his book, *Slouching towards Gomorrah*). So this is why I ran for political office twice in Hawaii: they were legislating immorality!

The first time I ran for County Council I was a fulltime preacher, part time Realtor and carpenter. But I ran for office to push Christian ethics (like against evolution in schools, abortion) and get a lot of free press. Afterwards, I wrote a Bible-based book on abortion, "A Mother's Son." I sent it to Rush Limbaugh in 1993, and he sent me a Postcard telling me he received it. Recently, on his radio show, Rush told me he had received the book. And, considering many of his stated views on the fact that a baby in the womb is a human being with a right to life, I believe he may have even read the book. I have offered this book free of charge to "Right to Life" groups. Why? Because, though it is about a social/moral issue, it still exalts Christ's word from cover to cover! Also, all my other "Biblical Books" on other religious issues are advertised on the back covers of my books. Plus, it reaches people who are not Christians or members of the Lord's church. The main reason we write books is to spread the Word!

The second time I ran for political office was when I ran for Mayor of the Big Island of Hawaii in 1998. I ran because I wanted to stop Same-Sex Marriage from being passed in this State. It didn't pass, and I wrote a book entitled "Homosexuality and the Bible." (See Research Sources for political clips and Rush's card.)

I'm not telling you any of this to toot my own horn, or shine a light on me, just the opposite. I'm telling you this because I believe "necessity is the mother of invention" and that, as a preacher and perennial participant in the Great Commission, I believe we should seize upon any opportunity to keep Christ and his Word before the public. Proof that I really didn't want to be elected for mayor can be seen by the following facts: **(a)** I didn't spend a dime to campaign for either office. **(b)** I took every media opportunity to tell people I was running to save an infant's right to life and biblical marriage in this State. **(c)** In the Mayoral campaign, I even told people that my opponent (Ray Yamashiro) would be the best fiscal Mayor.

Update: Though we carried the day by passing the Marriage Amendment to Hawaii's State Constitution, unfortunately, fifteen years later Hawaii's Governor Abercrombie (whom I once debated) and his liberal legislators passed same-sex marriage against the will of Hawaii's voters and in direct violation of Hawaii's Marriage Amendment. Eternal vigilance is a necessity when it comes to these issues!

Now this old evangelist will close this discussion on World Evangelism with two Psalms of David, two great songs and one scripture about our Lord's assistance in His Great Commission.

*I have been young, and now am **old**; Yet have I not seen the righteous forsaken, Nor his seed begging bread.... Yea, even when **I am old** and grayheaded, O God, forsake me not. Until I have **declared** thy strength unto the **next generation**, Thy might to **every one that is to come*** (Psalms 37:25; 71:18; See Judges 2:7-10 to see what happens when a nation fails to tell God's truth to the next generation).

Ring Out the Message

V.1—*There's a message true and glad For the sinful and the sad, Ring it out, Ring it out; It will give them courage new, it will help them to be true; Ring it out, ring it out.*
V.2—*Tell the world of saving grace, Make it known in every place, Ring it out. ring it out; Help the needy ones to know Him from whom all blessings flow; Ring it out, ring it out.*
V.3—*Sin and doubt to sweep away, Till shall dawn the better day, Ring it out, ring it out; Till the sinful world be won For Jehovah's mighty Son; Ring it out, ring it out.*
Chorus: *Ring out the word oér land and sea, Still far from Jesus many live in sin and doubt, Ring out the news that makes men free, To all the lost of every nation, Ring it ... ring it out* (James Rowe, Samuel W. Beazley).

Soldiers of Christ, Arise

V.1—*Soldiers of Christ, a-rise. . . And Put your ar-mor on; Strong in the strength which God sup - - plies, Strong in the strength which God sup-plies, Thro' His be-lov-ed Son.*
V.2—*Strong in the Lord of hosts. . . And in His mighty power; Who in the strength of Je---sus trusts, Who in the strength of Je-sus trusts, Is more than con-quer-or.*
V.3—*Stand, then, in His great might ... With all His strength en-dued; But take to arm you for the fight, But take, to arm you for the fight, The pan-o-ply of God.*
V.4—*Leave no un-guard-ed place,... No weak-ness of the soul; Take ev-'ry vir-tue, ev---'ry grace, Take ev-'ry vir-tue, ev-'ry grace, And for-ti-fy the whole.*
V.5—*That hav-ing all things done. . . .And all your con-flicts past, You may o'er-come thro' Christ a...lone, You may o'er-come thro' Christ a-lone, And stand en-tire at last* (Charles Wesley, Wm. B. Bradbury).

Ephesians 3:20-21

*Now unto **him that is able to do** exceedingly abundantly above all that we ask or think, according to the **power that worketh in us**, unto him be the **glory in the church** and in **Christ Jesus unto all generations for ever and ever. Amen.***

CHAPTER SEVEN
Sovereign Souls Choose Christ's Crown

CHRIST'S CHOICE

The only reason we have any hope in this world to ever receive any kind of afterlife or reward for trying to live a morally upright and divinely directed life on this earth is because Christ lived a sinless life, shed his innocent blood for our sins, was resurrected and ascended to his throne to wear His Crown of Righteousness ... and then imputed His righteousness to those who choose to accept his free gift of eternal life (Romans 3:21-30; 4:1-8; 6:23). In other words, the reason we have any hope of wearing Christ's Crown of Righteousness is because Christ Chose to wear a Crown of Thorns for us. And the only reason we know that Christ made this Crowning Choice for us in eternity and history is because Christ's Chosen Apostles wrote about Christ's Choice for us in their Epistles. And to them we now go.

It was Christ's imputed righteousness and ultimate *"Crown of Righteousness"* at the end of life that Christ's inspired Apostles preached and aspired unto throughout their Christian lives (I Corinthians 1:30; II Corinthians 5:21; Philippians 3:8-16; I John 1:9; 3:7). Here's what Paul said before his exodus from this earth:

> *V.6 For **I** am already being **offered**, and the time of **my departure** is come. V.7 **I** have **fought the good fight**, **I** have **finished the course**, **I** have **kept the faith**: V.8 henceforth there is laid up for me the **crown of righteousness,** which the **Lord, the righteous judge, shall give to me** at that day; and not me only, but also to **all them** that have **loved** his appearing* (II Timothy 4:6-8).

Notice that in this text Paul revealed unto us Five inspired Truths about his/ receiving Christ's Crown of Righteousness.

TRUTH ONE
The Crown is based upon Individual Life Choices

Paul used the personal pronoun *"I"* four times in this text, affirming his personal choice to live the Christian life that brought him to this point in his life. No one else made his choices for him. Though we know, from Acts 9:1-19, that Christ foreknew Saul's conversion (v.15), and worked miraculously in his behalf — appearing to him to get his attention, getting a Christian to help him (Ananias), and healing his blindness (vv. 3-9, 12-17) — it was still Saul's initial choice to accept or reject all of these miraculous signs and obey the Lord (v. 18; 22:16). Which is opposite of the choices Paul's Jewish leaders made when they rejected all of Christ's miracles and killed him (John 11:47-53).

Of course, the Lord would have foreknown that as well, and the story of "Saul, the Jewish Persecutor," who was renamed "Paul the Christian Preacher," would never have been written. Sometimes name-changes are helpful, especially when the old name was involved in much sinning! (Ahem. Jerry Neil Wright, *"You ain't nothing but a houndog"* without Christ!)

TRUTH TWO
The Crown Comes at our Departure (death)

The Crown comes at the end of our lives — at our *"departure"* — and not before. As Saul made his own choice to obey Christ and become a Christian, so he made his choice to fulfill his ministry even if it meant dying for Christ (Acts 20:22-27; 21:13). And he did. Here are the historical/scriptural facts that led up to Paul's martyrdom. **(1)** Christianity had become an illegal religion in Rome, under Nero, by this time in Paul's life, circa., A.D. 64-68. **(2)** Paul was already a *"prisoner"* in *"chains"* like some dangerous criminal, awaiting his execution in a Roman prison (II Timothy 1:8, 16f; 4:6). **(3)** Paul knew the only reason he was *"suffering"* this fate was because of his Christian teaching and preaching (Ibid. 1:8,11f). **(4)** Paul was still unashamedly preaching Christ in prison and preparing Timothy to carry on after his departure by writing him this letter and asking him to *"give diligence to come to me shortly,"* to see him before he died (Ibid.

4:9; 1:6-14; 2:1-3; 3:14 thru 4:5). **(5)** Paul knew he was already in the process of being *"poured out as a drink **offering***" as a sacrifice to Christ. **(6)** Paul knew the *"**time of his departure is come.**"* He knew his death was imminent. Time is of the essence. Work and write faster!

How stark the difference of the death of this soldier of Christ was from those Roman soldiers who slayed him. Commentator, R.C.H. Lenski's words about these "noble words" of Paul are better than mine, so I will quote them verbatim (emp. mine):

> ***Noble words!*** *The sun is setting blood-red but is shot through with **golden glory**. Indeed, so should **this great life close!** These words have left an indelible impression upon all future ages. **Socrates'** attitude toward the cup of hemlock has been admired; it is the best that paganism can offer. But how **pitifully empty** it is when it is placed besides these few **words of Christian triumph**, Christian assurance, which are looking up to the Lord, the righteous Judge, with all those who are loving his epiphany and awaiting **their crowning!*** **Lord, give me a death like this!** (R.C.H. Lenski's Commentary on Timothy, Copyright 1937, pp. 657f).

Well, said! And when you compare the final words of Paul, who was sacrificed for Christ, with the final words of Socrates, who committed suicide/self-murder, the divine everlasting glory of the death of one Christian outshines the fleeting flickers of human candlelight vigils like the Sun outshines a dying candle in the daytime. Just listen to the final words of Socrates to the jailor, named Crito, who administered the deadly dose of hemlock to him and monitored its lethal progress through his body: *"Crito, we owe a cock to Aslepius. Pay and do not neglect it"* (taken from Plato's *Phraedo*, 117e – 118a). "Asclepius" was the mythical Greek god of Medicine that Socrates wanted to thank for the drug (hemlock) that killed him ... I guess ... but who cares?

(7) Our choices for Christ should be as Paul's (I Corinthians 11:1; Philippians 4:9)! Let's continue with Paul's timely truths, and apply this "till death" goal after each one of them.

Truth Three
The Crown Comes after fighting the good fight till death

The mention of *"fighting"* over religion doesn't set too well with many people or preachers in modern churches, religions or secular societies. After all, remember, we're not supposed to "argue religion and politics." So why can't we all go along to get along ... agree to disagree ... or fondly sing and *"imagine a world without heaven, hell and religion, where the world will be one"* (*Imagine*, by Beatle, John Lennon)? After all, John Lennon did say the Beatles were more popular than Jesus. He was probably right in many segments of the secular, hippie and religious society of his day ... and maybe even worse in our day!

For it was during the heydays of the Beatles, in the 1960's, when the old "God is dead" movement of Frederick Nietzsche was resurrected by "Theologian" William Hamilton. Nietzsche was a Nineteenth Century German philosopher who repudiated the Bible, with its Creation and Morals, and advanced the rise of a super race ("Ubermensch," a superman) to control all of society. Nietzsche's "God is Dead" (German "Gott ist tot") movement influenced Adolf Hitler to practice what Nietzsche preached! And today's Atheistic, Socialistic and Evolutionary scientists and liberal preachers are preaching the same thing! And all of this proves the point I just made: many people do not like what Jesus, Paul and other Christians have to say about God our Creator, Jesus Christ our Lord and Savior, His New Testament as our moral and religious guide, heaven, hell or His conservative church!

Oh well, doesn't all of this venom and vitriol against Christianity appear to be completely ironic since the Christian religion does have the most loving Prince of Peace, God and Savior, and winsome message in existence to share with the world? Didn't angels announce Jesus' birth as being one that would bring *"good tidings of great joy which shall be to all the people ... And on earth peace, goodwill toward men"* (Luke 2:10-14, KJV)? Wasn't the appearance of the resurrected Christ so enthralling that the Apostles *"disbelieved for joy"* (Luke 24:39-41)? In other words, it seemed too good to be true. It's proof of the everlasting life for which every human longs (cf., Ecclesiastes 3:11). (It was disparaged by Karl Marx as the *"opium of the people."*) Isn't the peace that comes with trying to love our enemies, as Christ said, better than killing them (Matthew 5:44)? And didn't the Apostle Paul, the very man who just said he had *"fought the good fight,"* tell Christians to try to live at peace with all men as much as possible and to always speak the *"truth in love"* (Romans 12:18; Ephesians 4:15)? On and on we can go with this Gospel of Peace.

Besides all of these Christian contributions towards physical peace throughout the world, Christianity's spiritual contributions greatly exceed all the peaceful contributions of all other secular and religious beliefs put together. Christians refrain from all moral sins and crimes because of their love for Christ, respect for His laws, and their desire to please God rather than invite his judgment (Hebrews 11:6). Christians also put their divinely given and revealed spiritual souls, purposes in life (including sharing Christ's good news with their neighbors), promises of immortality and desire to go to heaven above their own physical needs and urges to covet, steal, seek revenge or harm their neighbors. You can't find any of these spiritual blessings and real-life incentives that promote self-restraint, love, peace, lawfulness, wellbeing and benevolence in the godless, "survival of the fittest," self-centered, purposeless and hopeless messages of atheists, evolutionists, or secular humanists—who tell people there is no God to save or judge them, and their only future is to become physical worm food and maggots' meals (see *The Supreme Scientist,* pp. 34-45).

Because of all of these positive peaceful aspects of Christianity, it is a historical fact that the Christian Religion is the greatest source and sustainer of civil peace and religious freedom on earth. For example, the U.S. Constitution guarantees our freedom of speech and religion. The Founders were all Bible believers, no atheists. And all those who signed the Constitution confessed the Lordship of Christ when they signed it on the *"Seventeenth Day of September in the **Year of our Lord** one thousand seven hundred and eighty seven."* Let's quote the most peace-promoting phrase in America's Declaration of Independence, which clearly attributes the equality and rights of all people on earth to the Creator of the Bible. *"We hold these truths to be self-evident, that **all men are created equal**, that they are **endowed by their Creator** with certain **unalienable Rights**, that among these are Life, Liberty and the pursuit of Happiness."*

As I said before, Christians are prohibited from using physical coercion, threats and actions to force people to listen to the truth about Christ and His Teachings, much less to make people accept and obey them. Christians don't pick fights with people who don't believe in what they believe, period! Christians don't hate and threaten and kill people who reject or seek to repudiate their beliefs or blaspheme their God and Savior. (A good example of this was the total absence of Christian riots when an artist, Andres Serrano', displayed a picture of the crucifix submerged in a jar of his urine!)

Christians get picked on by those in the world because amoral, atheistic, paganistic and anti-religion people don't want them to publically preach Christ and his love at all, especially if they do what Jesus did and point out the hate, evil and flaws in their godless lives and false religions (John 3:19f). That's why the Jews killed Jesus. He wasn't breaking any laws or forcing anyone to listen to him or follow him. He was a moral mirror they didn't want to have around to reflect their immorality.

Personally, I admit that I more enjoy teaching and discussing the Bible in peaceful and receptive settings, like during "Sunday School" and Sermons amongst my fellow brothers and sisters, than engaging in personal disagreements and debates with often inconsiderate, over-talking, cursing and hostile atheists, pagans and "Christian" cults. (I'll discuss more unpleasant confrontations when we look at "My Choice of Christ's Crown.")

That being said, I have to admit that it is simply not possible to always be pleasantly positive if we're going to be *"fighting"* or engaging in any spiritual *"warfare,"* as preached by Paul and practiced by Christ and all of his Apostles (see II Corinthians 10:3-6; Ephesians 6:10-17). One of the greatest Gospel Preachers I've ever had the privilege to listen to, Richard Rogers, said this about Norman Vincent Peale's all-positive philosophy: *"I find Paul appealing and Peale appalling."* I say: "I find Paul revealing (reality) and Peale concealing (it)." Or as America's Number One Broadcaster, Rush Limbaugh, often claims to be "The Mayor of Realville" and to live in "Realville," so do I also live in Realville. And things are not all roses in Realville. And sometimes you can tell how well you are doing at telling the truth by how many people hate you for doing it (Luke 6:26)!

Any fight for Christ that is allowed within Christ's Word is a part of the **good fight**: be it in defense of his Gospel (Jude 3); overcoming evil men, temptations and tribulations (Revelation 2:7,11,17,26; 3:5,12,21; 21:7); suffering persecution for preaching or practicing Christ's righteous laws and principles (John 3:20; 15:19; II Timothy 3:12); telling Christ's inspired truths about Him being the only true God, Savior, Way, Truth, Life and Church to anti-Christian zealots, political demigods (like the Caesars) and amoral and immoral near-do-wells (Galatians 4:16; II Corinthians 11:23-27; II Thessalonians 3:2). "Fight right, and fight with all your might!"

Before we move to the next timely truth, let's list some of the major "fights" that Paul was forced to engage in ... and won!

- He fought against Jewish plots against his life during his first visit as a Christian to Jerusalem (Acts 9:23-25). (He became a "basket case" in order to escape!) Before He took his second trip to Jerusalem, the Holy Spirit told him he would face more plots in every city (Acts 20:22f). But he went back any way and faced two more Jewish plots against his life (Acts 21:27ff; 23:12ff). The Lord used pagan powers to protect him!
- He fought against murderous "rock-throwing" Jews in Lystra (Acts 14:19).
- He fought against Roman Nationalists and mean magistrates, who beat him with rods and threw him in jail in Philippi (Acts 16:19ff).
- He fought against *"wild beasts"* — either real beasts or men who attacked him like savage beasts — in Ephesus and throughout Asia: so much so that he said *"we despaired even of life"* and *"had the sentence of death within ourselves"* (Acts 19:23ff; I Corinthians 15:32; II Corinthians 1:8ff).
- He fought against mutinous sailors and a shipwreck on his way to Italy (Acts 27:30ff).

So Paul preached and fought his way from Jerusalem to Rome — from town to town, village to village, country to country, jail to jail — and went through 101 battles in his blessed life for the Lord on the Road ... until he reached the end of his life under Nero's sword (II Corinthians 11:23-27; II Timothy 4:6). And not only Paul, but take a solemn look at the fate of the other Apostles.

DEATH OF THE APOSTLES AND LUKE

MATTHEW — was martyred by the sword in Ethiopia about thirty years after Christ (see Matthew 10:2f for List of Apostles).

MARK — was martyred by being dragged by a horse through the streets in Alexandria, Egypt.

LUKE — Though not an Apostle, Luke is included because he was a Gospel author, preacher, historian and partner with Paul until he died (II Timothy 4:11). Luke was hanged in Greece because of his successful preaching amongst the Gentiles.

JOHN — faced martyrdom when boiled in oil in a huge basin in Rome. He miraculously survived. Then he was sentenced to exile in the mines of Patmos by Nero or Domitian. He was freed and became a bishop in Turkey. He died naturally in Ephesus in A.D. 100, just as our Lord had foretold (John 21:21-23).

PETER — was imprisoned by Herod and miraculously released (Acts 12:3-11). He was crucified upside down in Rome under Nero, circa A.D. 64-67. Again just as Jesus foretold in John 21:18f.

ANDREW (Peter's brother) — preached in Archaia (Southern Greece) and Scythia (Ukraine, Southern Russia). He was whipped severely by seven soldiers and crucified spread-eagled on an X shaped cross. He preached all the way to the cross and upon the cross for several days. He rejoiced on the way to cross, saying: *"I have long desired and expected this happy hour. The cross has been consecrated by the body of Christ hanging on it."*

JAMES THE JUST (Son of Alpheus, Jesus' brother) — was a great church leader in Jerusalem. The Scribes and Pharisees threw him off the same 100 foot high pinnacle of the temple from which Satan asked Jesus to jump, for refusing to deny the faith. He survived, and they stoned him and then beat his brains out with a fullers club (see Matthew 13:55; Mark 6:3; Acts 12:17; 15:13; 21:18).

JAMES THE GREATER (Son of Zebedee, John's brother) — was beheaded in Jerusalem, A.D. 44, for refusing to recant (Acts 12:1f). The Roman officer, who watched his faith at his trial and walked to the place of execution with him, chose to declare his faith and die with him.

PHILIP — Preacher in Turkey, Phrygia, martyred in Hieropolis.

BARTHOLOMEW (Nathanael, John 1:45) — preached in Armenia (Turkey, Iraq, Iran), Egypt, Arabia, Ethiopia. He was flayed by a whip, then beheaded or crucified near the Caspian Sea.

THOMAS DIDYMUS ("Doubting") — preached in Parthia (Iraq and Iran) and Southern India. He was speared in India near

Madras on the East Coast of what is now "Mount St. Thomas."

THADDEUS — (Judas) brother of Jesus (Luke 6:16). He was shot with arrows for refusing to recant in Syria/Persia.

SIMON THE CANANEAN (Zealot) — No information on his death.

JUDAS ISCARIOT — hung himself for betraying Christ, not for denying Christ was God (Matthew 27:5; Acts 1:16-20).

MATTHIAS — replaced Judas as an Apostle in order to retain the "Twelve Apostles" (Acts 1:21-26). Paul confirmed Matthias' Apostleship amongst the "Twelve" in I Corinthians 15:5. Though we may assume Matthias was present with the "Twelve Apostles" in Acts 6:2, as well as in other places where the "Apostles" are mentioned, he was never mentioned by name after Acts 1:26. Since the history of his travels, ministry, persecution and martyrdom (stoned by Jews, then beheaded) are varied, we leave it at his being faithful till he was martyred. (Note: Most accounts of the Apostles' deaths are "varied" because they are derived from uninspired religious historians and traditions.)

We learn from the all of these mission efforts and martyrdoms that the Apostles didn't understand Jesus' Great Commission to only be something that they were to tell others to do, but something they should seek to do themselves. And if you look at all the mission fields where they preached and were martyred, you will see how true Paul's words — *"their words unto the ends of the world"* — were (Romans 10:18).

We can see how their refusal to recant their eye-witnessed testimonies of the resurrected Christ and deny their faith, even in the face of death, offers even more proof of the historical reality of the event. The Gestapo agents of Hitler — like Himmler, Goebbels, Eichmann — who thought he was a god of sorts, ran for their lives after Hitler committed suicide, hid their identity, told no one about their great leader and savior, and did not want to die for their belief in him. Most people put their lives above a dead god!

We are saved by the blood of Christ and built upon the blood of his Apostles. And since the Apostles never quit the fight because of the fright, nor should we. We must not be like Neville Chamberlain, who gained a bad reputation for seeking to appease Adolf Hitler before the War broke out; but like Winston Churchill, who once said to young students at their commencement at his old Alma mater, Harrow School: *"Never! Never! Never Give In!"*

Four more Learning Points: **(1)** We learn that Christians are not spiritual pacifists. We are to lovingly and aggressively preach the Gospel — *"with little or much persuasion"* — to every person who chooses to listen to us (Acts 26:29). **(2)** We Christians are not physical activists who are willing to resort to any kind of coercive or violent tactics to force people to become Christians. **(3)** We know, as did Paul, that preaching the loving and peaceful Gospel of Peace will often invite violent reactions from those who don't accept Christ's deity or demands. Jesus revealed this negative fact about preaching the truth in this world to all of his Apostles (John 15:19-21). And He revealed it to Paul at the beginning of his ministry and during his travels around the world (Acts 9:16; 20:23). **(4)** Since Jesus was persecuted and killed because of his preaching about his deity and world-wide kingdom, and knew and revealed that such would befall others who do likewise, Jesus would be the most malicious and greatest fraud of all time IF he wasn't who He said He WAS: God! This means no one can say Jesus was a "good man," if he then says "but he wasn't, and isn't, God." You can't be for Jesus on one hand and against him on the other. It's All Jesus or No Jesus! It's Sovereign Jesus or Solitary You (Matthew 12:30; also John 8:24, 58f; see "Why Jesus was Killed" in my *Killing Jesus* book)!

Truth Four
The Crown comes after Finishing the Course at death

Here Paul likened living the Christian life and being a Christian soul winner and soldier unto competing in a race or in the Olympic Games. He had done this before when speaking to the Christians in Corinth, who lived where the 'Isthmian' Grecian Games and races (named after the Isthmus of Corinth) took place in their public stadiums, before and after the Grecian Olympiads.

> **V. 24** *Know ye not that they that* **run in a race run all**, *but* **one receiveth the prize**? *Even so run; that ye may attain.*
> **V. 25a** *And* **every man** *that striveth in the games* **exerciseth self-control In all things.**

V. 25b *Now **they** do it to receive a **corruptible crown**; but **we an incorruptible**.*
V. 26 *I therefore **so run**, as not **uncertainly**; so **fight I**, as not **beating the air**:*
V. 27 *but **I buffet my body**, and bring it into bondage: lest by any means, after that I have **preached** to others, **I myself** should be **rejected*** (I Corinthians 9:24-27; cf., Ephesians 6:10-18; II Timothy 2:4-5).

Herein Paul compared all the similarities and differences between competing in the physical games and competing in spiritual games: from the runners, to the prizes, to the preparation and discipline required, to finishing the race and receiving the reward. There are **Five Lessons** to be gleaned from comparing our reception of the victor's crown at the end of the Christian Race with those who finish major races in the world's sports' arenas.

Lesson One: Verse 24 — We all run in the Spiritual Race for One Prize. Most serious and dedicated people like to excel in their chosen professions, pursuits and careers. Most don't plan to fail or delight in losing. This is especially true in professional sports or national Olympics. But the greatest, longest, most famous, powerful and successful life in the secular world or heathen arena doesn't compare with the lowest, shortest, simple life in Christ's spiritual kingdom. Consider "Dorcas," primarily known for her *"good works and almsdeeds"* in a little seaport town called Joppa (Acts 9:36-42). The fact that I and millions of other average Christian people know her name almost two thousand years later, when hardly a soul knows the name of a single contestant who won any great event in the Grecian Olympics then, or a hundred years ago, shows you how great being in Christ's Church and Christian Race is. There's no greater life to live than the Christian Life because it brings heaven into our earthly existence: our Christ is from heaven and in heaven; our message is from heaven, our goal is heaven and our prize is in heaven.

Because of our Preeminent Prince, Profession and Pursuit, each Christian should run the Christian race with all he's got to give and with the intent and intensity of coming in first place to win the only prize. (And, as we'll soon see, there is only One Prize!) He should seek to be perfect and seek Christ's kingdom first (Matthew

5:48; 6:33). Paul expressed this in Philippians 3:8f as per his preaching profession, and he said we Christians should do everything in our lives for Christ: *"And whatsoever ye do, in word or in deed,* ***do all in the name of our Lord Jesus****, giving thanks to God the Father through him"* (Colossians 3:17). So in the sense of giving our **all** to the Christian Race, it is similar to the Olympic Races of Life.

But, unlike worldly races, we don't have to reach the finish line first in time in order to receive but one prize for one winner. We all receive the **"first-place prize"** when we finish the Christian race! There are no second, third or lesser place finishes and rewards, because it is Christ's imputed righteousness that makes every contender qualified to enter, run, finish the race and receive His *"crown of righteousness."* Christ is our righteousness, and his victory over death is our victory over death (I Corinthians 1:30; 15:57). Sinners go to hell because they earned the *"wages of sin"* (Romans 6:23). Sinners don't ever get to go to heaven because they worked their sin debt off. But Saved Sinners go to heaven because they sought Christ's free forgiveness (Matthew 18:21-35). Christian's aren't perfect; they are perfected by the perfect law of liberty (James 1:25: 2:12). Lost sinners are infected. They need the Great Physician's blood to cleanse their sins and perfect their souls. Then they, as all of us saved and sanctified sinners, will receive the "Crown of Righteousness" that no sinner deserves or can earn by keeping some of God's law (Luke 17:10; 18:9-14; 23:41; Romans 3:9-28; Galatians 3:10).

Lesson Two: Verse 25a — We all must Train and Discipline for the Race. We spiritual Olympians must prepare our physical and spiritual beings in order to run and finish the race and win the prize. Paul pointed out how the reception of our reward at the end of this race is predicated upon our ***"exercising self-control in all things"*** and beating (***"buffet"***) our body into ***"bondage"*** or submission to our spirit (v. 27). In Romans 8:12f, he said we need to *"put to death the deeds of the body."* No one said discipline would be easy! Bethany Hamilton, a Hawaiian surfer who lost her entire left arm in a shark attack in 2003, was told any return to surfing wouldn't be easy. She replied: *"I don't need easy. I just need possible."* And she did return and excelled in the sport with one arm! Being an old surfer myself — who quit surfing after almost thirty years just because another guy was seriously bitten by a large Tiger Shark shortly before I went out at the Honoli'i surf spot in Hilo — I have a lot of respect for this lady's courage. Isn't it amazing how so many people are willing to endure such physical challenges and face such deadly risks for <u>what</u> they love? Can we do less for Jesus, <u>whom</u> we love more than our own lives?

Now Paul also needed to point out the need for Christian discipline of the body then, just as we need to today, because many of the Corinthians were prone to turning Christian Liberty and freedom from sin into a License to sin. The Grecian games were fraught with paganism, drunkenness and debauchery. Just as many or our "Star Athletes" (like Wilt Chamberlain and Tiger Woods) are drawn off into licentious lifestyles. So much so that sometimes it seems like many professional athletes expend as much energy running after sin as they do in their sports.

In like manner, many Christian "stars" of the pulpit and media (of all brands of Christianity) are not like Moses: who eschewed Egyptian royalty and chose to *"share ill treatment with the people of God, than to enjoy the pleasures of sin for a season"* (Hebrews 11:25). Rather they are often drawn away by their own sense of self-pride and greatness and fall prey to every sort of temptation and sinful pleasure (II Timothy 3:2-9). They, too, train for their lustful lifestyles by learning how to twist scriptures to sound like they support their ungodly lifestyles (Romans 3:8; II Peter 3:16f; see my book, *Homosexuality and the Bible,* for homosexual perversions of every Bible text into support for homosexual behavior). They also plan to make *"provision for the flesh, to fulfill the lust thereof"...* and have *"a heart that deviseth wicked purposes"...* and *"feet that are swift in **running** to mischief"* (Romans 13:14; Proverbs 6:18; cf., Micah 2:1). Peter said these lawless-liberated-lustful religious "leaders" enticed and seduced other new Christians and simple-minded souls into the same sins they were committing (II Peter 2:18-22). Read it!

Now, to be fair, stronger Christians are not exempt from these fleshly temptations and Satanic threats. They're usually Satan's Number One Targets. Remember Jesus was sorely and thoroughly tempted throughout his life and even upon the cross (Matthew 4:1-11; 26:36-40; 27:46; Hebrews 4:15). That's why Paul told Timothy the Evangelist to *"flee youthful lusts,"* just like Joseph had fled Potiphar's wife's sexual advances when they progressed from verbal requests of *"lie with me"* to a physical attempt to seduce him (II Timothy 2:22; Genesis 39:7-12). Sometimes running from sin is the only "way of escape" God provides (I Corinthians 10:13). Of course, we Christians have many more divine incentives to bring our bodies into control today than Joseph had then, or people in the world have today. And the best of all is next:

Lesson Three: Verse 25b — We seek the only *"incorruptible crown."* The rewards in physical races and careers — laurel wreathes, crowns, trophies, promotions, money — at best only benefit the winners until they die. They offer no hope for a better life beyond their glory days or demise. But our crown of righteousness will benefit each one of us forever. Jesus told us:

> *Lay not up for yourselves treasures upon the earth, where moth and rust consume, and where thieves break through and steal: **but lay up for yourselves treasures in heaven**, where neither moth or rust doth consume, and where thieves do not break through nor steal* (Matthew 6:19f).

That verse needs no explanation or verification. For we Christians know our greatest achievement and goal in life is not to look at a room full of trophies with our names inscribed upon them, but to reach heaven at the end of our life and see our names listed in the book of life. Jesus told his Apostles not to rejoice in their Spirit endowed miraculous powers, but rather to *"rejoice that your names are written in heaven"* (Luke 10:19f). He said this to His church members then and in perpetuity:

> ***He that overcometh*** *shall be thus arrayed in **white garments**: and I will in no wise blot his **name** out of the **book of life**, and I will confess his name before my Father, and before his angels. He that hath an ear, **let him hear** what the **Spirit saith to the churches*** (Revelation 3:5f; cf. 13:8; 17:8, 20:12, 15; 21:27). {Only Christ's churches can ***hear*** that!}

By way of illustration, I will now joyfully relate my visit to the World Golf Hall of Fame in St. Augustine, Florida. My wife and I walked around for several hours looking at all of the trophies, equipment and memorabilia of all the golfing greats over the past century: like Sam Snead, Ben Hogan, Jack Nicklaus, Arnold Palmer, Gary Player, et al. I was amazed that I had actually been on the course, as a marshal or spectator, in tournaments with many of these legends of golf. My wife was also on the course with them and got Arnold's autograph at his last tournament in Hawaii. (Arnold was our favorite older player. But in recent years, we also liked to walk with Freddie Couples, Davis Love, Ernie Els, Michele Wie and, especially, Tiger Woods.) Ironically, while in the Hall of Fame, I must admit that I was becoming more depressed as we went from each great player's exhibit to the other. That was caused by the fact that each one reminded me of the same thing: the vanity and futility of spending your life to acquire such fleeting fame and tarnished trophies. (Like old "laurel wreaths.")

But that depression soon gave way to joy when I reached the last exhibit of the day, Byron Nelson's Exhibit. Like the other great players, Byron was one of the greatest golfers of all time, and his record of winning eleven tournaments in a row and eighteen in one year (1945) still stands. But Byron was also a true and proud Christian. And the inscription that I saw written on top of his exhibit made the entire daylong trip and tour worthwhile. For Byron said that the greatest day in his life was when he was baptized and became a Christian. So Byron knew that all the corruptible trophies he won by playing well on the golf course did not compare with the incorruptible trophy/crown he was going to receive when he finished well on the greatest *"course"* that the Apostle Paul finished at the end of his life (II Timothy 4:7). And Byron once said this about his blessed life: *"I've been more blessed than anybody I know in golf."* "You're the man, Byron!"

Lesson Four: Verse 26 — We must run with complete confidence. We have confidence that, with Christ's help, we can and will finish this race and receive our reward. We don't run *"uncertainly"* in doubt about our ability to finish the Christian race as long as we are willing to run with Christ's help. Nor do we ever doubt that the reward is worth all the effort and risk. We are not just *"beating* {boxing} *the air"* and *"striving after the wind"* in vain physical pursuits, careers and races outside of Christ, where the physical effort and exercise are not profitable if not connected to our growth in godliness (Ecclesiastes 1:14; I Timothy 4:8).

We Christians have help in every one of our weaknesses or areas wherein we stumble, sin and fall short of perfection (I Corinthians 10:13). Even if all of our evangelistic converts fail to finish the race, and our efforts seem in vain, we still get credit for being faithful in trying to save some (I Cor. 3:14f; 9:22; Galatians 2:2). Because of that, we never lose our incentive and resolve to finish the race, knowing that every day our goal of *"salvation is nearer than when we first believed"* (Romans 13:11). As I grow older in the faith, I'm amazed at how much my optimism about finishing the Christian race has grown since that first night after my baptism in Bermuda when I told my wife: "I don't think I can do this!" Now I ask her: "Can you believe we've been Christians for over fifty years?" We're both still in the Christian Race!

Lesson Five: Verse 27 — We know we can't lose unless we cheat or quit. So Paul concluded this discourse by pointing out how he could fail to complete the race and receive his eternal reward if he didn't *"buffet my body, and bring it into bondage: lest by any means, after that I have preached to others, I myself should be rejected."* Just as many athletes don't finish races because they violate the rules or quit, we also can fail to finish the Christian race if we choose to leave Christ's Word or quit. The only person who can *"separate us from the love Christ"* is not mentioned in Romans 8:35-39 ... which is "you" and "I." It is up to each one of us "Sovereign Souls" to finish the race. There are a number of ways we can allow ourselves to be duped or drawn away from Christ before we lawfully finish the Christian Race.

1. We can be lost if we fail to follow Christ's rules. Just as it is crucially important that we complete the entire Christian Race — from Start to Finish — by beginning at the Starting Line by believing and obeying the essentials Gospel tenants to get through the only door into Christ's church, it is equally important that we remain faithful to all of Christ's Words and Rules of the Christian Race until we cross the Finish Line at our death. Paul put it this way: *"And if also a **man contend in the games**, he is **not crowned**, **except** he have **contended lawfully**"* (II Timothy 2:5). So it is up to each one of us "Sovereign Souls" to be "Sovereign Students" of Christ's Word/Rules, prove our faith, and not surrender our own intelligence and faith to others who don't know or obey the rules.

2. We can be lost if we listen to false teachers. If we don't maintain our vigilance and determination not to surrender our faith to others, as just presented, we will become more prone to allow false teachers to steal our faith from us. Just as there were false "Christian" teachers in the first century, there are false "Christian" teachers today. Just as these false teachers were able to keep people from becoming, or remaining, true believers in Christ and true members in his church then, so we have false teachers who do the same now. And, believe it or not, the false teachings they used then are the same ones they're using today. They just use modern or "progressive" terminology and religious clichés to disguise their anti-Christ/Christian teachings (instead of the old "Legalism, Gnosticism, Docetism, Arianism") and big church names, national organizations, personal titles, media productions and books to capture and captivate their converts. I will only list a few of the false teachers and teachings that have drawn away true Christians from their saving faith.

Legalism: Legalism is a false teaching which leads many Christians away from "faith working through love" to doing meritorious works to earn salvation. It has caused many Christians to either give up trying to live the perfect Christian life to be saved, and others to "feel" like they have done enough to earn some early earthly retirement from actively pursuing their faith and receiving their eternal reward. This menace is present inside the Lord's true church and many denominations, including the RCC, which has its members counting beads, saying Rosaries and doing the "Lent" thing every year to work off their wickedness for the past year or their latest celebration of Fasching or Mardi Gras.

We must maintain an attitude of gratitude and remember that all of our works are "works of faith" that prove our faith in & love for Christ and not our own quest for self-righteousness (James 2:18). There are NO acts of obedience or service — like repentance, baptism, commandment-keeping, acts of worship, evangelism, visiting the sick, etc. — that are meritorious, period (See "Faith Contains Obedience Passages" in my Baptism book, pp. 149-152).

Eternal Security: This false teaching is also called "Once Saved Always Saved," and it is similar to other self-righteous teachings like "Entire Sanctification," that teach that the person arrives at such a safe and holy status that he either doesn't sin or is in no danger of falling away because of his sin. They both create a sense of "False Security" that actually threatens their Eternal Security. All such teachings contradict the true teaching of the New Testament concerning our continuous need to fight against sin, repent and confess the sins we commit and be aware that there are sins we commit that we might not even know about. John was clear when he said: *"**If** we say **we** have **no sin**, we deceive ourselves, and the truth is not in us. **If we confess our sins**, he is faithful and righteous to forgive us of our sins, and to cleanse us from all unrighteousness. If we say that **we have not sinned**, we make him a liar, and his word is not in us"* (I John 1:8-10; see vv. 6-7 for Christ's continuous cleansing of our sins).

Also, these "False Security" teachings also contradict Paul's words in the Christian Race text we're discussing, wherein he stressed that he still had to *"buffet my body, and bring it into to bondage ... lest ... **I myself should be rejected**."* Paul also stressed over and over again in his writings that true Christians can fall away from the faith and be lost. Let's look at one that proves a true Christian can be led away from the truth by listening to false teachers.

> *Yea, I testify again to every man that receiveth circumcision, that he is a debtor to do the whole law. **Ye are severed from Christ**, ye who would be justified by the law; **ye are fallen away from grace**. For we through the Spirit by faith wait for the hope of righteousness. For in Christ Jesus neither circumcision availeth anything, nor uncircumcision; but **faith working** through love. **Ye were running well**; **who hindered you** that ye should **not obey the truth*** (Galatians 5:3-7)?

Notice the following facts: **(1)** These Galatians were Christians who had been ***"running well."*** You can't be running the Christian race/course at all if you never became a Christian in the first place. Plus, they were running it long enough for Paul to know they were *"running well,"* or according to the truth. **(2)** They had allowed someone to *"hinder"* them, and stop them from continuing to ***"obey the truth,"*** i.e., from continuing the race to the end as had

Paul. **(3)** The results of their lapse of progress in the race were *"ye are severed from Christ"* and *"ye are fallen away from grace."* This sure sounds like the Galatian Christians were fully saved and in danger of becoming fully lost. This sure looks like a total refutation of the false "Once Saved Always Saved" teaching.

For your later research on this critical issue, I offer you the following texts that prove any truly saved Christian can fall away from the truth, grace and Christ and be lost eternally if he/she does not repent before death.

- See Matthew 13:18-23 and Luke 8:9-15 for the "Parable of the Sower" where many accepted the truth and then fell away.
- See Matthew 26:24 with Acts 1:16-20 for Judas' Apostasy.
- See Luke 9:62 for putting the hand to plow and looking back.
- See I Corinthians 8:11 for causing a *"brother to perish."*
- See I Cor. 9:27 for the possibility of Paul being lost.
- See I Cor. 10:12 for one that standeth taking heed lest he fall.
- See I Cor. 15:1f for true believers falling away.
- See Galatians 1:6-9; 5:3-7 for Christian preachers and Jews falling away.
- See Colossians 1:21-23 for those reconciled to God having to *"continue in the faith"* and not be moved away from its hope.
- See Hebrews 6:4-8 where Jewish Christians, who saw miracles and received the Holy Spirit (Acts 2:38), being warned about falling away (see also 10:23f).
- See James 1:21-25 where it is only those who have received the *"implanted word"* and *"continue"* to be *"doers"* of the *"perfect law of liberty"* who will save their souls.
- II Peter 2:20f – Last state of apostates worse than before saved.
- II John 8f – Warning not to lose their reward by leaving word.

After telling his brethren they had *"obtained a like precious faith with us,"* and were becoming *"partakers of the divine nature,"* Peter told them to add all the Christian graces so they would be fruitful (II Peter 1:1-8). Then he added the following warning, admonition and promise in verses 9-11...

*For **he that lacketh these things** is blind, seeing only what is near, **having forgotten the cleansing from his old sins**.*

*Wherefore, **brethren**, give the more diligence to make your **calling and election sure**: for **if ye do these things**, ye will never stumble: for **thus** shall be richly supplied unto you the **entrance into the eternal kingdom** of our Lord and Saviour Jesus Christ.*

There's just no way any person can deny that this text proves you can be forgiven of your *"old sins,"* be one of Christ's *"brethren,"* be one who answered the Gospel *"calling,"* and became one of the *"election"* in Christ's spiritual kingdom ... and still only enter into the *"eternal kingdom"* {heaven} of our Lord *"if"* you continue to *"do these things"* that the Lord commanded, and continue to grow in the Lord's grace and knowledge till death.

3. We can be lost if we change with the times. As sure as the calendar is always changing, so are the "times always changing." And God's Bible-based Religions — Judaism and Christianity — have also been changed over time. Just compare Israel's religious faith in Joshua's days with the *"new generation"* that arose after his death, and you will see how God's people went from following God's laws to doing what was evil, idolatrous and *"every man did that which was right in his own eyes"* (compare Joshua 24:14-31; Judges 2:7-17; 17:6). Then there would be a temporary revival that would be soon followed by another defection. Their religious revival-to-ruin repetition continued until the total destruction of their holy city, temple, religion and nation in A.D. 70.

Modern "Religious Progressivism" is the new cliché for a form of religious liberalism that keeps up with the changing times and updates, or modifies, its practices according to popular opinions, practices and polls. As Solomon said, it isn't anything *"new,"* it's just how people with weak faith and moral fiber find new ways to justify old sins. Just like the Athenians loved to sit around and listen and talk about *"some new thing"* (Acts 17:21). The truth is: all of this "we-must-change-with-the-times" babble is just plain old bunk, Bible rejection and Christian apostasy!

Just because "times change" doesn't mean that Christ's Word, Ways and Church must be changed to fit the latest cultural model. In my life time, "sin has been sanitized" and "deviancy has been so defined down" by the religious progressive movement, that what was sinful in times past — abortion, drunkenness, smoking pot, "shacking up," pornography, sodomy, vulgarity, ad nauseam — is now not only considered to be "the right thing to do," it is the religiously right and lawful thing to do. Isaiah's declining national religious history has been repeated many times since he warned: *"Woe unto them that call evil good, and good evil"* (Isaiah 5:20).

Instead of simply giving you a few of the worst examples of today's historical repeats of Isaiah's "religious reversals," let's go **back in time** to when some of our "Old Sins" were beginning to be called "Old Fashioned" by the youth and college professors; but still had not yet been accepted by most religious people or politically legalized and defended as the lawful thing to do.

Back to 1986 ... when I wrote my book, *Sobering Questions,* and pointed out the dangers of Christians accepting alcohol as the "Drug Du jour." Which also included warnings that alcohol would be the gateway drug through which other drugs, like Marijuana, would be legalized. You know, **back before** "Pot" was legalized in many States and Countries today! And many want all drugs legal.

Back to January, 1996 ... when a Kansas Preacher, Joe Wright, delivered this prayer before the Kansas legislature:

"Heavenly Father, we come before you today to ask Your forgiveness and to ask Your direction and guidance. We know Your Word says, ***'Woe to those who call evil good,'*** *but that is exactly what we have done. We have lost our spiritual equilibrium and* ***reversed our values****. (Emp. Mine).* ***We confess that:***
— *We have ridiculed the absolute truth of Your Word and called it Moral Pluralism.*
— *We have worshiped other gods and called it multiculturalism.*
— *We have endorsed perversion and called it alternative lifestyle.*
— *We have exploited the poor and called it lottery.*
— *We have rewarded laziness and called it welfare.*
— *We have killed the unborn and called it choice.*
— *We have shot abortionists and called it justifiable.*
— *We have neglected to discipline our children and called it building self-esteem.*
— *We have abused power and called it political.*
— *We have coveted our neighbors possessions and called it ambition.*
— *We have polluted the air with profanity and pornography and*

called it freedom of statement {speech and art}.
— *We have ridiculed the time-honored values of our forefathers and called it enlightenment.*
Search us, Oh God, and know our hearts today; cleanse us from every sin and set us free. Guide and bless these men and women who have been sent to direct us to the center of your Will, and we ask it in the name of Your son, the living Savior, Jesus Christ. Amen.

Back to June, 1996, when Judge Robert Bork released his bestselling book about America's Decline, *Slouching Towards Gomorrah*. We're now way beyond just "Slouching Towards" it!

Back to June, 1998, when Merle Haggard lamented the passing of the good ole days by singing a song entitled, "Are The Good Times Really Over?," and opined: *"I wish a buck was still silver, It was back when the country was strong.... I wish* **coke was still cola, and a joint was a bad place to be***. It was back before Nixon lied to us on TV. Before microwave ovens, when a girl could still cook and still would.... Is the Best of the free life behind us now? Are the good times really over for good?....* **Are we rolling down hill like a snowball headed for hell?** *With no kind of chance for the flag or the liberty bell?...."*

Well, what can I say? Times have changed. Back in the 1950's, "Coke" was soda pop and a "joint" was prison; but now "Coke" is our drug culture's slang for Cocaine, and a "joint" is a marijuana cigarette that millions are using to get "high" and "stoned," others are using as a sacrament in their churches (e.g., "Religion of Jesus Church" in Hawaii), others are smoking to cure all ailments, and politicians are legalizing around the world. (Just as I predicted that alcohol would be the gateway drug for the legalization of "Pot!")

Back to 1998, when I ran for Mayor in Hawaii to oppose "Homosexual marriage" and push the Marriage Amendment protecting heterosexual marriage. Which was when I wrote my book, *"Homosexuality and the Bible,"* and about how accepting sodomy as the "Deviancy Du jour" would open Pandora's box to the acceptance of "Same-sex Marriage" and all the other imaginable "sexual orientations." Over 69% of Hawaii's voters passed the Marriage Amendment and Hawaii became the first state to do so. All was well in "Paradise" then ... But:

That was **back before** America's President (Obama) showed his true colors and pushed for "gay marriage" ... which was **before** Hawaii's governor (Abercrombie) shoved it down Hawaii's throats in November, 2013 ... which was **before** the SCOTUS passed it for all fifty states in June, 2015 ... which was **before** alleged "Christian churches" lined up to perform the ceremonies ... which was **before** America Sunk lower than Sodom and silently jumped in bed with legalized Homosexual Marriage! Now all we hear from political candidates for President in 2015-16 is how *"Same-sex marriage is the law of the land,"* and they will enforce it! Yeah, and that makes it right! That means God is rejoicing over this wholesale rejection of his entire Bible by the so-called "One nation Under God!" (Where's the National Christian Outrage over this Satanic Coup d' état?)

What do all of these radical changes mean to Christians? Besides the fact that the word "marriage" is morally meaningless, and the word "gay" no longer means "happy" and has no reference to *"Don we now our gay apparel"* on the holidays, it also means if you keep the latest laws and customs of the world, or the latest "fads of faith" espoused by some so-called Christian leaders and churches, you will probably have more worldly friends and attend larger churches ... but you will be lost! And this means we must be Stalwart Sovereign Souls and Scriptural Students who will not allow ourselves to be swayed like little children by these doctrinal "winds of change" or give any welcome, place or quarter to false teachers (Ephesians 4:13-14; II John 10f)! I rest my case on this point!

4. We can be lost if we lose patience. Some start their Christian life like a house on fire, patiently run for a while, and then *"lose their first love"* and "burn out" (Revelation 2:2-4). They become weary of their personal burdens of care, limitations, slow spiritual growth or continued temptations to sin, and choose to quit. They need to read and heed the words of James:

> *Count it all joy, my brethren, when ye fall into* ***manifold temptations;*** *knowing that the* ***proving of your faith worketh patience*** *{stedfastness, perseverance}. And* ***let patience have its perfect work****, that ye* ***may be perfect*** *and entire, lacking in nothing* (James 1:2-4).

Others add, to these personal feelings of inadequacy, their frustrations over their lack of success at converting others or even at the lack of fire or growth they see in their congregations. They fret at this, worry at that, and throw up their hands and quit. They've forgotten who they work **with** and Who they work **for**. The Hebrews writer highlights both of these oversights in an effort to light a fire under those who were in the process of losing faith.

> *Therefore let us also, seeing we are **compassed about** with so great a **cloud of witnesses**, **lay aside every weight, and the sin** that doth so easily beset us, and let us **run with patience the race** that is set before us, **looking unto Jesus** the **author** and **perfecter** of our faith...* (Hebrews 12:1-2a).

Notice we Christians are not only **working with** all of God's chosen people and citizens in His universal church/kingdom today, we are also historically and biblically working with — *"compassed about"* — the alumni of all of God's great successful people of faith since the beginning of time (Hebrews 11:4-40). This does not mean the departed saints are looking down upon us from heaven; this means we are looking at the biblical record of their faithfulness as a great cloud of witness overhead. I can't imagine leaving these present and past Spiritual Champions in the Greatest Race towards the Greatest Crown to be with any other group of people, regardless of who they are or what great things in which they claim to be involved.

Notice that one reason Christians lose patience in their ability to finish the Christian race is they do not *"lay aside every weight, and the sin that so easily beset us."* It is a lot easier to continue to *"run with patience* {perseverance} *the race set before us"* if we don't try to carry all of our emotional baggage and sins on our backs. Jesus asked us to give all of those burdens to him (Matthew 11:28f). Peter said: *"casting all your anxiety upon him, for he careth for you"* (I Peter 5:7). So we must not forget **who we work for** when we run the Christian Race. Then, as we discussed earlier at **Verse 26,** our knowing that Jesus is going to help us every step of the way frees us to run free, unencumbered, unburdened and unfettered by our failures, faults and fears. So when we're about to lose our grip on Christian Certainty and come apart, it's time to come apart and spend some time with Jesus in prayer. A few words of poetic wisdom from brother Jack Exum and Mary Stephenson might help illustrate this point further.

We mutter, we sputter, We fume and we spurt; We mumble and grumble, Our feelings get hurt. We can't understand it, Our vision grows dim; **When all that we need, Is a moment with Him** (Jack Exum, *This Will Kill You,* p.16).

"The Weaver"

Behind our life the Weaver stands, And works his wondrous will. We leave it in His all wise hands, And trust his perfect skill.

Should mystery enshroud his plan, And our short sight be dim, We will not try the whole to scan, But leave each thread to him.

The threads our hands in blindness spin, No self-determined plan weaves in, The shuttle of the unseen power Works out a power not as ours.

Not 'till the loom is silent, And the shuttles cease to fly; Shall God unfold the pattern, And explain the reason why.

The dark threads were as useful, In the weaver's skillful hands, As the threads of gold and silver, For the pattern which he planned (Exum, *How to Win Souls Today,* p. 115).

"Footprints in the Sand"

One night I was walking along the beach with the Lord. Many scenes from my life flashed across the sky. In each scene I noticed footprints in the sand. Sometimes there were two sets of footprints, other times there was only one.

This bothered me because I noticed that during the low periods of my life, when I was suffering from anguish, sorrow or defeat, I could see only one set of footprints.

So I said to the Lord, 'You promised me Lord, that if I followed you, you would walk with me always. But I have noticed that during the most trying periods of my life there has only been one set of footprints in the sand. Why, when I needed you most, have you not been there for me?'

The Lord replied, 'The years when you have seen only one set of footprints, my child, is when I carried you' (Mary Stephenson).

5. We can be lost if we lose focus. In athletic races the runners must keep their minds and eyes focused on getting to the finish line and not just thinking about the prize. In our race for the heavenly prize, we must not take our minds or eyes off the person who is going to get us to the finish line, **Jesus Christ**. We must never forget that Jesus didn't take his eyes off of Us and our redemption when he was nearing the end of his last day before his death. Continuing with Hebrew 12:2b, we read: *"looking to Jesus the author and perfecter of our faith, who for the **joy that was set before him** {the joy of saving us from our sins via his blood and finishing his march to the throne} endured the cross, despising the shame, and hath set down at the right hand of the throne of God."*

Because Jesus' living/dying example is ever before us, we can live the Christian life until the very end. Because of Jesus' declaration of **"Victory"** just before his last breath — shouting "Tetelestai," meaning *"It is finished, I have reached the goal!"* (not "I am finished") — we can die the victorious Christian death and not the vanquished Christian death (see John 19:30; *Killing Jesus,* pp. 111-113). Christianity is the only religion where dying faithful — whether of old age like the Apostle John or young age like James the brother of John — is the ultimate incentive, achievement and victory in life.

> *But when this corruptible shall have put on incorruption. and this mortal shall have put on immortality, then shall come to pass the saying that is written, **Death is swallowed up in victory.** O death, where is thy victory? O death, where is thy sting? The sting of death is sin; and the power of sin is the law; but **thanks be to God**, who giveth us the **victory through our Lord Jesus Christ**. Wherefore, my beloved brethren, be ye **stedfast, unmovable, always abounding in the work of the Lord**, forasmuch as ye know that **your labor is not vain in the Lord*** (I Corinthians 15:54-58). {Your labor and life outside the Lord is in vain!}

Victory in Jesus
I heard and old, old story, How a Savior came from glory,
How He gave his life on Calvary To save a wretch like me;
I heard about his groaning, Of his precious blood's atoning,

*Then I repented of my sins And won the **vic-to-ry**.*
Chorus: *O **victory** in Jesus, My Savior, forever, He sought me and bo't me with His redeeming blood; He loved me ere I knew Him, and all my love is due Him, He plunged me to **victory**, beneath the cleansing flood* (E. M. Bartlett).

Truth Five
The Crown comes after Keeping the Faith

Notice that Paul said he had **"kept <u>the</u> faith"** and not "his faith" as its author, nor "<u>a</u> faith" or "another faith" amongst the many other faiths in his day. Earlier in his ministry, He said *"there is <u>one</u> faith"* (Ephesians 4:5). It was this faith that Paul taught in every church (I Corinthians 4:17; 7:17). It was this *"pattern of sound words"* that he told Timothy to *"guard"* (II Timothy 1:13f). And then he told Timothy why he needed to guard it: which would be the rise of false teachers (3:1-13). Then he told him that only the inspired scriptures from God would enable him to repudiate and correct such false teachings and be a complete Christian *"man of God"* (3:14-17, which text we discussed in the previous chapter). So there is no doubt that Paul is referring to the complete Gospel and New Testament body of truth that was being delivered to the saints by all the Apostles, including Paul, once for all people and all time (Jude 3).

As far as the <u>Gospel Faith</u> is concerned, Paul preached every historical fact of the life of Christ: from His obedient and sinless life through His death, burial, resurrection, ascension to His throne, reign over His church/kingdom and our resurrection at the last day. As far as Christ's <u>Teachings in the Faith</u>, Paul taught every one of them: from the obedient faith, one faith, false faith, acts of faith (repentance, confession, baptism); doing good works, true worship acts like the Lord's Supper, giving, singing, praying, preaching, sacrificial living (Acts 20:7; Romans 12:1f; I Corinthians 11:20ff; 16:1ff; Ephesians 5:19); as well as all the offices in the church. On and on and on Paul **"kept the faith"** by delivering it, preaching it, practicing it, and most of all, defending it from false faiths.

Paul never told any Christians they had to keep any religious tenent of any other faith. Though he did teach and practice respecting <u>some</u> physical tenants and traditions of other religions that did not conflict with Christian liberty, as he demonstrated when he circumcised Timothy (Acts 16:3; I Corinthians 9:19-23); he also revealed to us by his teachings and actions, in refusing to circumcise Titus when the Christian Judaizers made it a test of faith, that Christians cannot accept or practice any teaching of any other "religious faith" that is imposed upon them if it in any way contravenes or contradicts any Christian liberty or law of Christ (Galatians 2:3-5).

Of course, Christians should never express any acceptance of any false religion or its false gods, saviors, prophets, teachers or teachings that repudiate Christ or any of his New Testament teachings. Why not? **First,** because Christ is our absolute *"authority"* and *"one Lawgiver"* (Matthew 28:18; James 4:12). **Second,** because we're *"under law to Christ"* and no one else (I Corinthians 9:21). Christ's New Testament regulates our lives and speech, period! **Third,** because Christ's New Testament condemns false religions, religious teachings, teachers and believers as being as sinful and lost as all other sinners. False religions are responsible for as much chaos and sinful, murderous practices as atheism, e.g., Islamic Jihad! **Fourth,** sinners are lost because their sins — moral or religious — are not forgiven by or within their Christless and lawless religions (Romans 3:9-23). **Fifth,** because Christ will be the judge of all men by his New Testament (John 5:22, 27; 12:48; Acts 10:42; 17:31; Romans 2:16; II Timothy 4:1). **Sixth,** because Christ charged Christians not to be a stumbling block to Christians or sinners by engaging in false, or even questionable, religious practices (Romans 14:1-23; I Corinthians 8:1-13; James 4:15-17). **Seventh,** because Christians love all people, regardless of their social or religious sins, and have chosen to accept Christ's Great Commission to seek and save all the lost in the world (Matthew 28:18-20). And that means we must try to capture them from the grasp of Satan, whether they're sinful atheists, hedonists, pagans, Muslims, Buddhists, Hindus, Jews, Cult Members, Protestants, Catholics, false "churches of Christ" and erring members of the true church of Christ:

> *But **ye, beloved, remember ye the words** which have been **spoken before by the apostles** of our Lord Jesus Christ; that they said to you, In the last time there shall be mockers,*

walking after their own ungodly lusts. These are they who make separations, sensual, having not the Spirit. But ye, beloved, **building up yourselves on your most holy faith**, *praying in the Holy Spirit, keep yourselves in the love of God, looking for the mercy of our Lord Jesus Christ unto eternal life. And on* **some have mercy**, *who are in doubt, and* **some save, snatching them out of the fire**; *and on* **some have mercy with fear**, *hating even the garment spotted by the flesh. Now unto* **him that is able to guard you from stumbling; and to set you before the presence of his glory without blemish** *in exceeding joy, to the only God our Saviour, through* **Jesus Christ our Lord, be glory, majesty, dominion and power, before all time, and now, and for evermore.** *Amen* (Jude 17-25).

Amen to you, Brother Jude! There's only one *"most holy faith"* whereby all sinners must be saved until the end of time. So, once again and finally, this Pauline prerequisite is like unto the previous one about his "finishing the course," and it means we, like Paul, must remain faithful to all of Christ's Word about himself, his church and teachings until we die: *"Be thou **faithful unto death**, and I will give thee the **crown of life**"* (Revelation 2:10).

How do we know the faith we believe and are keeping is the *"One Faith"* that was delivered in the first century, the one that Paul had kept and defended till his death, and that Timothy was to guard with his life? Here are **Four Ways** the first Christians did it and were told to continue doing it.

Read the Scriptures

In the first century, Christians were told to read and share the Apostolic Epistles that were being spread amongst the churches the Apostles had founded, visited or written (Galatians 1:6-11; 6:11; Ephesians 3:3; Colossians 4:16; I Thessalonians 5:27; Hebrews 13:22f; James 1:21f; II Peter 3:15f; I John 1·1-3; 2:12-14; 4:1,6; 5:13; II John 7 12; III John 9f, 13; Jude 3, 17. If you will take some time and read these quotes, you will see that the Apostles not only told them that they had received the essential gospel truths and all "the faith" in their epistles/letters (which became our New Testament books), they could also understand them alike and would be able to identify any of the false apostles and prophets that were seeking to overthrow the Lord's Apostles and their writings. A few quotes from the above will suffice.

> *For this cause I Paul, the prisoner of Christ Jesus in behalf of you Gentiles, if so be that **ye have heard** of the dispensation of that grace of God which was given me to you-ward; how that by **revelation** was made known unto me **the mystery, as I wrote** before in **few words**, whereby, when ye read, ye can perceive my understanding in the mystery of Christ; which in other generations was not made known unto the sons of men, as it hath **now been revealed** unto his holy **apostles and prophets** in the Spirit* (Ephesians 3:1-5).

> *I marvel that ye are so quickly **removing from him that called** you in the grace of Christ unto **a different gospel**; which is **not another gospel**: only there are some that trouble you, and would **pervert the gospel** of Christ. But though we {Apostles}, or **an angel** from heaven, should preach unto **any gospel** other than that which we preached unto you, let him be **anathema*** (Galatians 1:6-8).

> *These things have I **written** unto you, that ye may **know** that ye have **eternal life**, even unto you that believe on the name of the Son God.... For many **deceivers** are gone forth into the world, even they that confess not that Jesus Christ cometh in the flesh. This is the **deceiver and the antichrist**.... Whosoever goeth onward and **abideth not in the teaching of Christ**, hath not God: he that **abideth in the teaching**, the same hath both the Father and the Son. **If any one** cometh unto you, and **bringeth not this teaching, receive him not** into your house, and give him no greeting: for he that giveth him greeting partaketh in his evil works* (I John 5:13;   II John 7, 9-11).

So we Christians today can, in like manner, simply by reading the words of the Apostles, understand the original words of the *"mystery of Christ,"* the true Gospel, and all the teachings of Christ that will give us eternal life. And we can base all of our beliefs and practices upon them and know we are doing what Christ authorized us to do. We cannot keep the faith if we do not know the faith! We cannot keep the faith the Apostle Paul delivered and kept if we're keeping the faith of any later prophet, priest, preacher, religion or church. There was only one true faith and one true church then ... and will be until the end of time. Jesus said so! (Remember to read with an open mind and open heart!)

Plus, we can also use the Apostles' words and arguments to identify and correct or repudiate false faiths, teachers and teachings. You can simply write down the names, words, practices and teachings of any preacher, teacher or church and see if you can find them in the New Testament. If you can find them listed and approved in the New Testament, you know they're right. If you can't, you know they're wrong. For example, you can write down the words "Methodist/Mormon/Baptist/Roman Catholic Churches, Popes, Cardinals, Reverends, Infant Baptism, Same-sex Marriage, etc.," and then read every word of Christ's New Testament, and you will not find a single one of those words or phrases mentioned or discussed, much less being authorized. It is really that easy. And it is even easier if you have a Strong's Exhaustive Bible Concordance and can look for the specific words there. You will be able to easily find the smallest church of Philadelphia praised, the widows "mites" and Jesus getting a "piece of money" from the mouth of a "fish." But you won't be able to find the names or words identifying today's largest church and leader! You won't find a single Apostle saying he was Catholic, much less a Roman Catholic. You won't find a single evangelist or preacher calling himself or another leader "Reverend So and So." Would you call all of this Scriptural Inability to find or read your beliefs, or any religious denomination's "facts of faith," within the pages of the entire New Testament a lack of ability to "*prove your* {their} *own faith,*" which the Scriptures also require?

There are ways to enhance your reading of the Scriptures. A few pointers: Follow the Three R's of Scriptural Education: "Repetition, Redundancy and Reiteration." Read them out loud. Recite them over and over. Memorize them the old fashioned way: by rote repetition. (It is easier to memorize the King James Version and American Standard Version because they have a poetic flow that modern English versions don't have.) Recall them and their location on demand. Teach them. Preach them. Write about them. Declare them. Debate them. Live them!

Rightly Divide the Scriptures

*Give diligence {"study" in KJV} to present thyself **approved** unto God, a **workman** that needeth not to be ashamed, **handling aright the word of truth*** (II Timothy 2:15).

Paul wrote this charge to Timothy to encourage him to take the work of an evangelist very seriously and guard and transmit the *"same"* Gospel teachings Paul had bequeathed unto him to faithful men, who would teach others that same gospel also (II Timothy 1:13f; 2:2; cf. I Corinthians 4:17). This mantle of responsibility falls upon the shoulders of every person or preacher who would share Christ's word with others. Maybe we Christians should put a label on the cover of our Bible: "Handle With Care." It is not our word to manhandle. It is God's word that we must always *"handle aright."* That's what Paul said a divinely *"approved workman"* (professional) must do!

Now the Greek word that's translated as **"handling aright"** (**"rightly dividing,"** KJV) in this verse is the word *"orthotomeo,"* and it means: "to make a straight cut, to dissect or divide correctly." Timothy was told to *"**make a straight cut**"*— a clear division, separation — between inspired words and uninspired words and profane babblings (2:14, 16). Here's a list of other Bible Divisions we must recognize and rightly separate in order to be accurate students and preachers of God's Word.

Rightly Divide between Old Testament law and New Testament law. You cannot bind two different covenants (See my *Sabbatarian Concordance and Commentary*). Believe it or not, most divisions within the "Christian Religion" have come from people binding Old Testament law and practices upon Christians.

Rightly Divide between the Jewish laws, days and rites Jesus kept in Israel while he lived on the earth (as per the Gospels) from what He bound upon the World after He died and ratified His New Testament (as found in the book of Acts forward). Remember Jesus lived and died under the Old Testament law (Galatians 4:4 with Hebrews 9:15-17). Christians do not keep a single law of Israel — including circumcision, the Passover or Sabbath, etc. — because they were abolished and replaced with spiritual things in Christ's New Testament Church (Galatians 4:9f; Colossians 2:16f).

Rightly Divide between God's truths and Satan's lies. I know that saying the Bible has a good number of lies recorded in its pages comes as a shock to some people, but it is true. In fact the Bible's first book records the greatest lie of all time being told by the greatest liar of all time, Satan (compare Genesis 2:16-17 with 3:1-5; John 8:44). And the fact that it does is another proof that it is real history about good and evil and not one-sided propaganda.

Another classic Satanic lie, that is still being spread by *"men who speak lies"* about "Christ not yet being over the kingdoms of the world," is when they actually quote Satan's telling Christ he would give Him all the *"kingdoms of the world"* if he'd worship him (Matthew 4:8f; I Timothy 4:1f). Of course, they not only don't believe God has always ruled over all the kingdoms on earth, or that Christ does rule them as the *"only Potentate"* and *"King of kings,"* they also don't believe Satan was lying when he offered Jesus something that wasn't his to give (Daniel 4:17, 25; I Timothy 6:15)! *"Potentate"* means Christ is the Omnipotent, infinitely supreme Ruler above and over all spiritual and physical creatures and rulers, including Satan (Colossians 1:16)!

And I would be remiss not to mention that many fail to see the difference between Satan's *"lying wonders"* (like as practiced by Pharoah's magicians) and true miracles (II Thessalonians 2:9; see my *Now That's A Miracle*). A good question to ask yourself before you do any religious or moral thing is: "Who's going to approve and like what I'm about to do: God or Satan?"

Rightly Divide between Bible Facts and Fictitious Stories that have evolved out of those facts. These would include keeping of so-called "Christian Holidays" like Christmas and Easter, along with all the other added fictions, fantasies and false teachings that these holidays create: e.g., Santa Claus, Easter Bunny, partaking Communion (or "Celebrating Mass") on days other than the first day of the week, etc. Unfortunately, the KJV used the word "Easter" to translate the Passover in Acts 12:4. (We may keep parts of such traditions as long as we don't believe, obey or teach the falsehoods in them in the process. It is always wrong to lie!)

Other fictions are the "Immaculate Conception of Mary," which is a false teaching that asserts she was born sinless because she was chosen to be the Mother of God—which is based upon another false teaching, "original sin." (The Bible teaches all mothers and children are **born** without sin!). Another false teaching is that

Mary remained sinless; and yet another falsehood is the "Perpetual Virginity of Mary," which repudiates the Gospels that say Jesus had real blood brothers (Matthew 12:46; 13:55). Others include Mary Magdalene was a prostitute and not just demon possessed; Satan was "Lucifer" (Isaiah 14:12ff, KJV) rather than King Nebuchadnezzar; that the "Antichrist" is a person yet to come, rather than a teaching that denied Christ came in the flesh (I John 2:18-22; 4:2-3; II John 7). On and on we could go with the fictitious stories that need to be divided out, and excised from, the fabric of the Christian faith.

Rightly Divide between Scriptural History & Science and Secular History & Science. Quoting a thousand secular scientists who were not there at the Beginning of Creation will not replace God who was there, and who inspired Moses to write about it for mankind ever since. To quote a thousand secular historians who weren't there during the life, times, miracles, death and resurrection of Christ will not replace a single one of the Apostolic or historical witnesses who were there and recorded it accurately (Luke 1:1-4; Acts 1:1-4; I Corinthians 15:3-7; See *The Supreme Scientist,* also compare my *Killing Jesus—The History* with Bill O'Reilly's *Killing Jesus—A History,* as per secular historians).

Rightly Divide between Literal plain language and Figurative or Symbolic language such as allegories, metaphors, parables, similes, cultural idioms, Jewish numerology, etc. The teacher or text will usually tell you if his words, writings or books contain such pictures, parables and such; or the words themselves will obviously not be literal. Just like Jesus would tell his Apostles and sometimes his audience that he was telling a story/parable (Matthew 13:3-13). And when He called Herod a "Fox," he didn't mean he was a furry animal on all fours (Luke 13:32). Also John did say his entire book of Revelation was full of word-pictures and symbols when he said God's angel *"signified it"* in his introduction to the book (Revelation 1:1). On the other side of this dividing line, it is also obvious that the Genesis Account is literal, with literal days and events, and not an "Allegory" as claimed by so many "Theistic Evolutionary Bible believers." Moses didn't say it was an "allegory." And there's but one story (about Ishmael and Isaac) specifically identified as an *"allegory"* in the entire Bible (Galatians 4:21-31).

Rightly Divide between inspired Examples, Suggestions and Commands. Just because Paul circumcised Timothy and kept the Jewish Day of Pentecost amongst the Jews then does not mean we've been commanded to do that everywhere today. And just because Paul suggested it would be wise not to get married during the times of persecution and tribulation in which he lived, does not mean he commanded it, and even said so (I Corinthians 7:25-28).

Rightly Divide between Specific Commands and Generic Commands. Two Examples: **(1)** See generic on Lord's Supper (p. 82). **(2)** We've received the generic command to *"go into all the world and preach the gospel"* ... but not a specific command to **go** by walking, riding a donkey or by boat as in the time of Christ, which would eliminate going through radio, TV or the Internet. A Sovereign Soul and Student demands clear and specific commands in Christ's New Testament, in context, in order to be bound by any person or church to do anything. Remember: "Specific Detailed Demands require Specific Detailed Commands."

Rightly Divide between New Testament written fulfillments of Old Testament prophecies and later premillennial preachers' alleged fulfillments of Old Testament prophecies. Luke said the destruction of Jerusalem in A.D. 70 would fulfill all the prophecies concerning the coming of Christ's New Kingdom and the full end of the old Jewish Nation, Religion and Age (Daniel 2:44; Amos 5:2; Matthew 24:1ff; Luke 21:20-22; 24:44-47; Acts 3:24). When you find Peter saying *"this is that"* in Acts 2:16 — meaning the events recorded in Acts 2:1-15 is the beginning of the *"this"* which fulfilled *"that"* prophesied in Joel 2:28-32 (and quoted in Acts 2:17-21) — that is the end of the discussion: ***that's that!*** (See my *"End of the World: Jewish Calamity or Universal Climax?"*)

Rightly Divide between New Testament Christianity and New Age "Christianity," or between Christ's Gospel and all the later false Gospels, etc. If it's New it isn't True!

All of this means we must have clear New Testament Authority — Book, Chapter and Verse — before we believe or teach anything as being required by Christ in his church.

Research the Scriptures

There's a difference between casually reading the scriptures and researching them. Acts 17:11 tells us what that difference is.

Now these {Beroean Jews} were more noble than those in Thessalonica, in that they received the word with all readiness of mind, **examining the scriptures daily***,* **whether these things were so.**

The word *"examined"* (ASV) is translated as *"searched"* in the KJV. The Greek word (anakrino) means to "scrutinize and investigate" the Scriptures, and includes the ability to "interrogate" those quoting the Scriptures. Here we see it shows how the Beroean Jews knew how to do their own research into the Old Testament Scriptures and see if what they were hearing from Paul and Silas was consistent with what their Old Testament Scriptures literally said or prophetically allowed.

It is noteworthy that these Jewish Beroeans were "Sovereign Souls and Students" of God and His word. They didn't bow to Paul's Apostleship and surrender their right to do their own Scriptural Research of the Old Testament Scriptures on everything Paul cited in them to prove that Christ had fulfilled them. In like manner, we Christians must research all the Scriptures, Old and New Testament, so any person — regardless of his/her religious title or position — will have to prove their words and teachings are in harmony with the words of the Gospels and all New Testament teachings. That's what this book is about!

We Bible believers can be like the Noble Beroeans and do our own Bible research on any Bible text or teaching we believe, teach or confront in our daily lives of defending the faith, teaching others and, yes, correcting false teachings and refuting false teachers. We can learn how to do comparative studies between Old and New Testament history, law, prophecies and fulfillments. We can learn to do our own research into the original New Testament words in the texts, grammatically parse the words and sentences, exegete the texts, consider the contexts, identify the speakers and ones being addressed, and exposit the chapters and books. We can increase our abilities by going to Bible Schools ... but even there we need to understand that we all are students of Christ's word.

We can also do our own research at home. To expedite our research, it's helpful to read several standard Bible translations or versions. Be sure to include the two most reliable versions: the American Standard Version (ASV) and the King James Version

(KJV). The ASV had more manuscript evidence involved in its translation, and it includes these manuscript notes in its margins and later English words in its texts. The KJV is very important because the two major Bible Concordances — Strong's Exhaustive Concordance and Young's Analytical Concordance — utilize the English words found in the KJV. Both of these great Bible Concordances give you the original Hebrew and Greek words in their Lexicons.

Besides these two major versions and concordances, I would also recommend getting a Septuagint version (Greek) of the Old Testament and New Testament Interlinears and analytical lexicons by Zondervan for more indepth word studies. Other helpful aids would be: A Harmony of the Gospels, Bible Dictionaries, ISBE Encyclopedias, and Commentaries like Keil & Delitzsch's Hebrew OT Commentaries, R.C.H. Lenski's Greek NT Interpretations, Pulpit Commentaries, Sunset Teachers' commentaries, et al.

Repeat the Scriptures

*And the things which thou hast **heard** from me among many witnesses, **the same commit** thou to faithful men, who shall be able to teach others also* (II Timothy 2:2).

The Bible is not ours to revise and repair, but to read and repeat. Though many people "think" you need some sort of supernatural spiritual gift of knowledge or discernment to understand the scriptures, such is simply not true. It is just another way for people who claim to have such gifts to keep you from reading and understanding it yourself, and to get you to rely on their second-hand and superior interpretations. Again, remember that the pagan Ephesians could read and understand the simple Gospel words and mystery of Christ just as the truly inspired Apostle Paul understood them (Ephesians 3:3-5). And if they could thereby be saved by the truth, and united in the truth, by reading some of the Apostle's letters then — without all the other New Testament Gospels, books, lexicons and concordances that you and I have — so can you and I. (And I claim no supernatural gift of any kind.)

Read the scriptures over and over, remember them, and always repeat them as they are written before you accept or offer any elaborations or applications of the texts. If you find yourself or another person in conflict with the **sum** total of all the New Testament texts on any subject, then reconsider your and their teachings as being unworthy to repeat (Psalms 119:160)!

Require Scriptural Proof of all things

"prove all things; hold fast to that which is good" (I Thessalonians 5:21).

We've been told many times in Christ's New Testament that each one of us needs to prove his/her faith. We'll look at some of those passages shortly. But first we need to know that we would not have been told to prove all things if we, as uninspired individual Christians, couldn't do such by using the scriptures God has given us, or if there was no need to do it. If we could simply trust the authority and accuracy of another person's religious "credentials," testimony or teaching on the basis of his/her claims of sincerity, scholarship or superior miracle-working claims, we wouldn't need to investigate their motives or verify the authenticity of their claims or teachings. But Jesus' refusal to accept mere claims of working miracles as proof of keeping God's written will, and Paul's *"good conscience"* and sincere belief that killing Christians was the right thing to do, prove you can't put your faith in human sincerity, conscience, religious boasting and the human heart (Matthew 7:21-23; Acts 23:1; 26:9-10; Jeremiah 17:9). That's why we've been told, for the spiritual sake and safety of our own souls, as well as those we try to teach or correct, to *"prove all things."* Here's more proof of this point:

> Romans 12:2 — *And be **not fashioned** according to this world: but **be ye transformed** by the renewing of your mind, that ye may **prove** what is the good and acceptable and **perfect will of God**.*

> II Corinthians 13:5 — ***Try your own selves**, whether **you are in the faith**; **prove your own selves**. Or know ye not as to your own selves, that Jesus Christ is in you? unless indeed ye be **reprobate**.*

We earlier cited Acts 17:11 to show how we need to *"search the scriptures"* like the Beroeans in order to be sure what others tell us is *"so."* Now we will focus upon our need to be able to scripturally **prove** what we believe and say is *"so."* The Bible is not only accurate, it is harmoniously accurate. The Bible's New Testament fulfillments harmonize with the Old Testament prophecies. Paul's teachings harmonize with Jesus' and Peter's teachings. All church teachings must harmonize with Christ's finished New Testament teachings. And our individual teachings must harmonize with Christ's teachings. No contradictions can be allowed or tolerated. Otherwise, we must ask why did our Lord give us his infallibly written word at all? Why didn't He just tell us to make up our own doctrines and teachings? Why did He and his Apostles tell us to remember, study, teach and keep their inspired words or be rejected as *"reprobate,"* or unapproved? SO ... if my, or any person's or church's teachings, aren't scripturally *"so"* ... they must go!

Also, our scriptural **proof** is in the pudding: our fruit must match the *"perfect will of God"* and not the will, words or ways of the world. We must be *"transformed"* by God's word and not *"fashioned"* (or conformed) according to the world by twisting the New Testament teachings to conform to our beliefs and behaviors. Jesus said our righteous *"fruits"* prove our origin from, and presence within, the true *"branch ... good tree ... Vine"* (Isaiah 11:1; Matthew 7:15-23; John 15:5-8).

In regard to good fruit and bad fruit, we must note that in Christ's spiritual church and kingdom, the outward appearance of being a great fruitful church — like great temples, cathedrals, priestly array, elaborate services — is not biblical proof of bearing good fruit by a true church. No more than lovely leaves are always proof of the presence of fruit. Jesus made this clear when he entered into Jerusalem amongst much Jewish religious fanfare and outward religious trappings, and then on the next day cursed a leafy fig tree because it had no figs (Mark 11:12-14, 20-22).

Now some have questioned Jesus' character and the text itself, because verse 13 says *"It was not the season of figs."* But they fail to appreciate Jesus' use of natural things to demonstrate spiritual lessons about how religious pretense, pomposity and ostentatious physical trappings often accompany a religion bereft of true fruit. He often indicted the hypocritical Pharisees for hiding their inward rotten fruit behind their external and extravagant displays of religious piety and righteousness (Matthew 6:1-7; 23:1-36). When Jesus condemned and caused a leafy fig tree to die, He was simply illustrating how Jerusalem had all the religious appearance ("leaves") of having fruit and being blessed by God for centuries, but still had no real righteous fruit and proof of being God's faithful nation. Jesus spoke a similar parable to those in Jerusalem about a barren fig tree that was all show and no fruit, which was in imminent danger of being cut down (Luke 13:6-9). As far as the Jewish religious establishment was concerned, it was not only *"not the season of figs,"* it was also "not the season of leaves" which falsely advertised the presence of figs! Now let's look at how one of the most important fruits we can possess is *"the faith"* Paul was referring to in our previous proof-quote (II Cor. 13:5).

For we must try, or prove *"our ownselves whether we are in the faith."* Which is The One Scriptural Faith, which contains all the faithful beliefs and acts in Christ's New Testament (Jude 3). We must prove we are united with God's words of faith and not just united in our faith's words (John 17:21-23). We must follow Christ's teaching and doctrine and not any church's teaching or doctrine ... because no church has any authority to create or write any new or different teaching or doctrine (II John 9). We need to be sure we *"**keep** the unity of the Spirit"* in His word and not with man's words. We need to be sure we **believe** in the *"one body/church, one Spirit, one hope, one lord, **one faith**, one baptism, one God and Father of all, who is over all, and through all, and in all"* found in the New Testament and not in a single word found in any Catechism or Creed of man, woman or angel (Ephesians 4:3-6; Galatians 1:6-9). We need to be sure we *"stand fast in one spirit, with one soul **striving for the faith** of the gospel"* (Philippians 1:27). We need to prove all of this by **contending** *"for **the faith** which was once for all delivered to the saints"* (Jude 3).

We must speak where the Bible speaks and be silent where the Bible is silent. We must call Bible things by Bible names. We must do all things in love. We must be humble and not elevate ourselves as some sovereign authority above Christ. Our only sovereign authority in life is made possible by surrendering our stubborn wills to Christ's word. Then and only then can we be "True Sovereign Souls."

Here's the reality of Christian Unity: If you are not united with me in any biblical belief, then one of us must be wrong, or both of us could be wrong—but not God's word of unity. If your church is not united with my church, one of those churches is wrong, or both of those churches are wrong—but not God's word and true church. Let God be true and every man a liar before we accuse God of authoring the religious confusion within Big Tent "Christendom" (Romans 3:1-4; I Corinthians 14:33).

We must keep the Gospel Faith throughout our entire lives, and it will keep us in the bosom of "The Faithful and True Witness" when we depart this life (Revelation 1:5; 19:11). And so shall we live righteously by faith and receive a crown of life and righteousness by faith when we die (Ibid. 2:10; II Tim. 4:8). Our Christian life begins by faith, continues by faith, overcomes by faith and ends in faith: *"From faith unto faith"* (Romans 1:16f). As the song says: "Faith is the victory that overcomes the world!"

And I heard a voice from heaven saying: Write, **Blessed are the dead who die in the Lord** *from henceforth: yea, saith the Spirit, that they may rest from their labors; for their works follow with them* (Revelation 14:13). **And That's Why.....**

I CHOSE CHRIST'S CROWN

Sometimes the saddest words in a person's life are **"I could have."** Maybe **I could have** made something of myself if I would have listened to my parents and teachers and "applied myself." Maybe **I could have** been a doctor, lawyer, USAF Officer or President if I would've put my education and future above having fun and sowing wild oats every season of my younger years. Maybe **I could have** been a music star or professional golfer and been in the Hall of Fame somewhere if I had only practiced ... and if I had any talent! Since I've been playing golf & guitar poorly for 65 & 53 years respectively, I think I may have saved myself a lot of wasted time and effort by choosing a different career. And I thank God that I chose the only career that leads those who choose it to being listed in God's Hall of Fame, Book of Life and receiving an **Everlasting Crown** when it's over! And that choice also means I did become a Son of God, member of Christ's 'A Team' and an outspoken Sovereign Soul ... aka "Preacher."

Speaking of "outspoken," maybe the reason I am now a 'Professional Talker' was because I always talked too much in school. And maybe having to stay after school and write "I will not talk" on the blackboard a hundred times had something to do with my writing my talking in the newspapers and books. After all, when God asked me if I wanted good looks or good books, I chose good books!

In case you haven't noticed by now, I quickly learned that a homely-looking 'Southern Hick' has to have a lot of humor in life to keep from fighting or crying all the time! That's why I usually respond to any put downs about my less than attractive looks and questionable sanity with a verse from two of my favorite Country Music songs on such insults, and close by paraphrasing Brother Jack's humorous reply to such "ugly" charges: *"I was so ugly the doctor slapped my momma when I was born; then he took out his pocket knife and cut off my horns"* ... or *"I've always been crazy, but it kept me from going insane"* (Waylon Jennings). *"I know I'm not handsome, I'm not a movie star; but I'm behind my face, it's the one in front of it that gets the jar!"* (Jack Exum).

So we now return to where we started at the beginning of this book: which book covers from the womb to the tomb for all of us "Sovereign Souls." So let's wrap this book up by reviewing and comparing all my Choices with my Actions, see where I am when it comes to "Finishing the Course" and retake the "Sovereign Test." And I hope you take the test again with me and see how great you are as a Sovereign Soul. Personally, I think you had to be your own thinker and decision-maker or you wouldn't have read this far into this book!

I CHOSE: Christ as my Sovereign Creator. Christ's Covenant as my Sole Authority. Christ's Cross as my Supreme Sacrifice. Christ's Church as my only Spiritual House and Kingdom. Christ's Companionship as my Closest Friendship. Christ's Great Commission as my Career. Christ's Crown as my Life's Goal. I have tried to clearly state my acceptance of all of Christ's Choices. I have also tried to illustrate how my actions support all my claims of having accepted Christ's Choices. Now I will conclude this last Chapter and entire Book by briefly reviewing, one by one, those Seven Choices and attempts to practice those Choices.

I Chose Christ as My Supreme and Sovereign Creator

I Chose this because Jesus' New Testament clearly states that He was the Creator, Author of the Creation Account through Moses, and that He preached literal Creationism. Christ was the Supreme Creator and Creationist! So I chose to accept Christ's Word on the matter because He proved His claims by working miracles and being raised from the dead. Since He proved his Choice, I believe we have to prove our Choice of His Choice!

That's why I'm on record confirming my choice of Christ as My Creator, and his Genesis Account as the only inspired and accurate historical, scientific and religious account of how it was accomplished. I have taught and preached this Creationism since I became a Christian in 1963. I have discussed, debated and defended it personally and in print, privately and publically, in high schools, universities, church classrooms, political campaigns, church pulpits and magazines, newspaper articles, radio and TV media, and written a book, *The Supreme Scientist*. And I stand ready to continue preaching and defending Christ as my Creator and His Creation Account regardless of what anyone, or everyone, has to say to the contrary ... so help me God. When I made Christ's Creator Choice My Choice, Christ re-created this Sovereign Soul.

I Chose Christ's New Covenant as My Sole Authority

I have been involved in the same activities preaching and defending Christ's Sovereign Scriptural Authority as with His being our Supreme Creator. Every single article and book I've ever written is founded upon Christ's Word in His Old Testament history and His New Testament authority for His Church. None are based upon a single uninspired, ancient or modern, authority: whether he/she is an alleged prophet, pope, professor or president. Christ said it, that settles it! Period! And I stand ready to continue preaching and defending Christ's authoritative Word regardless of what anyone, or everyone, says to the contrary ... so help me God. When I made Christ's Covenant Choice My Choice, Christ made a life-long written Covenant/Contract with this Sovereign Soul.

I Chose Christ's Cross as My Sacrifice for Sins

I can say sincerely with the Apostle Paul: *"Far be it from me to glory, save in the **cross** of our/my Lord Jesus Christ..."* (Galatians 6:14). I was forgiven much, so I love him much (Luke 7:47). And I know I should love him much! So as a token of my love and gratitude for Christ's love and forgiveness, I have been preaching and writing about his loving sacrifice, saving blood and grace at every opportunity, with or without pay, since 1963. And I cherish my last book, *Killing Jesus – The History,* the most of all. Because the cruelty against our Lord was so severe, it was as tough on my emotions to write the biblical details of the Passion of Christ in that book as it was for me to watch Mel Gibson's movie, *The Passion of The Christ.* The Cross is why I'm a Gospel Preacher and plan and pray to be until I die ... so help me God. When I made Christ's Cross Choice my Choice, Christ made me his Saved Sovereign Soul.

I Chose Christ's Church as My only Church

I chose it because it is His Church, Body, Bride and Temple. He died for it, built it upon himself (The Rock), bought it with his blood, is its Head, Lord, King, Savior and will be with it until the end of time. I Chose it because Christ added me to it (Acts 2:36-47). And I will remain in it because He didn't offer any other churches from which to choose, then or now. And another visible evidence that proves I chose His Church is the fact that I have personally assisted other lost souls in getting Christ to add them to His Church: via preaching/writing about Christ's Plan of Salvation and Pattern of His Church, plus personally baptizing some of them. Though I, like Paul, being a local preacher for 3-4 years in each location, usually chose other native leaders or kinfolk in the church to perform the actual baptizing (I Corinthians 1:14-16). My prayers and plans are to be in it, work in it and be saved in it when I die ... so help me God. When I made Christ's Church Choice my Choice, Christ added this Sovereign Soul to His Church.

I Chose Christ's Companionship as My Closest Friendship

I chose Him because He is my Closest Friend, as well as because He was the closest friend of all my closest earthly friends in my life: George & Lucille Spurgin, (Joe Ann Spurgin) Jack Exum, Alvin Jennings, Sunset Teachers, Joe Buchanan, and most of all, my wife and two daughters, Stephanie and Melissa. I have been blessed with many great friends in my Christian life. My proof of friendship with them is that I still talk, write to and about them. My proof that Christ has always been my Best Friend is I have always talked about Him and to Him at every chance I get, including during my "Near Death Experience" and every night before I go to sleep. Plus all of my sermons, discussions, writings and books are about JESUS, MY BEST FRIEND. I'm glad He knows that! And I pray He knows I'll be His friend until I die ... so help me God. When I made Christ's Companion Choice my Choice, Christ made this Sovereign Soul one of His Best Friends.

I Chose Christ's Great Commission as My Career

I chose Christ's Great Commission as My Career because Jesus loves sinners, and so do I (a saved sinner)! I also chose it because He told me to choose it, and because it is the only Career with heavenly assistants, assistance and benefits. Though I have been involved in many occupations since becoming a Christian — the USAF, Carpentry, Real Estate, Politics, Salesman, Janitorial Service, on and on — I didn't consider any of them, or all of them put together, as being my primary vocation or career. I always knew they were a means to an end: earning money to preach and spread the Gospel. I've always been willing to work other secular jobs to pay for my evangelistic endeavors, even if it meant I had to preach for free or give away free tracts and books to those churches or individuals who could not afford them.

Historically speaking, I visited Hawaii in the summer of 1971 to investigate two open preaching jobs: one in Kailua, Oahu and the other in Hilo, Hawaii. Since the Hilo church was the smallest and needy of the two churches, I agreed to return in January of 1972 to preach fulltime there. My fulltime salary was to be from Hilo's small membership, plus raised support from other churches and free housing in a new "preacher's house" they were going to build before I arrived. I arrived as planned, and the preacher's house wasn't even started, much less completed. (200 inches of rain didn't help). So, though I had never built anything larger than a chicken house, I told them I'd help them build it. So a half-dozen of us members, counting my wife, built the house in six months, and my family and I lived in it for the next three years.

Then I was forced to leave the Hilo preaching position due to an unexpected loss of outside financial support to the church. So I suddenly found myself without a house or income. I considered taking another preaching job, but went back to the School of

Preaching for postgraduate work. After that I took a fully paid preaching job in Margate, Florida for three years. While there I bought me a "fixer-upper" house with a VA Loan, used my construction skills I had learned in Hilo to fix it up, and lived in it for three years while I preached fulltime there. Though my wife and I loved the people and work there, had some really great Christian male and female friends, and able church leaders like Joe Roles Sr. and Jr., I decided to return to Hawaii to do mission work again. The Margate church even provided some of my financial support in Hawaii for a year. Thanks brethren!

This time, though I fully understood that preaching is a work wherein the laborer is worthy of his hire, I decided I wanted to use the construction skills I had learned in Hilo and Florida to build my own home, which I would own free and clear, and then support myself financially by working with my hands rather than just by preaching (I Corinthians 9:6). So it was via the construction and real estate industry that I have been able to preach and write full time without the necessity of church support ever since. If tent-making and carpentry jobs were good enough for Jesus and Paul, they're good enough for me (Mark 6:3; Acts 18:3; I Corinthians 9:6).

So whatever work I have done, I always considered every job to be directly supportive of Christ's Choice of fulfilling His Great Commission as the greatest Cause on earth and greatest Career for everyone involved. And since our Lord appreciates all of our service to and for Him, we should express our appreciation to every Christian who contributes any part of his/her life or livelihood in service to our Lord. And I intend to pursue His Career till I die ... so help me God. When I made Christ's Career Choice my Choice, Christ gave this Sovereign Soul a Life!

I Chose Christ's Crown as My Full and Final Reward

The Lord does not expect us to sacrifice our lives for Him just to escape a conscious spiritual existence in hell at the end of our lives. Nor did Christ teach us to live righteously just so we can lose our personal identity, have no conscious existence and be absorbed into the "ALL," as do Hindus and Buddhists who seek Nirvana. Christians do not seek to live righteously because of their fear of judgment, death or decay; they live in hope of immortality in heaven (I John 4:18). They do not labor and suffer in vain for a great spiritual human being, like Ghandi. They labor in love for the Son of God and inherit His Crown of Life and Righteousness. And such is the prize I CHOSE to seek from my first step in Christ, throughout every step I've taken on His Christian *"Course"* until now—which goal/finish-line/prize is closer than I ever thought I'd get. And I know I'm still on the Course because of the following:

I'm still *"fighting the good fight."* As I stated in Chapter Two, my life as a conservative Christian preacher and writer in the liberal and pagan State of Hawaii has not been all "peace, love and tranquility in Paradise." I have been persecuted, defamed, libeled, slandered, assaulted and jailed over the past forty four years for doing nothing but preaching Christ's scriptural truths in love. I have been knocked down but never out (II Corinthians 4:8f)! Since I have not yet suffered unto blood, I thank God daily for his providential care (Hebrews 12:4). I also thank God for the privilege of suffering persecution for *"fighting the good fight"* and suffering for *"well-doing"* instead of suffering for *"evil-doing"* (I Peter 3:17). (Which I had just begun to suffer before I became a Christian!) I am also grateful that I don't have as many rounds left to fight as when I first entered into the fray.

I'm still alive and well on Christ's *"Course"* after fifty-three years. (And still on the same Muni Golf Course after 44 years!) Since I have not finished Christ's Course yet, I have no intention of stopping, retiring or slowing down. Though I don't do many physical things as fast and well as when I was younger, I've been pleasantly surprised that I can do the spiritual things (praying, preaching, teaching) better than when I was young. That's because wisdom comes with age. While it takes nothing but the passage of time "to get old" physically in this world, it takes continued faith-filled living, mental exertion, scriptural exercise and practice to "grow old" spiritually in the Lord. Here's the biblical formula for becoming wise: Like Solomon, pray for wisdom (James 1:5; I Kings 3:5-12). Then Read God's Word, Heed God's Word, Learn God's word, Share God's Word ... and grow old! You will also learn that most questions and problems we pray for God to answer and solve have already been answered and solved in his Word!

I have also *"kept the faith"* for a long time. And since it is my last precept in this book, but in no way the least, I'm going to take a little longer to deal with it. As I've said before, you can't keep what you don't know. And it does take a fair amount of time to <u>grow in knowledge</u> of God's Word: taking the time to do the necessary reading and research in all the moral and doctrinal issues, commandments, liberties, false teachings, figures of speech, literal speech, parables, grammatical structure, on and on. And it takes even more time to <u>grow up in Christ's wisdom</u> by learning to teach and act like Christ, and apply his teachings and principles to your life and other situations and religions. So becoming an "old seasoned Christian citizen" is good because we have had the opportunity to learn and memorize much of the New Testament, and we have also spent decades living Christ's teachings to gain the wisdom, experience and evidence to appreciate them and illustrate those teachings in our own lives.

Of course, we New Testament Christians can do all of the above faster than those in false religions because we have but one book, the New Testament, that we must learn and obey to "Keep the One Faith." Thus we do not need to waste valuable time reading and learning church manuals, creeds, catechisms, liturgical rituals, etc., or keeping unnecessary religious rules and rites, or seeking assistance in such matters from any clergy as to what is the wise or right and wrong thing to do. It is not only difficult to keep many of the extra-biblical and extraneous rules and restrictions that permeate, and actually create, modern faiths, it is impossible to keep your knowledge of their many different doctrines and ongoing updates current. In my Public School cafeteria years, it was eat "fish on Friday" because of the RCC (so I didn't eat there on Fridays!) ... but that passed after I got out of school. Now Public School students have to "Eat Veggies" every day because of our new National Socialist "Green" Religion! Not on my plate!

Also, unlike the false faiths I dabbled in when I was young, which I found to be more and more scripturally flawed as I studied the New Testament, I have found that the more you read ***"the faith"*** that Christ gave to us in His New Testament the easier I found it was to learn, retain, teach and keep His faith. As John said: *"For this is the love of God, that we keep his commandments: and **his commandments are not grievous**"* (I John 5:3). I found that I didn't need to give up a single thing that was "good" in order to remain faithful. Unlike how you often have to give up things that were pronounced good by Christ (like sobriety), and accept things that were prohibited as bad by Christ (like drinking wine or using marijuana in the Lord's Supper) to be considered simpatico with many "faiths" and "churches" today.

I also discovered during my long faithful journey that becoming an old married priest in Christ's Faith is sexually easier than being a young celibate priest in the RCC (like "Father Meade"). And I have really enjoyed eating all of God's tasty, protein-packed, meats for fifty years without a guilty conscience, including putting them on the outdoor BBQ grill on the "The Lord's Day" (Sunday) at His Faithful Church's Potluck dinners. It is so much easier and more enjoyable than depriving myself of all this thanksgiving to God than eating a Vegan Diet or keeping the Sabbath-restrictions of Sabbatarians. Or the diets and holy days of the Jews and RCC.

And who could forget all of the religious chaos that many of the religious cults and "pre-millennial churches" put us through when they regurgitated their revised prophetic puzzles and charts and ran here, there and everywhere with their "Bad News-Spiel" about the "End of the World" and "The Late Great Planet Earth." First the world was going to end with the invention of the Atomic Bomb ... then with the rise of Russia ("Gogg & Magog") ... then with the swarms of Cobra Helicopters (Lindsey's *"locusts"* in Rev. 9:7) ... and now with the rise of Islamic Jihadism and threats against Israel. On and on and on the denominational "drones" and doctrines have flown around inside their heads and around the world since I became a member of the faithful kingdom of God— that they still insist has not yet come (Colossians 1:13; Revelation 1:9). Indeed, Christ's 2000 year old, scriptural and spiritual kingdom is easier to understand, enter and live in than their made-up earthly Messianic Regime, that has not yet materialized.

Since we are discussing "keeping the faith," I can tell you it is a historical fact that when false faiths base their credibility on such fear-mongering and "The-End-is-Near" preaching, their members have left in mass when their predictions failed to come to past. It happened in 1975 when a large percentage of the Jehovah Witnesses left their church when their prediction of the end of the world failed to come to pass. And it happened in 1981 when the same sort of exodus from Lindsey's persuasion occurred when all of his false predictions failed to come to pass. And it will fail every time they build a modern church and faith upon a "kingdom yet to come" rather upon the "kingdom that already came" as per "the faith once for all delivered to the saints" (Hebrews 12:28).

Yes, I chose to "keep the faith" and have tried not only to keep it one day at a time, but also to share it one day at a time. Sharing the faith is a vital part of keeping the faith. And creating faith in others is good for enhancing your faith and expanding the faith. And I have asked the Lord of my Life to extend my life as long as I can preach His Gospel, glorify His Name and save lost souls ... so help me God. I will now close this part of the book by taking the same **"Sovereign Soul Test"** I asked you to take at the beginning.

1. **Do I believe I have a divinely created soul?** YES!

2. **Do I believe my soul is unique amongst the billions of souls who have lived/live on earth?** YES!

3. **Do I believe I am the highest creature in the Universe?** YES!

4. **Do I believe my soul is worth more than all this world's treasures and pleasures?** YES!

5. **Do I believe I am as important to God as any person on earth today?** YES!

6. **Do I believe I am equal in authority to all religious and moral authorities on earth today?** YES!

7. **Do I believe my soul will survive the death of my physical body and receive an immortal body?** YES!

YES, I believe all of this because Jesus and His Bible told me so. And I have presented many scriptural confirmations of all these facts. And, because of what My Heavenly Father, Messianic Friend and Indwelling Spirit have revealed unto me in their Scriptures, I intend to walk and talk like "The Sovereign Soul" I was Created to be, Told to be, Intend to be and shall be Judged to be ... so help me God!

Since this is the first book I've written with pictures outside and inside the covers, I think it would be appropriate to finish with the most important Picture of All: a written Portrait of what a Sovereign Soul looks like in action. Hope it looks like you!

"Portrait Of The Sovereign Soul"

The Lord's *"Sovereign Soul"* **is any sinner on the earth:**
- Who has believed, confessed and obeyed the authorized, historical New Testament Gospel (Matthew 28:18ff; Mark 16:15f; John 3:16, 36; Romans 1:16; I Corinthians 15:1-3).
- Who has repented of his/her sins and been forgiven by being washed in Christ's blood by being *"born again of water and the Spirit"* (John 3:3-5; Acts 2:38; 22:16; Romans 6:3-6; Titus 3:3-7; Hebrews 10:22; I Peter 3:18-21)
- Who has received the *"gift of the Holy Spirit"* — the Holy Spirit as an indwelling gift, *"seal"* of sonship and *"earnest"* (guarantee, down payment) of divine inheritance (Acts 2:38; Romans 8:9; Galatians 3:26 thru 4:6; Ephesians 1:13f; 4:30).
- Who has been added by the Lord to **His** One True Church (Matthew 16:18; Acts 2:38-47; Ephesians 4:4f).
- Who is growing in faith, grace, love (of God and for man) and knowledge of God's word by feasting upon a steady diet of God's word (II Peter 3:18; II Timothy 3:14-17).
- Who is becoming more like the Christ that he/she imitates — in heavenly words, thoughts, deeds, desires and goals — and the word *"Christian"* is the best word to describe him/her.
- Who is determined to be the faithful servant, student, soldier and saint the Lord wants each of us to be until we die (II Timothy 4:8; Revelation 2:10).

I pray that will be the case with you. And I pray that you have learned something from my presentations of Christ's Word, and my attempts to apply it to my life — with all of its bad choices and good choices, sins, shortcomings, stumblings, struggles and victories — and better imitate Christ than have I. May God bless you to be all you can be as God's Saved and Sovereign Soul! Keep the Faith and it will keep you. Keep on Keeping On. God speed. Aloha and Agape. *Gerald N Wright*

Supplemental Studies

CONTENTS

MAN'S SOUL AND SPIRIT .... P. 273
JESUS IS JEHOVAH TEXTS .... P. 274
PRES. OBAMA INDICTS XITY .... P. 277
JESUS IS THE ROCK .... P. 287
PETER NOT THE FIRST POPE .... P. 290
MEMORIES OF KAIMU .... P. 296

"Man's Soul"

<u>Soul as man's physical life principle</u>:
Hebrew *Nephesh* — (Leviticus 17:11; 24:18; Numbers 6:6).
Greek *Psuche* — (Matthew 2:20; Luke 12:22; Acts 20:10; Revelation 8:9; 12:11).

<u>Soul as man's immortal body</u>:
Hebrew *Nephesh* — (I Kings 17:21f; Psalms 16:10; 49:8, 15; cf. Genesis 2:7).
Greek *Psuche* — (Matthew 10:28; Hebrews 10:39; 13:17; James 1:21; I Peter 1:22; Revelation 6:9).

"Man's Spirit"

<u>Spirit as man's (or animals') physical breath</u>:
Hebrew *Ruach* — (Genesis 6:17; Job 12:10; Psalms 104:29).
Greek *Pneuma* — (John 3:8; Hebrews 1:7 ("winds"); Revelation 11:11).

Spirit as man's spiritual inner being (or God's Spirit and spirits):
Hebrew Ruach — (Genesis 6:3 – can't mean *God's "breath"* was striving with men; 41:8, 38; Exodus 31:3; Numbers 14:24; II Chronicles 18:20; Psalms 31:5; Ecclesiastes 12:7; Isaiah 42:5; Ezekiel 11:19; 13:3; 36:26; Zechariah 12:1; Malachi 2:15).

Greek *Pneuma* — (Matthew 28:19 – can't mean to baptize in the *"name of God's breath or force;"* Luke 8:55; 23:46; Acts 7:59; 23:8; I Corinthians 5:3, 5; Hebrews 12:9, 23; James 2:26; I Peter 3:19). See my book, *The J.W. Bible*, pp. 58-67, for more discussion on this subject.

"Jesus Is Jehovah Texts"

That Jesus Christ was the "Jehovah" of the Old Testament (along with the Father and the Holy Spirit in the "Godhead") can be seen by looking at the Old Testament statements and prophecies speaking of "Jehovah," yet fulfilled by Christ in the New Testament. This same approach can be used to show how the other Old Testament names for God — like *"Elohim, Elohe, Holy One"*— were also applied to Christ in the New Testament. **Jesus was He** (John 8:24)! Consider the following comparable texts.

1. **Exodus 3:14f** — **Jehovah** is the Great "I Am," or the *"Ego Eimi"* (LXX).
   John 8:58 — **Jesus** said he was *Ego Eimi*.

2. **Exodus 20:10** — It is **Jehovah's** Sabbath.
   Mark 2:28 — **Jesus** is the *Lord of the Sabbath*.

3. **Exodus 31:13** — **Jehovah** sanctifies men.
   I Corinthians 1:30 — **Christ** sanctifies men.

4. **Deuteronomy 10:17** — **Jehovah** is *Lord of lords*.
   Revelation 17:14 — **Christ** is *Lord of lords*.

5. **Deuteronomy 32:4,15,18**
   I Samuel 2:2; Isaiah 44:8 — **Jehovah** is the only *Rock*.
   I Corinthians 10:4 — **Christ** is the *Rock*.

6. I Kings 8:39   Jehovah knows men's hearts.
   Luke 5:22; John 2:25   Christ knows all men's hearts.

7. Nehemiah 9:6   The angels worship **Jehovah**.
   Hebrews 1:6   The angels worship **Christ**.

8. Psalms 24:10; 29:3   **Jehovah** is *Lord/king of glory*.
   I Corinthians 2:8   **Christ** is the *Lord of glory*.

9. Psalms 89:8f   **Jehovah** alone stills the sea.
   Matthew 8:23-27   **Christ** stilled the sea.

10. Isaiah 8:13   Do not fear men but sanctify **Jehovah** in your heart.
   I Peter 3:14f   Do not fear men but sanctify **Christ** in your heart.

11. Isaiah 40:3   John was to prepare the way for **Jehovah** (Malachi 3:1).
   Matthew 3:3   John prepared way for Christ.

12. Isaiah 42:8   **Jehovah** did not give his glory to another.
   John 17:5; 1:14   **Christ** possessed God's glory.

13. Isaiah 43:11, 25; 45:21   **Jehovah** is Savior from sins.
   Mark 2:7; Titus 2:13f   **Christ** is our Savior from sins.

14. Isaiah 44:6   **Jehovah** is the *first and last*.
   Revelation 1:17   **Christ** is the *first and last*.

15. Isaiah 44:24; Nehemiah 9:6; Jeremiah 10:11)   **Jehovah** is the only *Redeemer* and *Creator*.
   John 1:1f; Col. 1:16; Luke 1:68; I Peter 1:18   **Christ** is the *Creator* and has *Redeemed* us.

16. Isaiah 60:1-3   **Jehovah's** glory to shine as a light to the nations.
   John 1:4; 8:12   **Christ's** glory lights the world.

17. **Jeremiah 23:5f** — *Jehovah our Righteousness* to be the name of the Messiah.
    I Corinthians 1:30;
    II Corinthians 5:21 — **Christ** is the Messiah and our *Righteousness*.

18. **Ezekiel 34:11-24** — *Jehovah* to be our *Shepherd*.
    John 10:11; Hebrews 13:20; I Peter 5:4 — **Jesus** is the *Good Shepherd*.
    Note: The Shepherd to come was to be the anti-type of David (Ezekiel 34:23). Jesus was the anti-type of David and the Shepherd (Acts 2:29-34; See also Zechariah 13:7).

19. **Joel 2:32** — Those who *call on the name of Jehovah to be saved.*
    Acts 2:21, 36; 4:12; 22:16 — *Calling on the name of Christ brought salvation.*
    Note: This "calling" and "salvation" likely includes the physical salvation of Christians who fled Jerusalem as per Christ's prophecy in Luke 21:20-21.

20. **Micah 4:7** — *Jehovah* to rule as King in Zion.
    Hebrews 1:8; 10:12f; 12:22; Ephesians 1:20-23 — **Christ** rules as King in Zion, which is the church.

21. **Habakkuk 1:12;**
    I Samuel 2:2 — *Jehovah* is the *Holy One*.
    Acts 2:27 — **Christ** is the *Holy One*.

22. **Zechariah 12:10** — *Jehovah* to be pierced.
    John 19:37 — **Christ** was pierced.

23. **Zechariah 13:7** — *Jehovah's fellow* (or equal) is the *shepherd*.
    Matthew 26:31;
    Philippians 2:6 — **Christ** is *equal* to God and is the *shepherd*.

24. **Godhead/Trinity Passages** — See *The JW's Bible* Page 53.

"President Obama Indicts Christianity"

NEWSBREAK! While I was typing Chapter Two of this book, which is about how LOVE for Christ and His Word is "Vindicating" for all Sovereign Souls, President Barack Obama, while at a prayer breakfast (2/5/15), indicted Christianity by saying there's some moral equivalency between what Islamic terrorists (ISIS) are now doing to innocent people in the **"name of Muhammad or Islam"** (like cutting off heads and burning and drowning them alive in cages) and what people did **"in the name of Christ"** during the Crusades (which were actually against Islamic Conquest) and Inquisitions. Christ's word says otherwise, and as we'll see, it completely vindicates itself and all who follow it. First, here is some of Obama's speech, verbatim:

> *Unless we get on our high horse and think that this {ISIS/Islamic terrorism} is unique to some other place, remember that during the* **Crusades and Inquisition**, *people committed terrible deeds* **in the name of Christ** (emp. mine)... *In our* **home country**, **slavery and Jim Crow** *all too often was justified* **in the name of Christ.** *So it is not unique to one group or one religion.*

This is pure obfuscation. This is seeking to obscure the clear and unassailable Bible teachings of righteousness and peace that Christ commanded all Christians to seek and share by emphasizing evil things that only biblically ignorant and disrespectful people can be found doing, ostensibly, *"in the name of Christ."* While it is true that the sinful things many people claim to be doing *"in the name of Christ"* run the gamut from A to Z — from aborting babies, adultery, alcohol consumption ... to polygamy, same-sex marriage, smoking pot to zenophobia — it is not true that they were scripturally done *"in Christ's name."* Just as you can't do anything "in my name" if I didn't authorize you to do so. And Mr. Obama does not even speak for me as a Christian, much less Christ. Thus this is not only a blatantly false accusation, it is an indictment and attack on the Christian religion. There's not a word of truth in any of his indictments. First, let's discuss President Obama's accusation of **Christian Racism** — *"slavery"* and *"Jim Crow"* segregation — then we'll discuss his **Religious Beliefs.**

Obama's Charge of Christian Racism?

Christ never remotely authorized any kind of **racial discrimination**. You'd think Christ's loving words in John 3:16, and his absolute "authority" and loving Great Commission to preach to every "creature" and "ethnic group," would have proved that to any Christian who had only read the Gospels. And if he had read the Book of Acts, he would have read how the Apostles and Church were to preach the Gospel to everyone equally, Jews and all those *"afar off,"* the Gentiles (Acts 1:8; 2:39). Then we find Philip preaching and baptizing a high-ranking **black** "Ethiopian" man (Acts 8:27ff; see Jeremiah 13:23). Then, after Christ corrected Peter's Jewish racial bias in Acts 10-11), we find him preaching full racial equality for all and baptizing Gentiles, saying:

> *Of a truth I perceive that* **God is no respecter of persons**; *but in every nation he that feareth him, and worketh righteousness, is acceptable to him* (Acts 10:34-48).

It is true that some with anti-Christian biases point out how Paul did not condemn **"*slavery*"** outright, and did tell servants to be good servants of their masters for Christ's sake (Ephesians 6:5-9). But they don't point out how Paul told the "masters" to remember that God was: *"both their Master and yours in heaven, and there is* **no respect of persons** *with him"* (verse 9). And they don't point out how Paul's teachings about loving all men in the world equally, and especially in Christ's church, served to reduce slavery in the world. Paul had this to say to a Christian brother, Philemon (vv. 1-7), concerning his run-away servant, Onesimus, who was also Paul's convert who was assisting Paul in his imprisonment:

> *Wherefore, though I have all boldness* **in Christ** *to enjoin thee that which is befitting. yet for* **love's sake** *I rather beseech, being such a one as* **Paul** *the aged, and now a prisoner also of* **Christ Jesus**: *I beseech thee for* **my child**, *whom I have begotten in my bonds,* **Onesimus**... *For perhaps he was therefore parted from thee for a season, that thou shouldest have him forever;* **no longer as a servant, but more than a servant, a brother beloved,** *specially to* **me**, *but how much rather to* **thee, both in the flesh and in the Lord** (Philemon 8-16).

So Paul, by converting Onesimus, turned him into his Christian brother like Philemon, which also turned him into Philemon's beloved brother instead of just a servant. So the sinful slavery President Obama said has been done "in the name of Christ" is exactly opposite of what Christ's authorized scriptures teach and have accomplished in the church and world from His day onward.

I highly recommend reading Dr. Thomas Sowell's books on Racism and Slavery, or look up his quotes on the Internet, wherein you will learn the true history about slavery. You will learn how many nations besides America, including European, African and Asian nations, enslaved their own people and were involved in the slave trade with Africa. You'll learn how blacks enslaved as many blacks and whites as whites enslaved blacks; how many black slave owners in America were against ending slavery; how America is the only nation that ended slavery so quickly; and how slavery of all races is still going on today. So it was/is the "powerful" who enslaved the less powerful: be it via big business, government or religion. This is why President Obama's charge that slavery is a part of "America's DNA" is prejudicial, unhistorical and untrue. What's in the DNA of all divinely unrestrained people is the propensity to sin against their fellow man for pride and personal gain. This is why we willing and joyful "slaves of Christ" all need to teach all nations of God's creatures to be Christ's Sovereign Souls who treat others like Sovereign Souls!

Now to Obama's charge that acts of **personal racism** have also been done *"in the name of Christ."* From my pre-Christian days in Roanoke, I didn't understand what the entire "color of skin" conflict was all about. I had black caddy friends and motorcycle friends. I became a Christian in Bermuda, which was populated by about sixty percent black people, and had black friends in the church there, and in the military and amongst the local people. When I completed my tour of duty in Bermuda, I returned for a thirty-day leave to my hometown of Roanoke with a new religion and daughter. I don't know how it came up, but my dad, who was rather racial in his preferences, asked me if *"I'd allow my daughter to marry a black person."* I told him I didn't care if she married a purple person, as long as that person loved and didn't abuse my daughter. So even little old "Jerry" had no racist DNA!

Of course, the more I matured as a Christian and Bible student, the more new "Gerald" couldn't understand how Christians could discriminate against any race of people. For some reason, being "in Christ" and trying to "be like Christ" by doing everything *"in the name of Christ,"* made this "Southern Soul" see all souls — "red, yellow, black or white" — as equal and precious in God's sight, and not inferior and deserving any less love than anyone else, especially from Bible-believing Christians. I mean, for me, there was no debating Christ's Scientific/Scriptural Credentials on Race: Christ created all the colors and races as one "human race," and said they all have *"one blood"* (Acts 17:26 KJV; see my *The Supreme Scientist,* p.187). And though they can change their minds and sexual "orientations," they cannot change their race or skin color. Even old Jeremiah knew that: *"can an Ethiopian change his skin"* (Jeremiah 13:23)? Which prompted me to ask, *"why should they want to?* Furthermore, isn't it Bible rebellion to do as Aaron and Mariam did when they opposed Moses' marriage to a "Cushite" (ASV), or "Ethiopian" (KJV) woman, who was of dark-skinned African descent (Numbers 12:1ff)?

And finally, the man **Jesus** was a "Semitic" Jew and not an "Arabian" Jew, or "Aryan" Jew. That means he was an olive or light brown-skinned, ordinary-looking Jew with dark eyes and hair; and not a black-skinned Jew as pushed by the modern "Black-Jesus" movement; or the lily white-skinned, blue-eyed, blond-haired, good-looking Jew as pushed by Hollywood and the Aryan Movement (see Isaiah 53:2). So I guess that means we can't blame Christ our Creator, or his Authorized Bible, or Christians for any of the racist DNA President Obama accused me — a red and white (albeit sun-tanned) American born, Bermuda born-again Christian of Scotch-Irish-Indian descent — and all white American Christians of possessing!

Now, may I add to all of this, my **"Hawaiian Heritage?"** President Obama may have been born in Hawaii; but he acts and talks more like a "malihini" (newcomer) Hawaiian than like a "kama'aina" (old-timer) Hawaiian, especially when it comes to his constant drum-beating about one race of people: so-called "African-Americans." (I don't like dividing Americans by calling them hyphenated-Americans anymore than I like dividing Christians by calling them hyphenated-Christians!) Now I'm not Hawaiian-born or of the Hawaiian Race, but I have lived in Hawaii almost four times longer than Obama has. And one big reason why I chose to live and preach in Hawaii was because it is a "Melting Pot" of all races, mixed-races and cultures. (See "Memories of Kaimu" for more on this missionary attraction.) It is truly a "Rainbow" society that sees beauty in all the colors of the beautiful rainbows and races of people who live here ... and they talk about this and have a lot of pride in this. This is one of the main attractions of Hawaii Nei. "All Colors Matter here, not just "Black Lives Matter," as is presently being debated in America. (This book is about **"My Life Matters"** as a "Sovereign Soul," as well as all other individual human beings in all races on earth.)

Since Hawaii is still a "Rainbow Society" — which now has "Rainbow" music, sports teams, radio shows, clothes, waterfalls (Hilo), and Rainbow minded people — it has not yet adopted the new politically-correct "color-neutral" copout which says: *"I don't see a person's color, I just see a person."* Well, since I'm not blind, when I see a black person, I see a black person. And I have no problem telling them "I love you black people!" Just like I can identify a native Hawaiian person, Japanese person, Filipino person, Korean person, Chinese person, et al., by his/her appearance, and tell them the same thing! But back to black-raced people. What's wrong with being black? "Black IS Beautiful!" What's wrong about calling a black person, a "black person?" They're always calling themselves "black persons" or "persons of color." They often call me a "white person." (Inspite of the fact that I'm not colorless!) They have even called me a "honky." And here in Hawaii, I've been called a "haole" (a "white person") a million times! Now get this, I have no problem with black people lovingly calling me a "honky." (I didn't like them calling me a "cracker" or "cracka" as much as I liked eating white crackers with sardines on them!) And I don't have a problem with Hawaiians lovingly calling me a "haole," either. Or as they say, *"I don't care what you call me, just don't call me late for dinner!"*

Besides all of this natural and cultural use of racial idioms and slangs to identify different races, the Bible often identifies people by their race and color. And sometimes by their bad traits: As Jesus called some of the Jews "serpents and vipers," and he called Herod a "fox" (Matthew 23:23; Luke 13:32). As Paul cited how a Cretan prophet said: *"Cretans are always liars, evil beasts, idle glutons"* (Titus 1:12). It's the context that determines the truth!

Now let's apply this Hawaiian **"Rainbow"** philosophy to Gerald and Brenda Wright's extended family and see how we now have all the colors of the racial rainbow — **red, yellow, black and white** — in our family! (Or "Tribe!")

- **White Fathers** — Harold Wright and Bill Meredith. Brenda's Stepfather, Bobby Bird, was half Indian (not in bloodline).
- **White-red Mothers** — Beulah Wright (her mother was part Indian.) Alma Meredith/Bird was of German descent.
- **White-Red Daughters** — Stephanie and Melissa Wright married "People of Color" (next).
- **Black/Brown/Yellow Son-in-Laws** — Stephanie married a dark-skinned Micronesian, Peter Ngirngotel (his mother was also part of the yellow Japanese race). Melissa married a Filipino (also mixed with Chinese-Japanese), Nester Tamayo.
- **Red/Yellow/Black and White Grandkids** — Stephanie and Peter gave us a Red/Yellow/Black and White girl, Samantha. Melissa and Nestor gave us two Red/Yellow and White boys, Sergio and Justin Tamayo, and one girl, Tori Tamayo. (All of our grandchildren favor their fathers' as per skin color.)
- **Red/Yellow/Black/Brown and White Great-Grandkids** — Sergio married a Samoan lady, Melinda, who brought more light brown color into our family. Their two daughters, Penina and Eva Tamayo, brought more Red/Yellow/Black/Brown and White into our family. Justin married a Japanese lady, Janee, who brought more Yellow into our family.
- **Jewish Race** — All those in my family who have spiritually married Jesus Christ by becoming members of his church/bride — my parents, wife, daughters, Son-in-law and granddaughter (Peter & Samantha Ngirngotel) — have brought the Jewish Race, as well as Divine Kinship, into our Family.

So our family is a typical "Hawaiian Mixed Plate!" And when you mix our Biblical bloodline and spiritual kinship all the way back to Adam, we are a worldwide family ... which is a part of the Heavenly Family (Hebrews 12:22f; see "Biggest Church")!

Listen, the more races the better I like it! Besides enjoying all the lovely colors and cultures in Hawaii, no one race can get "traction" here by playing the "race card." If an "African-American" (a "Popolo" in Hawaiian language) complains about how his color and culture isn't getting any special social privileges here, ten different "peoples of color" will say: "so what's the big deal about that? Join the crowd?" This is how it ought to be in a free and equal society. Though the science of Cultural Anthropology supports how each one of the different races in Hawaii (as well as in other mixed-race societies) tend to be "cliquish" — meaning each race usually socializes more within its own culture, ethnicity, foods, music, relationships, etc. — it can't be denied that Hawaii has more racial integration and harmony than most anywhere in the world, and that it has not had the religious or racial strife, segregation and riots that always seem to be seething in places where there are only two or three different races and cultures.

And all of this Hawaiian racial/cultural education prompted me to write a short book entitled "The Bigot" about ten years ago — to point out all kinds of prejudice against a person's race, looks, size, accent, religion — but I never got around to publishing it ... yet!

Barack Obama's Religious Beliefs

There is no comparison between Jesus and Muhammad, Christianity and Islam or the New Testament and the Koran. Here are the facts.

(1) Islam's prophet, **Muhammad**, was a man of war and not peace. Muhammad's claim to fame and power was, according to his own words: *"I have been made victorious with fear/anxiety/ terror."* **Jesus Christ** did drive criminal money-changers out of his Father's temple by brandishing a whip; but he never lifted a sword or finger to hurt a single ignorant or unbelieving *"infidel,"* not even his worst enemies. He didn't kill them; they killed him (see my *Killing Jesus*)! He is called the "Prince of Peace" by free and freed people all over the world.

(2) Islam's Bible the Koran (or Quran), and other writings, like the Hadith, in fact advocate conquest and killing infidels and unbelievers who won't convert or Muslims who renounce Islam (Check "Koran/Quran and Jihad, or Terrorism" on the Internet). **Christianity's Bible**, the New Testament, not only tells us to love our enemies and do good unto our persecutors, it disallows any coercion (scare or fear tactics) or force in conversion and any physical punishment of anyone who falls away from the faith, or renounces his faith and blasphemes and curses the Christ (Matthew 5:43-48; Romans 12:17-21). Here's a good illustration of the difference between Christian Peacemakers and Islamic Persecutors: Since the Islamic terror attack on America on September 11, 2001, through September 11, 2015, there have been 25,544 Muslim attacks and Zero Christian attacks over religion! *"Blessed are the peace-makers: for they shall be called sons of God"* (Matthew 5:9).

(3) *"In the name of Christ"* means you have clear New Testament teachings where Christ authorized his Apostles or anyone else to put his signature on an act or practice (Matthew 28:18-20). Jesus and the Apostles restated this inviolable fact all through his New Testament (see Acts 2:21, 38; 4:12; 10:48; 19:5; 22:16; Colossians 3:17). Furthermore, Jesus made it clear that just saying *"Lord, Lord"* does not mean He approved/approves of the claims or deeds being practiced in his name (Matthew 7:21-23).

And that applies to President Obama's oft-repeated confession that he is a "Christian." It is not Mr. Obama's (or anyone else's) ***"call"*** as to whether or not he is a Christian; it is entirely Christ's call. Christ gave us the requirements on how to become a Christian and how to remain one. You can't claim to be a "Christian" on one hand and deny it on the other by direct statements: like *"there are other ways to God than Christ"*; or praising Muhammad by saying *"The future does not belong to those who slander the prophet of Islam"* ("My Muslim Faith," Barack Obama, 9/7/08); or by saying *"The Muslim call to prayer is the most beautiful sound"* you ever heard. Nor can you claim Christ or Christianity allows or tolerates Mr. Obama's pushing abortion, same-sex marriage, incessant lying about Islam being a great and peaceful religion, racism, as well as about every other anti-Christian thing that comes into play in the social and political arena. (See President Obama's legal and financial support of national and universal "gay rights," including marriage, in my *Homosexuality and the Bible"* book, pp. 193f.) So Obama's Christian fruits are either absent or rotten!

President Obama doesn't get to insert and interject any of his Muslim beliefs or skewed Bible verses into Christ's teachings.

He's just a humanly elected "president" of a country, not God like Jesus. Or the new *Messiah* like Chris Rock proclaimed. I've met the Messiah in Bible History, and Barack Obama is no Messiah! He is a slave to his own personal narcissism, and not a "Sovereign Soul/Servant" of Christ. He has my agape, sympathy and prayers.

Point being: there's absolutely no authority from Christ in his entire New Testament allowing Christians to engage in personal vendettas, vengeance, holy wars, Crusades, Inquisitions, racism and lynchings, *"in his name."* Surely, if you need written words and approval to do anything, no matter how trivial, in Gerald Wright's name (as power of attorney or executor of my last will and testament), you must have clear, positive, written authority from Christ to do anything in Jesus' name. And I think I have presented that need to have Christ's written authority in all I/You say and do, as well as for everything I have presented as being required by Christ. If not, please present it and I will either present His Authority or remove it from this book.

Now, rather than summarily indicting President Obama as being deliberately anti-Christian, I'm going to be longsuffering and publish a few more of President Obama's quotes to demonstrate how he, sadly, just doesn't know that much about our Lord's New Testament or Christianity.

> *Our **job** is to be true to him {God} and his words and we should assume, **humbly**, that **we're confused** and don't always know what we're doing ... **We're staggering and stumbling** towards him, and have some humility.... First, we should start with some basic **humility**. I believe that the **starting point of faith is some doubt**. And not be so full of yourself and so confident that **you're right**. And that God speaks only to us, and that God doesn't care about others, and that **we alone are in possession of the truth**.*

Not to be nit-picking, but why would anyone call our blessed privilege to know and serve our Lord a *"job"*? Oh well, I can agree with Mr. Obama's words that he is *"confused ... staggering and stumbling"* in his "Christian" walk, and also that he is full of his self-confessed *"doubt,"* and not full of Christ's truth and faith, as Jesus desires of his most humble servants (John 8:32; Acts 6:5). Again, we Christians are not supposed to wander around doing things we have ***any doubt*** about (Luke 12:29; Acts 10:20; 11:12; Romans 14:1, 23). Yet, I doubt Mr. Obama ever read those verses. Personally, I have **no doub**t that if the resurrected Son of God, Jesus Christ, is not the only *"way, truth and life,"* as He said in John 14:6 (which Obama repudiates), that my faith is vain, and so is every other person in every other non-Christian, resurrection-less religion (I Corinthians 15:14).

Proof that President Obama is not ***"in possession of the truth"*** about Christ's being and delivering all truth in his New Testament can be found again in Obama's own words: *"**I believe** there are **many paths** to the same place." And that "**All people of faith** — Christians, Jews, Muslims, Animists — everyone knows the same God. There are **other ways** of salvation besides Christianity!"* President Obama not only believes there are other religions (especially Islam) that offer salvation besides Christianity, he ignorantly and falsely indicts Christianity every time he's afforded the opportunity!

Having said all this, I'm forced to say: I didn't ask for President Obama's approval of Jesus's Sovereignty as our only Savior. Because Christ is Supremely Sovereign above all human kings, presidents (including President Obama) and all other religious leaders on earth. And He, and only He, has vindicated this messenger and his message every time it agrees with Him and His Vindicated Apostles and their Message. HAIL JESUS!

"Jesus is The Rock Foundation"
(Matthew 16:13-19)

*13 Now when Jesus came into the parts of Caesarea Philippi, he asked his **disciples**, saying, **Who do men say that the Son of man is?*** Comment: This was for the disciples' benefit and not Jesus.'

*14 And they said, **Some say John the Baptist**; some, **Elijah**; and others, **Jeremiah**, or one of the **prophets**.* Comment: Notice that all these were great religious icons ... but also mere human beings.

*15 He saith unto them, But **who say ye that I am?***

*16 And **Simon Peter answered** and said, **Thou art the Christ, the Son of the Living God.*** Comment: Peter did not here represent all the disciples in his answer. This is another of the many examples where Peter's aggressive and outspoken personality is on full display (see at verse 22; also Matthew 26:33; John 18:10). The Lord understood and accepted this as being Peter's personal confession of Christ's Deity (Matthew 10:32a).

*17 And Jesus answered and said unto him, **Blessed art thou, Simon Bar-Jonah**: for flesh and blood hath not revealed it unto thee, but my Father who is in heaven.*

Comment: First of all, Jesus reciprocated Peter's confession with his personal confession of Peter's faithfulness and factualness, as he had promised to do for him and all who confess him (Matthew 10:32b). Notice he addressed Peter by his given name: *"Simon Bar-Jonah,"* which means "son of Joanes/John." Next, in verse 18, we'll see that Jesus will address him by the name *"**Cephas** (which is by interpretation, **Peter**")* — which means a *"rock or stone"* — which is the name Jesus gave him when he first became Jesus' disciple (John 1:42, see margin note). Notice how Jesus was contrasting human wisdom versus divine wisdom in all of these questions and answers: man's opinion as to who Christ was is juxtaposed with his Father's revelation of who He was.

*18 And I also say unto thee, that thou art **Peter** {Greek, **Petros**, masculine gender, meaning "a detached rock, stone"}, and upon* *this rock* {Greek ***Petra***, feminine gender, meaning "a mass of rock, ledge, shelf"}, ***I will build my church; and the gates of Hades*** {death} ***shall not prevail against it.***

Comment: Again the contrast is between Peter, as a single <u>male</u> **human-stone**, and his divine confession of faith in **Christ the Bed-Rock** foundation of the church. Peter cannot be the object of Jesus' confession. Jesus did not say "I will build my church upon **you**," which He surely would have if, indeed, Peter was the foundation. Peter cannot be the object, or *"this rock,"* of Christ's declaration. Christ is <u>this</u> *"Rock"* ... which is the same Greek word *"Petra"* used of Christ in I Corinthians 10:4. So Christ was/is the bedrock *"Rock" foundation.* Peter is never called the *"Petra."* So Peter cannot be the **Foundation Rock** of Christ's church (I Corinthians 3:11f; Ephesians 1:22f; Colossians 1:18).

Christ's church was *"built upon the foundation of the Apostles and prophets, Christ Jesus himself being the **chief corner stone**"* (Ephesians 2:20). The word *"of"* is possessive: Jesus is the only foundation the Apostles accepted/possessed as their foundation, and the only one we may accept. Notice this also says the foundation of which Paul speaks includes all the *"apostles and prophets"* and not just Peter, which would be the case if Peter were the foundation. Also the *"chief corner stone"* is the key stone in the foundation — which determines all the correct lines and angles of the building — and is that which is often referred to as the foundation itself: *"therefore thus saith the Lord Jehovah, Behold I lay in Zion for a **foundation a stone**, a tried stone, a precious corner-stone of sure foundation...."* (Isaiah 28:16). Jesus built his church <u>upon</u> himself, <u>off</u> of himself, and according to his specifications, pattern, or blueprint (II Timothy 1:13). Jesus is the builder of his church: *"Except Jehovah build the house, they labor in vain that build it"* (Psalms 127:1). Jesus is the only One who went through *"Hades"* (the unseen realm of disembodied spirits) to build it. Peter, as the stone he was, was built into the church and upon Christ its foundation (I Peter 2:4-10).

To even suggest that a mere human being is the foundation and head of the church of God is objectionable. To say Jesus built his church upon a man (Peter) contradicts all the prophecies and fulfillments about how the Messiah would be the divine ruler, king and high priest over his government/kingdom/priesthood (Isaiah 9:6f; Ephesians 1:22f; Hebrews 8:1). To say a man who did not shed his sinless blood to purchase his church would have his name on its title of ownership or identity is absurd (Acts 20:28; Romans 16:16). To say the Lord Jesus would appoint any man and his human successors — who are prone to corruption and physical death (as was Peter!) — to be the "Papal" heads and authorities over his church is asinine. The sinful history, changing beliefs and dead bodies of past "Popes" (some that "lie in state" in the Vatican and in other Cathedrals!) prove their fallibility and the fallacy of this entire heretical teaching (read *Catholicism Against Itself,* by O.C. Lambert). The RCC church goes for days and weeks being "headless" as they await the right color of smoke to signal the election of each new pope! Which procedure is clearly revealed and regulated in Matthew 66:6 and Acts 29:1000! (Check those two references out now...if you can!) This Papal Bull is beyond false; it is ridiculous! (It would be funny if it were not so serious!)

19 I will give unto thee the keys of the kingdom of heaven: *and whatsoever thou shalt bind on earth* **shall be bound in heaven;** *and whatsoever thou shalt loose on earth shall be loosed in heaven.*

Comment: This shows the words *"church"* and *"kingdom"* are used interchangeably, and are thus describing the same thing. Those in the church are in the kingdom (Colossians 1:13-18; Hebrews 12:22-28; Revelation 1:9; 5:9f). More proof of this is how Peter, who had been given the **"*keys of the kingdom,*"** is not the one who established the kingdom, but was given the entry information (**"*keys*"**) to open the door into the kingdom: as he did when he preached the first gospel sermon on the Day of Pentecost and 3,000 Jews entered into the *"church"* in one day (Acts 2:36-47). If Peter did not use the **"*keys of the kingdom of heaven*"** on Pentecost, when did he use them? If the *"kingdom"* of prophecy has not come, Peter has not used the keys for almost 2000 years! (So Jesus was wrong!) If he used them anytime during his life, the kingdom has come. Acts 2:38 is the fulfillment of Matthew 16:19 to any person not blinded by false teachings.

Peter's being told that whatsoever he would **"*bind...loose*"** on earth shall be **"*bound...loosed*"** in heaven has been badly abused as papal authority due to their failure to mention that the terms *"shall be bound/loosed in heaven"* are perfect passive participles, which literally mean: *"shall be as having been bound or loosed"* in heaven. Peter did not originate the dictates. He was inspired by the Spirit to know them and enforce the ones that came from the One on the throne in heaven! Christ has all authority in heaven and on earth, not Peter (Matthew 28:18) ... *"And **the key** of the house of David will I lay upon his shoulder; and he shall open, and none shall shut; and he shall shut, and none shall open"* (Read Isaiah 22:22; 9:6-7). **Note**: Peter was a married man at home and not a celibate pope living in any religious city or separate quarters (Matthew 8:14; Mark 1:30; I Corinthians 9:5). See next subject.

"Peter Was Not The First Pope"

In this short treatise, I will present the arguments the RCC has published supporting Peter as the First Pope, along with the scriptural proof that their claims are invalid.

1. The number one text the RCC uses to push Peter as a Pope is Matthew 16:13-19, which we just disproved in the previous exposition of that text. It clearly and undeniably proves just the opposite. Christ carefully chose his words so every average, honest person would know His Church would be built upon His Eternal Deity and not upon any man's dying & dead body (Acts 2:27-35).

2. The RCC claim that the reason Peter is seen acting as the leader and spokesman for all of the Apostles in the Book of Acts was because he was the Pope, is also false. **First**, because many of the texts they cite show all of the Apostles speaking and not just Peter (Acts 5:12, 29; 8:14; 15:2, 6, 22f, 16:4). **Second**, Peter was always the most outspoken person amongst the Apostles because that was his nature from the beginning. And many times it got him into trouble: as it did right after he confessed Christ in Matthew 16:22f; and as it did when he contradicted his own boast of superior faith over the other Apostles and ended up denying the Lord three times (Matthew 26:31ff; John 21:15-23). **Third**, being a spokesman for the Apostles did not make Peter a higher Apostle or Pope. This will become more and more evident as we progress through this study.

3. Peter never claimed to be the head or foundation of Christ's church. Nor do we ever find Peter seeking any primacy over his Apostolic peers by claiming any such higher appointment by Christ in Matthew 16:13ff, as is alleged by the RCC. In fact, since Peter was very outspoken, He would surely have proclaimed his superiority over the other Apostles if Christ had given him such! Also, Peter never called himself "the rock" or "stone" (or "chief shepherd") when referring to the foundation or corner stone of the church; he called Christ that (I Peter 2:3-8). But Peter did admit that he was a True Apostle because he met the qualifications of an Apostle and was hand-picked by Christ to be an Apostle. He also told us that he was married, stayed married, had believing children, and was therefore a fully qualified Elder in Christ's local church (see at #8). And if Peter were on earth today, he would be the first person to tell the RCC to stop using him as their example of usurpation of His Lord as the only Foundation and Head of His Church of Christ (not "Saint Peter's Church").

4. None of the other Twelve Apostles, New Testament prophets or writers (like Luke) ever elevated or referred to Peter as being the head or foundation of the church, or as being above or over them as per their inspired authoritative words in Christ's church.

5. The Apostle Paul never called Peter the foundation "rock" upon which Christ's church was built. But he did call Jesus ***"the rock"*** (I Corinthians 10:4). To be sure, Paul was a humble Apostle who didn't elevate himself above any of the Apostles, and he did recognize that James, Peter and John (not just Peter!) were *"reputed to be pillars"* in the church in Jerusalem (I Corinthians 15:9f; Galatians 2:9). But He did not elevate any of these three "pillars," or any of the other Apostles, as being above or over him (II Corinthians 11:5). In fact, he rebuked Peter for his sin of dissimulation (Galatians 2:11-21). Which sin was contrary to Christ's building of his church upon Himself with people of all races (Matthew 28:19f; Acts 10:34f; Galatians 3:26-29).

6. Also, Paul did say that he, as a master builder, had *"laid a foundation"* and that ***"other foundation can no man lay than that which is laid, which is Jesus Christ"*** ... and ***"the rock was Christ"***... and that the only ***"foundation of the apostles and prophets"*** was ***"Christ Jesus** himself being the **chief corner stone"*** (I Corinthians 3:10f; Ephesians 2:20). So Christ is the

Original Foundation upon which all of the Apostles and prophets were built upon, as well as the only Foundation which the Apostles continued to lay and build upon via their inspired preaching. How can you get any clearer than that? All of the later human stones Christ added to his church after being baptized into Him were built upon that same original foundation which the Apostles' laid down via their words. There's not a single scripture that says the church's foundation **is the Apostles**, or the church was built "upon the **"foundation of Peter!"** There can only be One Foundation of the Church. You do not lay another foundation on top of the original foundation, especially an inferior human foundation on top of a Divine Foundation. That would be like building the walls directly upon a sand foundation instead of upon the Bedrock Foundation of Christ!

And, furthermore, Paul said Christ was also the *"chief cornerstone."* Just as a physical corner stone governs all the correct lines and angles of a building, so Christ is the Chief Cornerstone of the Church when it comes to governing all of its correct teachings as per adding us as spiritual stones into His spiritual church. His Church had to be divinely designed and constructed according the divine pattern so God's spiritual *"temple"* would be *"fitly framed together"* for a *"habitation of God"* (Ephesians 2:21f). Peter wrote the same thing (I Peter 2:5).

So the Scriptural-historical truth in all of this is that on the Day of Pentecost the Apostles were the first stones the Lord added to His Church and laid upon Himself as their Foundation. And they were also laid squarely off of Him as their Chief Cornerstone. Then they were inspired with Christ's Divine Directions so they could assure that all later Christians would also be laid upon Christ as their Foundation and in straight Scriptural lines as their Chief Cornerstone. Not a one of the Apostles, or all them together, could qualify as being the Foundation Rock or the Chief Cornerstone. But they could reveal or lay it down before us. There are no flawed or accidental spiritual stones in the Lord's church. He chose them one by one, perfected them one by one, added them one by one, and then set them within the righteously straight walls of his sanctified and holy sanctuary.

If you want to be built into Christ's true Church/Temple, you must choose to allow Christ to be your Divine Architect, Designer,

Builder, Foundation and Perfecter of your faith. Christ can do this to you and for you! You can no more accomplish this by choosing to allow any fallible, flawed, fleshly human being to do it for you (like a Pope) than you can do it all by yourself. Peter was a sinner like you and me (and every Pope). Peter preached Christ's Words and Church Pattern, not his. Peter said Christ would add you to **His** Church, not "Saint Peter's Cathedral!" Listen to what Peter said about Christ and His Church, not about what others say about Peter and his church! Peter is my brother in Christ's Church!

7. There is no scriptural mention of any "Mother Church" or "Church Headquarters" being over all of Christ's autonomous churches anywhere in his word (Acts 14:23). (The Lord's Church is the "Bride of Christ," not the "Mother of Christ!") A brief New Testament history of the founding of the first church and its growth in members, congregations and maturity as per its leadership, will completely eliminate any notion that a single Apostle, including Peter, was remotely involved in setting up any Mega-church Headquarters in, of all places, Rome!

First, **Jerusalem**, not Rome, was the historical birthplace and gathering place of the Apostles to get the first congregations organized during the first few decades after the church was founded on Pentecost in A.D. 33 (Acts 1:4f, 8; 5:12; 8:14; 11:22; 12:25; 13:13; 15:2-6, 22; 16:4; 20:16; Galatians 1:17f; 2:1).

Second, remember it was **Rome** that carried out the execution of Jesus; that declared Christianity to be "religio illicita" (illegal) under Nero; that became the number one enemy of the Church throughout the rest of the first century ... and thereafter.

Third, there is no scriptural evidence that Peter was ever in Rome. (Saying the word *"Babylon"* in I Peter 5:13 is symbolic of Rome is questionable.) Though there is abundant scriptural evidence Paul was in Rome, and wrote many of his thirteen NT Books from Rome (as a free man, or under house arrest or in prison), for some reason he was not considered to be a Pope by the RCC. (Probably because the RCC did not exist in the days of the Apostles!)

Fourth, the only reason the RCC (versus the Greek Catholic Church) has its headquarters in Rome is because the apostasy from true Christianity gained its greatest power by organizing its pyramid-of-power structure upon the Roman Government's pyramid-pattern of government: with a monarchial Caesar/Pope at the top and his archbishops, cardinals and priests in descending order below him.

Fifth, the Lord said his Twelve Apostles have been sitting upon twelve spiritual thrones in heaven, judging in Christ's church via their word, ever since they left the earth (Matthew 19:28). Which is far better than sitting on any throne in Jerusalem or Rome!

8. Christ never elevated Peter above the other Apostles. He did liken Peter to Satan right after the RCC says He anointed Peter as the "Rock" and foundation of His church (Matthew 16:23)! The RCC claims that Jesus installed Peter as the Chief Shepherd over His entire earthly flock when he told him to *"feed my sheep"* before He left the earth (John 21:15ff). Never mind that this is adding something to Jesus' words and not reading it out of them. For Jesus did not say, as he easily could have clearly said by simply saying: "Peter you are the Chief Shepherd in and over my church/flock." But He didn't. Also, Peter never said Jesus said that; nor did he ever say he was the Chief Shepherd of Jesus' church-flock. But he did say Jesus was and is the *"one shepherd"* of the *"one flock"* and the only *"great, chief shepherd"* of the church (I Peter 2:25; 5:4). Which is what Jehovah said in the Old Testament when He prophesied He would be the "one" Shepherd in the Messianic Kingdom; which is what Jesus claimed to be in his New Testament (Ezekiel 34:11,15, 23; John 10:11-16; Hebrews 13:20). You have to have some serious and sinister help to miss these scriptural truths!

Could it be that the reason Jesus told Peter to *"feed my lambs, tend my sheep, feed my sheep"* three times after he had denied Him three times was to get Peter's eyes off of himself, as he did in his denial, and on to the needs of the members in Christ's church-flock? Especially since Peter would soon become a *"fellow-elder"* (who are called *"bishops and shepherds"*) in the local church of Jerusalem, not Rome (I Peter 5:1; Acts 15:4-6; 20:28). (Notice in Acts 14:23; 20:28, that *"all the flock"* elders are to oversee is within the local church.) A "fellow-elder/bishop" means an equal elder and shepherd with the other elders/shepherds, and not a chief elder or shepherd above them like the Pope would be...and claims to be today. Every which way you turn within the Roman Catholic Church's Worldwide Pasture — whether it's with their Chief-

Shepherd (Pope) in Rome, their Arch-Bishops scattered amongst the world's Big Cities, or even its elevated local shepherds (aka., "Priests, Monsignors, Cardinals") trolling the hills and valleys — you will find them to be unscriptural wolves in sheep's clothing!

9. Christ included no qualifications or instructions in His New Testament for the office of "Pope." As we saw in Chapter Four, Christ gave us clear and specific instructions as to how any responsible adult sinner can become one of His church members; then clear and specific qualifications as to how a member who is widow can become an enrolled widow (supported by church), or man can become a deacon, local elder or evangelist in His Church. He also gave us detailed instructions as to how to discipline every doctrinally erring and sinful member and remove him/her from any office and church fellowship if he/she doesn't repent. But we're asked by the RCC to accept their Pope is over every member, work and office of their alleged Universal Church without so much as a single word from Christ, the absolute sovereignty of the Lord's heavenly-earthly kingdom/church, that there ever was to be such a lofty position, much less any instructions as per any qualifications or instructions as to how to install, discipline, remove or replace their alleged Vicar of Christ and Head over their alleged True Universal Church if he turns out to be less infallible and sinless than they allege him to be! Good Grief, that's harder to believe than to say!

10. There's only one conclusion we Christians can come to about the RCC and its Pope: this church is not operating "in the name of Christ!" And I, as a Sovereign Soul, Saint and Priest in Christ's Church will not accept their distorted view of Matthew 16:16-19. Let them debate it. I'm available! Furthermore, I will also personally demand that they present all of the missing evidence for their other false miraculous claims about Mary, their Super Saints, Fatima, the Shroud of Turin, ad infinitum. Let the Bible Speak or, please, for Christ's sake, let them be silent ... or silenced!

Memories of Kaimu Black Sand Beach

As I stated earlier in this book, I, as a new preacher and missionary, chose to move to Hawaii because I was offered a pulpit position there while still in Bible School. I also admit that living in Bermuda created an affinity in me for Island Life. Before going to Hawaii to physically check out the work, I wrote a thesis on Hawaii and was further attracted by the fact that Hawaii was a "Melting Pot" of so many races of people (Matthew 28:19). Plus God's Great Commission includes all places where people live, including the *"islands"* of the seas (Isaiah 42:12). As I also stated earlier, I chose to go the Big Island of Hawaii rather than Oahu because of the needs of the smaller church in Hilo.

Now let me tell you that another reason I chose the Big Island over Oahu was because of Kaimu Black Sand Beach ... which was the first Big Island Attraction that I visited during my investigation trip in the summer of 1971. Here's what I found. Kaimu Black Sand Beach was one of the most unique and beautiful places I had ever seen. The word Kaimu means "Gathering at the Sea," which means Kaimu attracted people near and far to look at its unique beauty, powerful surf and surfers. Kaimu consisted of a beautiful blue bay, black sand beach, warm water, rough waves, swaying coconut palms, swimming dolphins and views of an active volcano which drew Islanders, tourists and surfers from around the world. Movies were made there. God's physical handiwork was on full display. The place itself was captivating!

But, to me, as a missionary considering moving to Hawaii, the Hawaiian people that lived down in what was "Old Hawaii" was the number one spiritual attraction. There was one Hawaiian Family, the Keliihoomalo Ohana ("Family") of thirteen that lived right across the narrow road around Kaimu Bay and Beach. Though, from my childhood visits to my Grandmother "Maw's" house in Hampton, Virginia, I always liked going to the beach and playing around in the waves, I had never really considered body or board surfing. That is until I watched all the local Hawaiian "Braddahs" surfing at Kaimu. I have to admit it, the lure of this piece of Hawaiiana, especially it's fun-loving people, had some influence on my final decision to move to the Big Island. (I also learned in "Missions" at Sunset that you should choose to go where you will incur less culture shock! And, believe me, Hawaii is different, in many ways, not all good, from where I had lived most of my life, in Mainland America. It is a physical "Paradise" which has many natural wonders and "risks" (active volcanoes, earthquakes, tsunami's, hurricanes, cliffs, black-green-white sand beaches and dangerous surf). It is a great place to live.

To make what could be a book on Kaimu shorter, here's a list of a few of the memories I experienced at Kaimu. Becoming friends with the Keli'iho'omalu Family and learning all of their sons' and daughters' names. I loved the father (Makua Kane) "Robert Keliihoomalu," his lovely singing wife, "G-Girl," and surfed with their younger sons (keiki na kane) and daughters (keiki na wahine) until they became lovely ladies (na wahine) and surfer dudes, or men ("Kane"). My two girls went to school in Pahoa with them. I also surfed with Billy Kenoi, even hauled him around a few times in my surf buggy, who is now Mayor of the Big Island. I made a goofy T-shirt about Kaimu, I loved to talk story with Clarence "Aku" Hauanio, the lifeguard. And I even have a great story about meeting Big Bad John Kealoha out on the high seas all by myself. To put it candidly: "This haole boy paddled faster than a motorboat to outrun him across the Bay!" (We're still friends!)

I was going to move down to the Bay when I sold my house ... but my wife didn't want to live that far from Hilo. Turns out she was right ... since I now only have memories of Kaimu Black Sand Beach. I didn't leave Kaimu; it left me! For in 1990 the ongoing lava flow from the Kupaianaha Vent finally filled in Kaimu Bay. When I knew this end was inevitable, I watched one of the fallen palm trees, that had been being rolling around in the surf for a week and had become a five foot long smooth pedestal, and decided to collect it for memory's sake (see picture below). I also paddled across the Bay a day or so before the flow covered the Bay and had a fellow surfer snap a telephoto picture of the event. The slow-moving pahoe-pahoe lava was already in the water, which was so hot it melted the wax on my board. To my knowledge I was the last surfer at Kaimu (see pictures below).

And so ends the "good ole days" at Kaimu. But not all the memories, nor all of the people who still live there. (Uncle Robert, G-Girl and one of their sons have passed away. Sigh!) So now I include a few of my memorable pictures of Kaimu.

My Daughter and Grandson, Melissa & Sergio Tamayo, at Kaimu Beach before covered with lava

Jerry Surfing during Lava Incursion
(Surf, Fire and Smoke)

Jerry, Stephanie & Samantha on top of Lava that now covers Kaimu Bay (2016)

Goofy Kaimu T-Shirt and Last Stump Standing

RESEARCH SOURCES

DOCUMENTS AND PICTURES: Before presenting the documents and pictures referenced and included in this book, here's a list of some that were not included to illustrate how I sought to reach people in all types of public and political places to share the truth and fulfill the Great Commission. **Postcards** thanking me for sending them one of my books: Nancy Reagan ("Just Say No" campaign) and Candy Lightner (MADD) for my *"Sobering Questions"* book; Pat Buchanan for my *"A Mother's Son"* book against abortion. **Letters** from The Johnny Carson Show and James Randi (a magician who was on the show) rejecting my request they pay me $10,000 for accepting Mr. Randi's $10k challenge to anyone who could prove any miracles have ever occurred, as I did in my Miracles book. Abigail Van Buren's lengthy handwritten answer of my letter in her defense of her "Dear Abby" claim that people are born homosexual. She apologized for her sloppy writing, which was also in red ink, by saying she was under the hair-dryer at the beauty shop! Letter from the Federal Election Commission (Jan. 1988) telling me how to register for President of the United States (I qualified! But didn't want to step down from being a Preacher, like President James Garfield!) An attached Hawaii Tribune Herald newspaper article entitled: "For President," by Gerald Wright.

All the Research Books used in the writing of this book will be included after these Documents and Pictures.

Elvis on 1956 KHK Harley and Unused Concert Ticket

Jerry Neil III Golf Bag at Home

Challenger Letters

October 30, 85

President Ronald Reagan
White House
Washington, DC

Dear Mr. President,

Aloha. Please don't think I'm crazy, but I have a crazy sounding request to make of you, or somebody in NASA. I would like to go up on one of the shuttle flights!

There are many reasons why I would like to do such and why I felt writing and requesting such was not actually so outlandish: (1) Other seemingly common people, from various professions (women, journalists, even monkies!) have been chosen to go to share their perspectives; (2) No preachers, of which I am one, has gone so far, and I sincerely believe a biblical apologist and historical, scientific Creationist would learn and be able to share some things, uniquely so, from such as experience and outside world vantage point; (3) I have been preaching for about 20 years, debating creation for longer, writing books, dealing with the logics of Creationism via lectures; etc. (4) I have spent eight years in the USAF and am, I think, healthy and fit enough to do such (being 43 years old and athletic).

Thus, Mr. President, if such a person is ever considered for a shuttle flight, how would I get "in the hat," so to speak? How could I be considered? I would jump at the chance to see and study God's world from space. I would love to write of such and teach of such. I would also enjoy lectures or articles praising our country for its vision, power and ability to engage in such grand endeavors as space travel.

So, Mr. President, could you or your staff give me a little direction in this regard? I am serious. I am ready, willing and able. I sincerely believe a person from the number one profession when it comes to looking at creation ought to be considered as a candidate for a shuttle mission — that is a Bible teacher and Creationist. "Here I am...send me!"

Aloha and mahalo,
Gerald Wright
P.O. Box 1706
Pahoa, Hawaii 96778

NASA

National Aeronautics and
Space Administration

Washington, D.C.
20546

Reply to Attn of: ME

FACT SHEET
SPACE FLIGHT PARTICIPANT PROGRAM

Due to the tremendous public interest in flying on a space shuttle mission, this fact sheet is being distributed in lieu of answering each letter with an individual response.

NASA has established the Space Flight Participant Program as a means to offer periodic opportunities for private citizens to fly on space shuttle missions. As you may have heard, the first citizen who will participate on a mission under this program is Christa McAuliffe, a secondary school social studies teacher from Concord, New Hampshire who was selected through the Teacher in Space Project. She is now scheduled to fly on mission 51-L in January 1986.

The Journalist in Space Project was recently announced as the second Space Flight Participant opportunity. This competition is open to full-time working media representatives (U.S. citizens) with five or more years experience covering or commenting on the news for U.S.-based audio, video, or print media.

Eligibility requirements for subsequent Space Flight Participant opportunities will be announced through the media and through organizations affiliated with the selected category. The next Announcement of Opportunity outlining eligibility requirements for a third category will not be released until next year. In the meantime, we are not taking names, there is no waiting list, and we will not retain unsolicited applications. While NASA appreciates the public's enthusiasm and dreams to fly on a shuttle mission, it must be remembered that the Space Flight Participant Program is but a small step in the evolution to increase flight opportunities beyond the traditional astronaut corps. In the near term we envision 2 or 3 Space Flight Participant opportunities per year.

Numerous individuals have written to suggest that NASA establish a separate category for "senior citizens." Since there are no age restrictions connected with the Space Flight Participant Program, senior citizens are already able to apply for flight opportunities provided they meet other eligibility requirements. Therefore, it is not likely that age factors will be included as requirements for Space Flight Participant opportunities.

If you have additional questions not answered in this Fact Sheet, please contact:

>Alan Ladwig
>Manager, Space Flight Participant Program
>Mail Code ME
>NASA Headquarters
>Washington, DC 20546
>(202) 453-2537

Council Flyer

The Boldest Candidate ✓ **Openly Against Abortion**

GERALD WRIGHT
Puna Council - District 5

WE NEED:
* Puna Coast Highway - for alternative access and jobs.
* People rewarded for getting off welfare rathar than rewarded for staying on welfare.
* MORE recreational facilities, fields, and activities for youth.
* Hilo Beach clean-up.

Mayoral News Clip

Gerald Wright

A self-described fiscal and social conservative, Republican mayoral candidate Gerald Wright says promotion of traditional values is the cornerstone of his campaign.

"I primarily ran to oppose same-sex marriages," he says. "I think it's going to be a bad, bad thing for the Big Island."

Wright, 53, is a practicing Christian minister with the Hawaiian Church of Christ and makes his home in Pahoa. He works as a real estate broker, and also has experience in the construction industry and is a published author of seven books relating to religious issues.

Legalizing same-sex marriages would harm Hawaii's tourism industry, while also contributing to the further erosion of the nuclear family, Wright says.

"I'm against the recreational use of all drugs," he says of alcohol and more traditional drugs like marijuana and cocaine. Abortion, homosexuality and gambling are other social issues Wright notes he opposes.

Unemployment is the major issue facing Big Island voters, he says, adding double-digit jobless figures are actually much higher due to the exclusion of many welfare recipients and others not seeking employment.

"I would support what I think the Kona side needs — a huge amusement park between Waikoloa and Kona," Wright says. "I think Hawaii is the place where we ought to have one."

A private water or theme park would create jobs and provide recreational activities he said are lacking in West Hawaii.

Wright cites the need to realign Saddle Road by making the cross-island link as straight and fast as possible to improve commuter routes. He suggests incorporating the private sector through the development of hotels, gas stations and other amenities along the realigned Saddle Road.

Wright vows he would work toward improving tourism and establishing localized industries to aid the economy.

Steve Yamashiro

Combating crime, implementing a more-equitable real property tax system and improving recreational

Rush Limbaugh Postcard

The Rush Limbaugh Show
EIB Network
2 Penn Plaza/17th Fl.
New York, NY 10121

Thanks for the book.

Thanks for listening.

My best,

Gerald Wright
15-2775 Papio St
Pahoa, Hawaii
96778

BIBLES: American Standard Version (ASV) used in all quotes; Also King James Version (KJV); New American Standard Version (NASV); Revised Standard Version (RSV); The Septuagint Greek-English Old Testament (LXX); The Hebrew-Greek Key Study Bible (Spiros Zodhiates, TH.D.); Hendrickson's Interlinear of The Hebrew-Aramaic Old Testament (Vol. I-III); George Ricker Berry's Greek-English Interlinear of the New Testament; A Harmony of the Gospels (Kerr, based upon ASV text); A Harmony of the Gospels for Students of the Life of Christ (A.T. Robertson).

BIBLE STUDY AIDS: Strong's Exhaustive Concordance of the Bible; Young's Analytical Concordance of the Bible; Arndt & Gingrich's Greek-English Lexicon of the New Testament; Bullinger's Lexicon and Concordance of the English-Greek New Testament; Gesenius' Hebrew Lexicon; Thayer's Greek-English Lexicon of the New Testament; Vine's Expository Dictionary of New Testament Words; Zondervan's Analytical Greek Lexicon; Zondervan's Pictorial Bible Dictionary; International Standard Bible Encyclopedia, 'ISBE,' (Vol. I-V); Webster's Third New International Dictionary (Vol. I-II).

BOOKS: *Catholicism Against Itself,* O.C. Lambert; *Christianity A Clear Case of History; The Church of Christ,* Edward C. Wharton; *Cults And New Religions – Jehovah's Witnesses II* (my "JW Bible," pp. 263-342), Garland Publishing; *Customs and Cultures,* Eugene Nida; *Early Christians Speak,* Everett Ferguson; *Eusebius' Ecclesiastical History; Evidence That Demands A Verdict,* Josh McDowell; *Father Smith Instructs Jackson,* Noll & Fallon; *God Among the Nations,* Ed Wharton; *If God Came,* Jim McGuiggan; Edward Young; *Introduction to the New Testament,* Henry C. Theissen; *John The Gospel of Belief,* Merrill C. Tenney; *Josephus Complete Works; Killing Jesus – A History,* O'Reilly & Dugard; *Man's Religion,* John B. Noss; *The Apostolic Fathers,* J.B. Lightfoot; *The Four Major Cults,* Anthony A. Hoekema; *The Life and Times of Jesus the Messiah,* Alfred Edersheim; *The New Testament Documents are they reliable?,* F.F. Bruce; *Mormonism – Shadow or Reality.* Jerald & Sandra Tanner.

COMMENTARIES: Keil & Delitzsch, Old Testament Biblical Commentaries (24 Vol.); R.C.H. Lenski's New Testament Commentaries (12 Vol.); Pulpit Commentaries (Spence & Exell); Adam Clarke's Commentary, Old and New Testament; Barnes' Notes On The New Testament; *The Daily Study Bible*, (Barclay).

BIBLICAL BOOKS by Gerald N. Wright referenced in this book: *Homosexuality and the Bible; Killing Jesus—The History; Now That's A Miracle; Sabbatarian Concordance and Commentary; Sobering Questions; The End of the World or The Jewish Age?; There Has Always Been One Baptism; The Prejudices and Perversions of the New World Translation* (The JW Bible); *The Supreme Scientist.* **Tracts:** *Three Strikes And You're Out; Everything You Wanted To Know About Religion But Were Afraid To Ask; The Meaning Of Life* (See www.Biblical-Books.com).

www.ingramcontent.com/pod-product-compliance
Lightning Source LLC
Chambersburg PA
CBHW071650090426
42738CB00009B/1475